Designing Garments
— *on the* —
Knitting Machine

Designing Garments
on the
Knitting Machine

JANET NABNEY

B. T. Batsford Ltd, London

Dear John – it's jam every other day, jam tomorrow and jam yesterday, but never ever jam today

I am extremely grateful to Brother Ltd and Pfaff Ltd for the loan of knitting machines. Also to Anita Gilliard for her kind help and support.

ISBN 0 7134 6164 0

Typeset by Servis Filmsetting Ltd, Manchester and printed in Great Britain by The Bath Press, Bath, Avon for the Publishers B. T. Batsford Ltd 4 Fitzhardinge Street London W1H 0AH

Contents

Common abbreviations

AH	armhole
alt	alternate
beg	beginning
BP	bust point
carr	carriage
CB/CF	centre back/centre front
CB NP	centre back neck point
cm	centimetre
CO BH	cast-on by hand
COL/COR	carriage on left/carriage on right
Con Col	contrast colour
dec	decrease
FNP	first needle position
FNR	full needle rib
g	gramme(s)
HP	holding position
inc	increase
K	knit
KH/KR	main bed/ribber bed
MT	main tension
MY	main yarn
nd/nds	needle(s)
NWP	non-working position
RC	row counter
rpt/rpts	repeat/(s)
rw/rws	row/rows
SNP	side neck point
SP	shoulder point
st/sts	stitch/(es)
T	tension
tog	together
TUH	turn up hem
UA	upper arm
UP	underarm point
UWP	upper working position
WP	working position
WY	waste yarn
×	times

Introduction

The modern knitting machine has given the present-day knitter the ability to produce unlimited and extraordinary creations with great ease, yet most knitters seem to be afraid to experiment with shape, colour or design. I think this is largely because of the fear of making mistakes. There is no such thing as right or wrong – if something 'works' and is pleasing, then it's right; if it's jarring or you don't like it, then it's wrong. You can't make an omelette without breaking an egg and you can't design exciting and original garments without experimenting; you win some and you lose some. You must have the courage to take chances. You may not succeed initially, but on the other hand you may make a marvellous new discovery. You don't get something for nothing – there is certainly no such thing as a free lunch. All designers put a considerable amount of time and effort into their creations. Remember, we only see their successes; their failures wind up in the bin! Perhaps one of the differences between a professional and an amateur is that the professional is less afraid of making a mistake.

Sometimes knitters have unrealistic expectations. They feel that unless the garment they have made looks exactly like a shop-bought one they have produced a failure. They lack self-confidence and are easily defeated by small mistakes, whereas the more confident amateur can often convert these small mistakes into design features. A knitter might say, 'Oh, I can't be bothered doing all that handwork,' or 'I haven't got the time to be doing all that messing about trying all those different ideas. I just want to knit a jumper' (sometimes in two hours). What I think she or he is really saying is, 'I'm frightened of making a mistake,' or 'I'm frightened of being wrong.' Well, all I can say is – *don't be frightened!* You will make errors from time to time, but the important thing is to learn from your mistakes. Sometimes, what doesn't work in one place may find a happy home elsewhere, if you save the sample. You will only be truly defeated when, out of boredom, you knit the same 'brown paper-bag jumper' over and over again, only varying it by changing the colour of the yarn or by using a different punch card pattern on your knitting.

In designing garments there are two elements: the designer who has the vision (the colour, the shape, etc.) and the technician who can make the knitting machine 'sing'. This book will help to bridge the gap between them and make them one.

As a designer you will learn how to focus on the visual elements around you in order to use them in your work. You are not a camera, so you are not required to produce a totally accurate reproduction of what you see. The object of making a drawing is to have a visual rather than verbal record of colour, shape, etc., *not* to produce an absolutely slavish record of the idea that appears in your mind. What you will be recording will give you sufficient visual information to use as signposts when you want to complete your garment. In other words, your drawing is only a tool to be used in your designing process. You are simply describing your garment in pictures rather than words.

I am not asking you to sit down in front of a blank piece of paper and create a wondrous garment. There are ways, systems, recipes (if you like), methods, and techniques which will lead you from simple basic principles on to more complex creations and help you to form your own ideas. You can use various devices, such as tracings, photocopies, rubbings, cut-outs, and photographs, to help clarify your ideas and to convert them into pictures.

The elements that go into making up your garment are:

1. **The fabric.** The stitch pattern and type of yarn.
2. **The garment shape.** This is based on your own shape and what will look good on you. You can use your design doll to try the proposed garment on and decide where the design lines should go to make the garment compliment your figure. Then transfer the resulting information to your basic block. Finally, draft your garment pattern.
3. **The construction of your garment.**

1 and 2 are mutually dependent, and you can really start from either. Once you have established the groundwork you are ready to go on to 3.

When you have determined your ingredients you must make your game plan. You will now have to decide what kind of edges and finishing you will require; how many tension swatches of fabric you will need; and the plan of how you will actually knit and assemble the garment.

Only when you have made all these decisions can you actually begin to knit the garment. You should try out all your ideas on little sample pieces. It's no good knitting the front as far as the neckline and then deciding that you are not really sure how to get the pattern back for the second shoulder.

It is very easy to be intimidated by magazines, sales ladies, and friends, into thinking there is something wrong about taking two or three days to knit a garment. This is a myth. Don't lose your sense of perspective: if you were knitting this garment by hand, it would take far longer! Don't be prejudiced about time wasting, either in using hand tooling techniques or in making samples, or about wasting yarn. You would waste far more yarn if you knitted a jumper which didn't fit anyone or didn't work out quite right.

It can be as easy to design your own garments as to follow a printed pattern in a magazine. Designing your own garments frees you from the dictates of a printed pattern and you can knit in the colour, yarn, stitch pattern and size to suit you.

Designing is just a question of doing everything in the right order. The task may seem daunting, but the trick is to break it down into manageable sections and then deal with each one separately. The whole thing will then fall into place effortlessly. How often have you found that a garment doesn't fit because the pattern in the book or magazine has been designed to fit a mythical beast and *not you?* Where does the mistake lie? With you or with the pattern? Possibly it's because you didn't look carefully to see if the garment

measurements corresponded with the measurements you had in mind. For example, the pattern might come to the hips on the model, but you might happen to be long-waisted and so find that the garment finishes at your waist! Or the amount of ease on the pattern might be more (or less) on you than you had anticipated. Pattern writers cannot read your mind, nor can they legislate for the person who is convinced she is a (slightly generous) size 12, when she is really a size 16! Printers and pattern checkers can also make errors. So why make other people's mistakes, when you can make your own? At least you will learn by your own.

Making a garment is like following a recipe. Gather all the ingredients together *first*, before you start mixing and cooking. Then, when you are mixing the ingredients, put them together in the right order. When you cook you should taste constantly to see if the seasoning is right. When you knit you must make little samples to check your ideas and to see whether they fit in with the larger concept. If you put too much salt into your cooking early on, it is difficult to retrieve your mistake. If you put the wrong cast-on edging on the beginning of your garment, you may be sorry later.

Fashion principles which have been used by designers for years are often ignored by domestic machine and hand knitters: it is so much easier to knit simple brown-paper-bag shapes which make few demands on the knitter. Moreover, if the garment shape is sufficiently casual it can fit almost anyone. But nothing in fashion is constant, and there is no reason why the principles of pattern cutting, long used by the fashion industry in making garments from woven fabrics, cannot be adapted to knitted textiles. But when 'pattern drafting' for knitted fabrics, you can also incorporate all the special techniques that can be manipulated by knitters, such as stretchability, the possibility of constructing the fabric in several different directions, and the ability to incorporate various qualities or different stitch patterns in one piece of fabric.

By looking at how garments were made in the past, you can learn various ways of making your own garments much more interesting and exciting. You can pick up tips from garments made from woven cloth, as well as from the construction methods used by 'old knitters.' You can develop ideas for both the shape and construction of a garment, and also for ways of embellishing and adorning your knitting to make it more distinctive and original. *No more brown paper-bag jumpers!*

1

The design doll

The knitter's first reaction to the suggestion of designing is usually 'I can't draw!' As a designer you are not necessarily a painter, draughtsman, or indeed a camera. The bottom line of your work is the garment, not the drawing or scribbling that led up to it.

As a designer, you need to have some visual record of your ideas, such as the colour, shape, appearance and form of a garment. You need to be able to assess whether it will hang correctly and look pleasing, and, more importantly, make the wearer look attractive – which is, let's face it, the object of the exercise!

Since it is very difficult to fit knitted garments once they have been completed, it would be useful to devise a method that would enable you to try the garment on *before* it is made up. In other words you need a way of visualizing accurately what the garment will look like on the body before you make it. If you can't draw, you will have to do something else to get a visual image. Some artists can put an abstract idea down on paper, but most artists don't just sit down in front of a blank piece of paper and create a masterpiece. You have to be resigned to making the odd mistake too. Don't forget that artists spend years drawing and sketching, looking at and analysing what they see around them, and storing up visual images in their minds ready to be called upon when they have to sit down and do a design. Even so, these designs don't always live up to preconceived expectations. Often a sketch must be altered or even discarded several times before the artist is satisfied. You have to be prepared for trial and error.

For non-artists (keen amateurs) there are various devices or 'tools' that will make the job easier. There is nothing wrong with using these if they help to make designs easier to do, more accurate, and consequently more exciting. Some people have great difficulty visualizing their ideas accurately, so if they can easily make a visual record on paper which will be a true representation of their idea, they will have less room for error when planning the garment itself.

It is difficult to stand in front of a mirror and assess accurately what sort of figure you will be designing for, and then to translate these ideas into a series of flat pattern shapes which, when put together, will make up a garment that will fit around a three-dimensional object (the body). If you look at a globe and also at a projection of a map of the world, you will see what I mean (*fig 1.1*). A globe gives the appearance of a ball. You know that this ball is a three-dimensional object, even though you can't see all sides of it at once. The silhouette gives an idea of the amount of space it displaces, but you know from experience that this idea is not totally accurate.

1.1

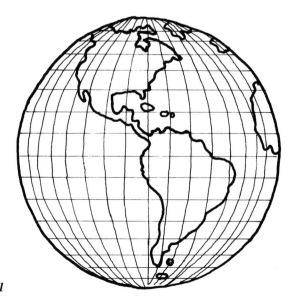

1.2

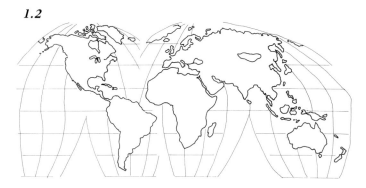

If you take a globe and cut it up, you can then see the part you couldn't see when it was whole (*fig 1.2*). It is, strictly speaking, more informative, but not necessarily more accurate. The shapes of the land masses, for example, are subject to varying amounts of distortion, depending on their position on the globe relative to the way the globe has been dissected.

If you wanted to do some designing for a round object, you would have to 'cut it up' to be able to represent all the sides at once. But as a result the object would be distorted. So it follows that, when designing a garment for a three-dimensional body, it is impossible to get an accurate idea of what it will look like from the flat pattern because, in making it flat, the appearance has been distorted. You must see what it will look like on the three-dimensional figure before you can assess whether it will be complimentary or not. So your designing must be done on a representation of the appearance of the body, not on the flat pattern pieces, which are necessarily distorted. In other words, as I have said, you need a way of 'trying on' your ideas before making up garments. This is a very easy thing to do.

The magic answer is a 'doll' much like the paper ones you may have played with as a child (*fig 1.3*). Remember the paper 'outfits' that could be cut out and perhaps coloured, with little tabs at the shoulders that you could hook over the doll to hang them on it? You could even make up your own outfits by using the paper doll as a model to draw or trace around.

You are now going to use your own measurements to make a paper doll, to one-fifth scale. It will be a literal representation of your own figure, including all your good and bad points, so be prepared for the truth. The most important thing is that it won't lie! You may not like the look of your doll, because it will be totally realistic and not the vision you have of yourself in your mind's eye. But it will be a great help in our designing.

To make your paper doll, you will need a blank

wall, a large set square, a tape measure, and a good friend. Mark your outline on the wall using the set square to note the critical points (*fig 1.4*). There is no need for a large sheet of paper. If you have a plain unpanelled door you can mark the points on this. Use a piece of chalk which can be removed when you have finished, or the small sticky paper labels that come in packets from the newsagents or an art store. You should wear basic undergarments and flat shoes (or bare feet) for accuracy. The more points you can mark, the easier it will be to make your doll accurate, and the easier your designing task will be.

MARKS (both sides of the body) (*fig 1.5*)

1. Top of the head (one mark)
2. Base of the neck
3. Shoulder tips
4. Armpits
5. Elbows
6. Wrists
7. Height and width of bust (at widest point)
8. Waist
9. Leg break (where the leg bends from the body)
10. Hips (at the widest point, even if it is the top of the thigh)
11. Knees

Use your set square and get a helper to measure you. When you step away from the wall your outline will be there in dots. Now measure between them in

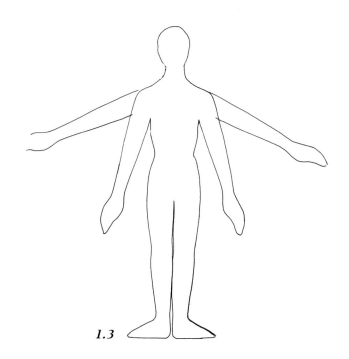

1.3

centimetres. Measure between the points at either side of your body to find your width, and between the points and the floor to find your height. You can also measure vertically between the points to find the relative length of each section of your body (e.g. to see if you are long-waisted).

To convert this information into your scale doll, use the following method. Multiply each number by 2, and then move the decimal point one place to the left. For example, if you measure 38cm from shoulder tip to shoulder tip, calculate $2 \times 38 = 76$. Then move the decimal point to get 7.6. Therefore, your doll will be 7.6cm wide at the shoulder (*fig 1.7*).

Your doll will be used to 'try on' your garment.

Measuring using a set square against a wall

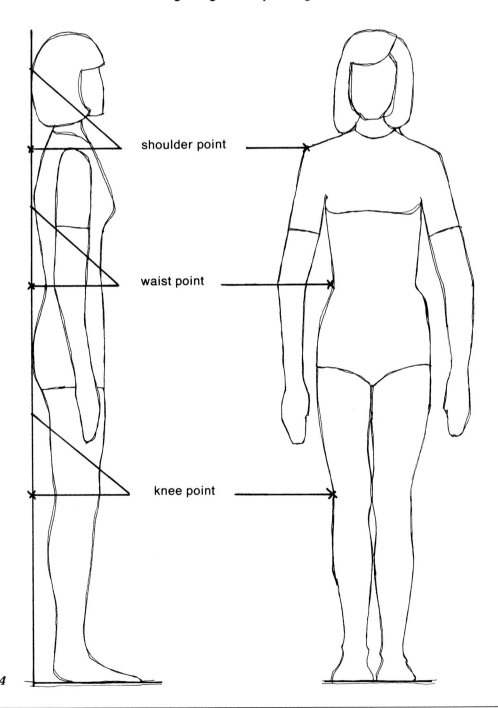

shoulder point

waist point

knee point

1.4

Measurement points for design doll

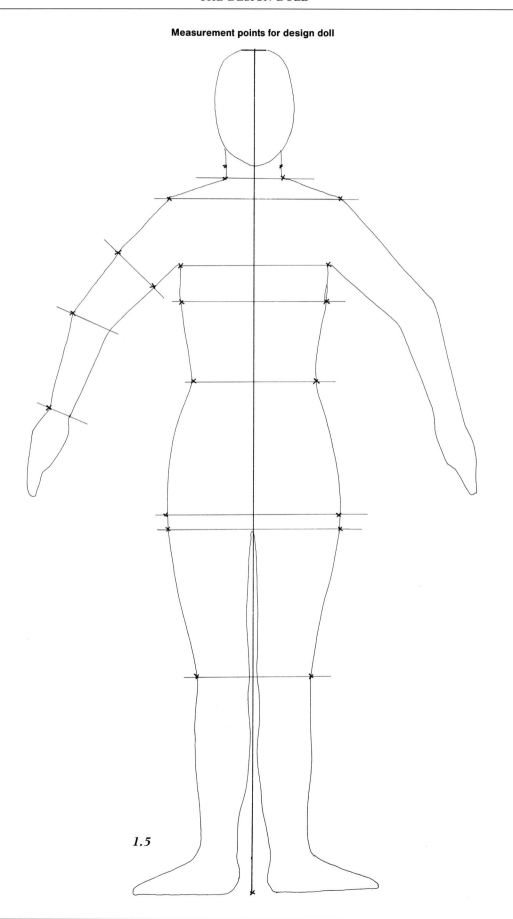

1.5

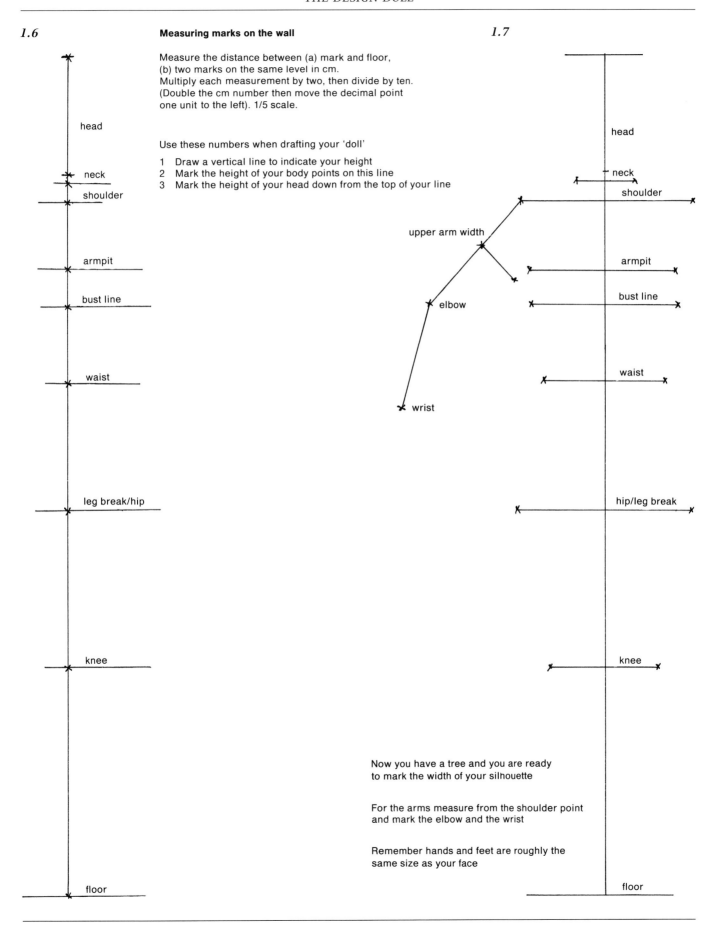

1.6

Measuring marks on the wall

1.7

Measure the distance between (a) mark and floor,
(b) two marks on the same level in cm.
Multiply each measurement by two, then divide by ten.
(Double the cm number then move the decimal point
one unit to the left). 1/5 scale.

Use these numbers when drafting your 'doll'

1   Draw a vertical line to indicate your height
2   Mark the height of your body points on this line
3   Mark the height of your head down from the top of your line

head

neck

shoulder

armpit

bust line

waist

leg break/hip

knee

floor

upper arm width

elbow

wrist

head

neck

shoulder

armpit

bust line

waist

hip/leg break

knee

floor

Now you have a tree and you are ready
to mark the width of your silhouette

For the arms measure from the shoulder point
and mark the elbow and the wrist

Remember hands and feet are roughly the
same size as your face

However, because it is two-dimensional, it will not give you the shapes you need to knit to make your garment: you will have to rely on altering your basic block to do that. The doll *will* give you quite a good idea of how long or wide to make your garment. Use it to draw an outline of your shape, and then draw the garment you want to knit over the outline. In this way you are 'dressing your doll'. You will then be able to measure some of the garment features, such as the length from the waist to the chosen hemline, and you can use the measurement between your body and the garment to help to determine the amount of ease you might add to your basic block, and how much you will need to alter it. It will also help you to establish design lines and to visualize features such as centre panels, collars, neckbands and sleeve lengths.

2

How to record the knitting of a garment

Before beginning your journey, you must learn how to make a record or map of where you have been, otherwise when you arrive at your destination you will have forgotten the route you took to get there, which means that you will not be able to repeat the process or learn from your mistakes. Remember the story of Hansel and Gretel, who left a trail of crumbs behind them on their journey through the forest.

You can only record the knitting of a garment once you have decided on a finished design, so even before you begin to make your record, you must 'sample-up'. That is, you must try out various different yarns, stitch patterns, hems and edges before you are in a position to make a considered evaluation of the steps needed to take to make your garment. It is unwise to make decisions without knowing all the facts, and it is taking a chance to experiment on your garment rather than on a sample. (As part of your record you might consider keeping any samples which you find unsatisfactory.) All too often a knitter will get to the middle of a jumper without having considered exactly how she or he wants to construct the neckline. The middle of a jumper is *no place to experiment*. You must get used to making your mistakes on samples, not in the middle of your garment. Once you get into the habit of working out the procedures you intend to follow *before* you begin, you will find that it is not only easier in the long run, forestalling any panic which might occur when you reach a point where you suddenly realize you don't know exactly what comes next, but that it also helps a great deal when planning your next garment. You can always refer back to previous notes and records, and even if it seems to be time-consuming, this will save you time in the long run. It looks simple

when you see designers turning out garment after garment, all looking absolutely wonderful. What you don't see are all the rubbish and mistakes that have been discarded on the way.

If you decide to embark on a teaching career or to go into business knitting garments to order, it is also a good idea to keep a photographic record of your work. This will not only enable you to show samples and swatches, but will also give a record of the finished garment along with all the necessary details. If you are planning to market your work at craft fairs or some other retail outlets, photographs of your work are essential.

The record

1.   Note carefully the type and brand name of yarn (where applicable), the sources (address), and unit cost (cost per kilogram, pound, etc.). Note also the care directions for the yarn (warm-wash, dry-clean only, etc.). *Weigh all yarn* before beginning to knit. Attach samples of yarn to your record.

2.   Knit a sample strip to determine the tension you wish to use.

3.   Knit a tension swatch and measure it. Calculate how many sts/rws are in 1cm. (Either use the Knitmaster Green/Blue ruler or divide the number of sts/rws by what they measure in cm.)

4.   Measure the body (use this technique if you plan to knit a very simple garment):

A: Body with ease divided by 2
B: Length of garment
C: Centre back to wrist
D: Closed fist (loose)
E: Closed .fist (snug)
F: Around armhole (snug)
G: Around body at hem (snug)

5. Draw garment shape with all measurements.

6. Hem and cuff: Knit a sample (40sts × 20rws) and measure it, stretching slightly.

Using the body measurements (see step 4) calculate the number of sts and rws you will require for your hems.

7. After the garment is finished, weigh the remaining yarn and subtract from the weight of the yarn at the beginning. (This method is very good if you are using more than one yarn.)

8. It is wise to make a note also of the construction techniques used. When planning your garment remember that you are like an architect or engineer building a bridge or a house: you must follow an orderly system so that at the end of the day:

(*a*) the item is soundly constructed so it will not fall apart – each section must fit together and be suitable and well balanced

(*b*) you haven't forgotten any critical parts, like pocket linings, that must be knitted in advance and then added while knitting the front of the garment. *Think ahead.* Do you want to take your shoulders off on to waste yarn or to cast them off?

You must work at making your particular system idiot

proof. You have a number of decisions which should be made *before you begin.* So write your record not after the garment is finished, but before it is begun.

Once you have mastered the basic techniques of recording necessary details and go on to designing more sophisticated projects, your plan should also consider factors like:

1. Shape of the garment – the fashion outline. Use your *design doll;* your *basic block;* and your *garment design* – the pattern shapes you must knit. You must bear in mind that the shapings and techniques you use to achieve your 'vision' will affect the stitch pattern, or the stitch pattern might limit your choice of shape.

2. Type of fabric – the filling in of the outline. Consider your yarn – its source, colour, quality, price, etc. – and your stitch pattern – the number of different stitch patterns that might be used, and their sources (manual or automatic or both).

For flat pattern knitting, look at colour-ways (and variations or alternatives), which may be indicated in swatches and/or wrappings; and also the direction of knitting, e.g. horizontal, vertical, diagonal or a combination. You may want to use techniques such as short-rowing or needles in NWP to incorporate a third dimension within a knitted shape, such as a mitten or sock.

3. Construction – the 'picture frame.' Make samples of hems, joinings, edges, and shaping details, e.g. decreasing techniques. Do not forget seaming details, facings, cuffs and collars, and other relevant dressmaking techniques that may be applicable.

4. Getting it together – your plan of action.

3

The record sheet

Pattern for a plain jumper

The easiest way to keep a record of your knitting is to establish a system. This is like a filing cabinet; you can automatically slot all the relevant information into the correct drawer at the appropriate time. This way the chore of keeping notes that you can refer to becomes simple. You won't be scratching your head at the sight of a handful of scrappy pieces of paper with illegible jottings on them, asking, 'I wonder if 10 refers to the tension dial or to the number of rows?'

What follows is a typical set of instructions for knitting a very simple garment. These include all the sampling and trying out you will need to do if you are a designer-knitter. At the end you will find the **record** of the garment. When you have followed through the information, you will then be able to work out your own system for recording your designs.

'BROWN PAPER-BAG' JUMPER

The knitted fabric

1. Knit a strip sample on approximately 20 needles, to decide on the tension that you feel will be suitable for the garment (*fig 3.1*).

2. Knit a tension swatch in the desired stitch size (see photo on page 18).

3. Leave the swatch to rest. (Wash it if necessary, e.g. if the yarn used is in oil on the cone.) Place the swatch on a carpet tile *or* piece of sandpaper and measure it.

Standard gauge:

$$40\text{sts} = y \text{ cm; therefore } \frac{40}{y} = \text{number of sts in 1cm.}$$

$$60\text{rws} = x \text{ cm; therefore } \frac{60}{x} = \text{number of rws in 1cm.}$$

Chunky gauge:

$$20\text{sts} = y \text{ cm; therefore } \frac{20}{y} = \text{number of sts in 1cm.}$$

$$30\text{rws} = x \text{ cm; therefore } \frac{30}{x} = \text{number of rws in 1cm.}$$

3.1

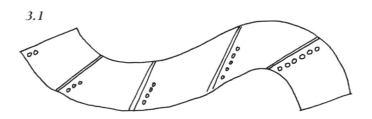

3.2

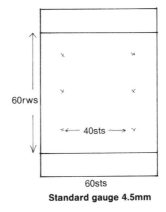

60rws

×— 40sts —×

60sts

Standard gauge 4.5mm

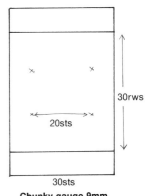

30rws

20sts

30sts

Chunky gauge 9mm

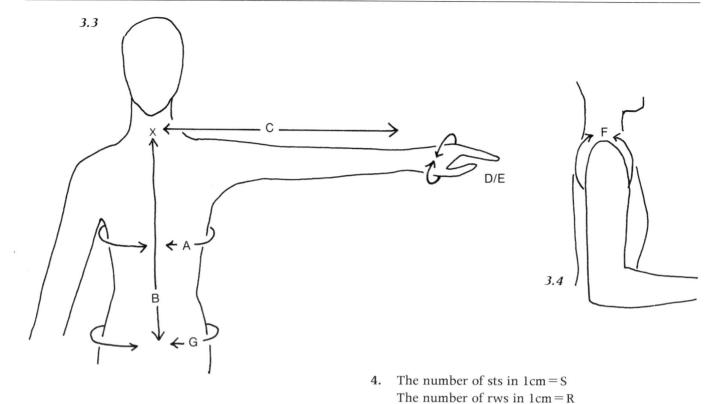

Tension swatch and edge sample from the
'brown paper-bag' jumper

4. The number of sts in 1cm = S
The number of rws in 1cm = R

Measurements of the body

A = Front or back. Measure the chest loosely and add
2-6cm ease. Divide by 2

B = Length. The desired length of the garment to its
edge or hem

C = Centre back to wrist

D = Around closed fist (loosely)

E = Around closed fist (snug)

F = Around armhole (snug) (*fig 3.4*)

G = Bottom edge. Measure around the body at the
bottom of the jumper and divide by 2

Design

Design the shape of the garment from the
measurements.

Calculating the garment shape (*fig 3.5*)

1. Body 1.

   A × S (number of sts in 1cm) = number of sts to cast
   on.

   B × R (number of rws in 1cm) = number of rws to
   knit.

2. Sleeve. For the basic shape:
   F × S = number of sts at the top of the sleeve.

$(C - \dfrac{A}{2}) \times R = $ number of rws to knit.

$D \times S = $ number of sts at the bottom of the sleeve.

Shapings   To get a shaped sleeve (wider at the top than at the cuff), you must increase if you cast on at the bottom or decrease if you pick up the sleeve head from the shoulder and knit downwards.

(*a*) Determine the difference between the number of sts you need for the top and bottom of the sleeve. Number of sts at top − number of sts at bottom = number of sts to lose.

(*b*) To find the number of times you must increase or decrease, and because these shapings are done in pairs (one at each end of a row), divide the number of sts you have to lose by 2.

(*c*) You have to knit a given number of rows to make your sleeve the correct length. Therefore you have a given number of opportunities to make these shapings. Divide the number of rows by the number of shapings to obtain the number of rows between shapings. (If you have a number of rows left over when you have finished dividing, on a simple garment you can safely put them at the top of the sleeve, instead of distributing them evenly between your shapings.)

Note: All sections of the jumper are to be knitted beginning and ending with a section of knitting in waste yarn.

Edges

1.   Do samples on 20×20 needles to determine the style of the edges.

2.   Stretch the sample and measure the 40 sts. This measurement need not be totally accurate but should

be done to give you a fair idea of how the edge would look when fitting neatly on the body. 40 sts = y cm.

3.   Hems.

(*a*) Calculate the number of stitches required for the hem at the bottom edge of the garment.

$\dfrac{G}{y} \times 40 = $ number of stitches needed for the hem.

(*b*) Knit the hem and leave it on the machine. You are now going to pick up the sts from the bottom of the garment on to the machine. To put the bottom of the garment on to the hem you will have to reduce the sts evenly across the row by putting two sts at a time on to some of the needles.

(*c*) Calculate the number of decreases needed to put the bottom of the garment on to the hem. Number of sts on the body − number of sts on the hem = number of sts to lose.

(*d*) To decide how many needles you must have between each decrease (2 sts on 1 needle), divide the number of sts on the hem by the number of sts to lose to obtain the number of needles between each decrease. To make it easier to arrange your decreasing before you put the garment back on to the needles with the hem on them, pull out to holding position the needles on to which you will pick up two sts. You can then check visually whether you are decreasing the correct number of sts, and if they are evenly spaced out across the row.

(*e*) Pick up the garment on to the needles with the hem. Either pull the garment sts through the hem sts and cast off loosely, or knit 1 row through all the sts and cast off loosely.

4.   Cuff.

(*a*) Calculate the number of sts needed for the cuff.

$\dfrac{E}{Y} \times 40 = $ number of sts for cuff. Knit cuff and leave on needles.

(*b*) Calculate the number of decreases needed to put the bottom of the sleeve on to the cuff. Number of sts on bottom of sleeve − number of sts on cuff = number of sts to lose.

(*c*) Calculate the number of needles between each decrease. Divide the number of sts for cuff by the number of sts to lose to obtain the number of needles between each decrease.

3.5

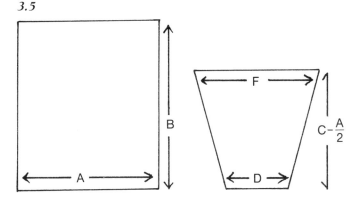

(d) Pick up the bottom of the sleeve on to the needles with the cuff sts and finish in the same way as the hem at the bottom of the garment.

The neck edge can be finished as you choose, or you can put a simple boat neck on the garment. You will probably not need to decrease at all at this point.

3.6

RECORD SHEET.

1. WEIGHT OF YARN

		GREEN	WHITE
BEFORE		350	280
AFTER		50	260
YARN USED.		300	20

2. MEASUREMENTS: (PERSONAL)

A: 50 CM.   D: 26 CM   G: 45 CM
B: 54 CM   E: 20 CM
C: 62 CM   F: 46 CM

3. TENSION SWATCH: T6 – 40 STS = 11·6 CM   60 RWS = 15·2 CM
1 CM = 3·4 STS   1 CM = 3·9 RWS.

HEM T4, 2×1 MOCK RIB ||o||o||o||
KNIT:
15 RWS T4.   41 NEEDLES = 14 "RIBS".
1 RW T8   HEM MEASUREMENT:
15 RWS T4.   S = 16 CM   R = 4 CM.

4. GARMENT:

156 STS.
46 CM
+ 1 ST EACH
END EVERY

210 R   54 CM   37 CM   144 R.   4 RWS.

50 CM   26 CM
170 STS.   88 STS.

COLOUR NOTES:

FRONT/BACK AT RC 20   6 RWS W   SLEEVE AT RC 100   2 RWS W
2 " G   2 " G
4 " W   2 " W
2 " G   2 " G
2 " W   4 " W
2 " G   2 " G
2 " W   6 " W

5. CONSTRUCTION
a. KNIT ALL SECTIONS STARTING WITH W.Y.
b. NECK BAND: KNIT 40 RWS MOCK RIB (2×1) T4
AT TOP OF FRONT AND BACK
c. CAST-OFF SLEEVES.

6. HEMS: PICK-UP GARMENT SECTIONS FROM W.Y. AS
2×1 MOCK RIB. DECREASE EVENLY ACROSS ROW.

FRONT/BACK 116 STS.   SLEEVES 56 STS.

T4 KNIT 40 RWS. TURN-UP HEM. LATCH-OFF.

4

Historical and ethnic fashion

This is an attempt to show a personal approach to researching information with a view to using this material as a source of ideas and inspiration. We can learn a great deal by looking at the way other people have clothed themselves both throughout history and in other countries.

'Begin at the beginning,' the King said gravely, 'and go on till you come to the end; then stop.' (Lewis Carroll, *Alice's Adventures in Wonderland*) It would be folly if, when looking at fashion and designing, we ignored their history. Whilst we may not find bustles, hoops and other historical paraphernalia relevant to modern fashion, we can often see, in the Paris or Milan collections, the ghosts of times past as well as echoes of ethnic influence.

When we design or choose our clothing we are also making a very important statement about ourselves, how we think and work and about our values. So, to begin this review of historical and ethnic costume at the beginning, body coverings were originally made from skins tied across the shoulders (*fig 4.1*). The idea of wrapping woven fabric around the body in a similar way can lead to several interesting variations.

The cardigan (*see over*) was inspired by the idea of knitting one very large piece of fabric and then 'folding' it around the body. In order to obtain the required width, a tuck stitch pattern is used and knitted in a very large stitch size. In this way a piece of knitting wide enough to go from wrist to wrist on an adult is produced. The pattern is 1 × 1 tuck stitch (double length), and is knitted on a standard single-bed machine, using a single end of standard 4-ply acrylic. The garment is cast on from waste knitting, and knitted to the underarm line. Some stitches are taken off each end on to waste yarn, and then the work is mounted

on the needles, again using pieces of waste knitting. The sleeves, neckline and upper fronts (yoke) are knitted. All stitches are removed on to waste knitting. The two sides are folded around to the front and joined to the upper fronts by grafting. The underarm join is made by grafting. The hems are then knitted separately and joined to the garment. You would only cast off if you chose to join the edges to the garment by this method.

4.1

'Lion-skin' cardigan

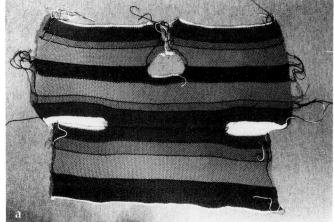

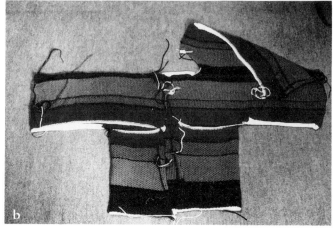

'Lion-skin' cardigan (a) spread out as it comes off the machine and (b) folded

4.2

'Lion skin' cardigan

Tension 10, Card 1. Double length tuck stitch 4 ply yarn.
40sts = 25cm   16sts in 1cm
60rws = 10.4cm   5.8rws in 1cm

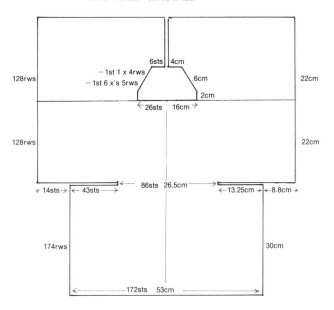

128rws

6sts | 4cm
− 1st 1 x 4rws
− 1st 6 x's 5rws   6cm
2cm
← 26sts   16cm →   22cm

128rws   22cm

86sts   26.5cm
← 14sts → ← 43sts →   ← 13.25cm → ← 8.8cm →

174rws   30cm

← 172sts   53cm →

Knit two rows in stocking stitch in black yarn between each colour change.

Colour changes

R.C.	Rws	Colour
58	58	dark purple
116	58	light purple
144	28	blue
174	30	red

Knit several rows in WY on 43sts each end for the sleeves
Cast-on 14sts at each end

214	40	red
232	18	blue
282	50	light purple
302	20	dark purple

Divide for neck shaping

322	20	dark purple
372	50	light purple
390	18	blue
430	40	red

Remove on to WY. Graft underarm sleeves and front.

Neck shaping:

R.C.
302 Divide for neck, 26sts for back neck.
Knit 12rws straight.
Inc. 1st at neck edge 6 times every 5rws.
314
319   Edging: Tension 5, 20rws
324
329   Sleeve: 44sts
334
339   Hem: 86sts
343 Inc. 1st at neck edge once in 4rws (+7sts).
348 Inc. 6sts at neck edge.   Neck: 120sts

Repeat for the other side   Front bands: 130sts

22

4.3

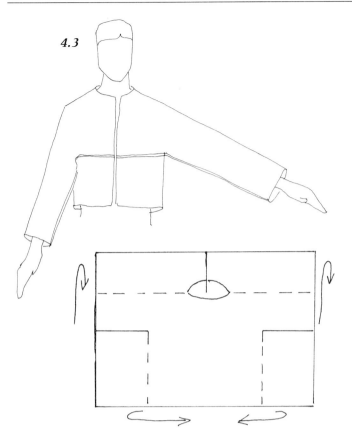

piece of woven fabric four to six yards long and approximately two yards wide. It was laid down on the ground on top of a belt, and was gathered in pleats or folds to fit the waist of the wearer, with two sections at either end left unfolded. The man lay on top with the selvedge at about knee level, brought the fabric up and folded it about himself, fastening it around his waist with the belt. The excess on top could be draped about his shoulders in the cold. Women wore fabric folded about themselves in a similar way, but the selvedge was worn lower down, well below knee level. A modern knitting machine could certainly produce fabric two yards wide, and a skirt made from a gathered knitted fabric would be extremely easy to make and comfortable to wear. It would also be possible to knit a pattern at one edge of the fabric width, giving a border at the hem if needed.

There are many other examples of unsewn (draped) garments in both historical and ethnic contexts. The Ancient Greeks, for instance, wore the *himation* (*fig 4.5*) which had a diagonal drape, and the *exemis*, which left one shoulder uncovered. Today in countries of South and Central America, the *poncho* (an overmantle) is worn.

It wasn't long before the simplest clothes, made from fabric woven on a loom, began to appear. These lengths of fabric were made with minimal sewing, and then draped, folded, wound and tied on to the body. In Greek and Roman times the wealth of the wearer was indicated by the fullness of the folds of his toga (*fig 4.4*).

Once clothes were made on a loom, the width of the loom, rather than the body beneath, became the skeleton of clothing construction. Garments made from loom-woven fabric were constructed in such a way that the selvedges would be used to save sewing hems and to give added strength where needed. The earliest garments had the most simple cut and showed fewest seams. Later on, complicated garments could be reduced to a characteristic core which remained when all decoration indicated by seaming was removed. In the thirteenth and fourteenth centuries Europeans started adding gores and godets to modify the shape of the simple basic garment.

Modern-day equivalents of the wound and draped type of clothing are the sari worn in India and the Scottish kilt. Originally foreigners accused the Scots of wearing their bed linen as clothing. The kilt was a

4.4

4.5

4.6

4.7

The simplest sewn garment was the *chiton* (*fig 4.6*), which was long and formed by sewing two pieces of linen together at the side, leaving openings at the top for the arms and neck. The garment was fastened at the shoulders by a pin or brooch.

The Romans adapted the basic principles of simple garments from the Greeks, but made their garments bigger and wider. A Roman swathed in the many folds of his garments was an impressive figure indeed. Some *togas* (similar to the *himation*) could be as much as three times the height of the wearer in length. The Romans invented many varied ways of draping and twining their clothing about their bodies.

The study of costume design shows that one of the constant factors that appears in the development of clothing design is the body, with its need for movement. Climate is another factor, though it is not always as important as the occupation of the

population. Even here the ancients were vulnerable to the influence of fashion. For instance, after the Ancient Persians conquered their neighbours, they, being susceptible to foreign influence, adopted their clothing fashion, which consisted of garments that were typically long and wide with long pointed sleeves (*fig 4.7*). As such, they were totally unsuitable for people who were mostly horsemen and warriors.

Often all social classes wore garments that were similar in shape and construction. The variations that indicated affluence and class were usually the amounts of decoration and embellishment found in the weaving of the cloth and added to the garments. Fringing can be seen as an echo from the times when skins were used to cover the body.

Terrain or activity (e.g. horseback riding) also became increasingly important in the variation of garment design.

One of the geographic influences on costume and design was the width of the loom. In the Mediterranean area, looms were quite wide (approximately 56cm), but in the east they were much narrower, which meant that garments had more seaming, were much narrower and more fitted.

Nowadays we tend to take cloth manufacturers very

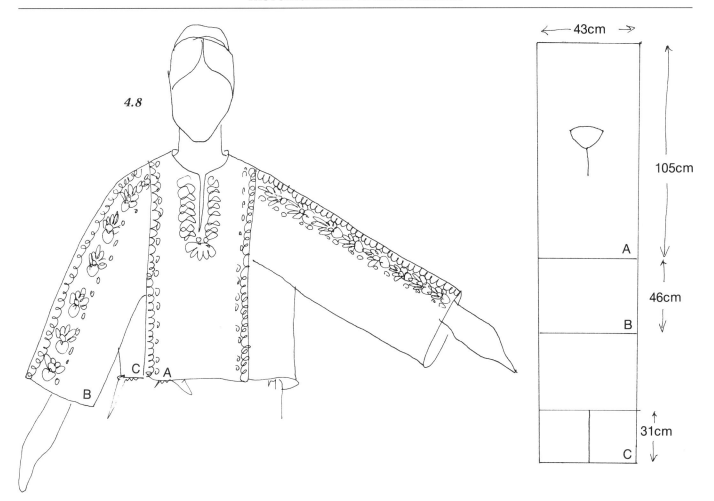

4.8

much for granted, and think nothing of wasting fabric when cutting out a garment to make a better or more fashionable fit. But when you are closer to the means of production, as a machine knitter or a weaver is, cutting into your precious length of fabric (or knitting) can be a very frightening prospect indeed. You might be afraid that the stitches will run and thus spoil all your hard work, and having spent time actually producing the knitting you might find it a painful process having to throw pieces away! People who wove their own cloth, and didn't have the advantage machine knitters have of weaving the *shapes* they require for their garments, practised an extreme economy of material when they planned their traditional garments (*fig 4.8*). They didn't necessarily make them skimpy or fitted, and often used fabric lavishly, but if they cut a bit off the width or length in one place, they would add it for effect somewhere else. Nothing was thrown out or wasted – an attitude which I am sure appeals to many machine knitters.

The simplest form of sewn garment was a variation of the *poncho*, which not only appears in antiquity but also today amongst the people of the Americas. It

consists of a simple short length of fabric with a hole in the middle for the head, but when the sides are sewn up it becomes a simple shirt. In some South American tribes where the men and women wear similar garments, it was important to differentiate between the two, so, in the man's case, stripes ran up and down the body, and the seams ran centre front to centre back and up each side leaving openings for the head and hands. On the woman's garment stripes ran horizontally across the body, and the seams across the top (leaving holes for the head and hands), sideways across the middle, and up one side (*fig 4.9*).

Historical garments can be used to inspire modern ones. Here are ideas for two ponchos. Both are based on the rectangular shape. The first is truly an 'unsewn' garment. The second is still basically a poncho, and, although there are two seams, it is merely draped on the body and doesn't have any shaping (*fig 4.10*).

The poncho is just a rectangle of knitting. It has been knitted in a double-bed tuck stitch fabric, which has very important qualities. It doesn't roll at the edges, it is firm, and has weight and stability. Any fabric with similar qualities, such as single-bed tuck

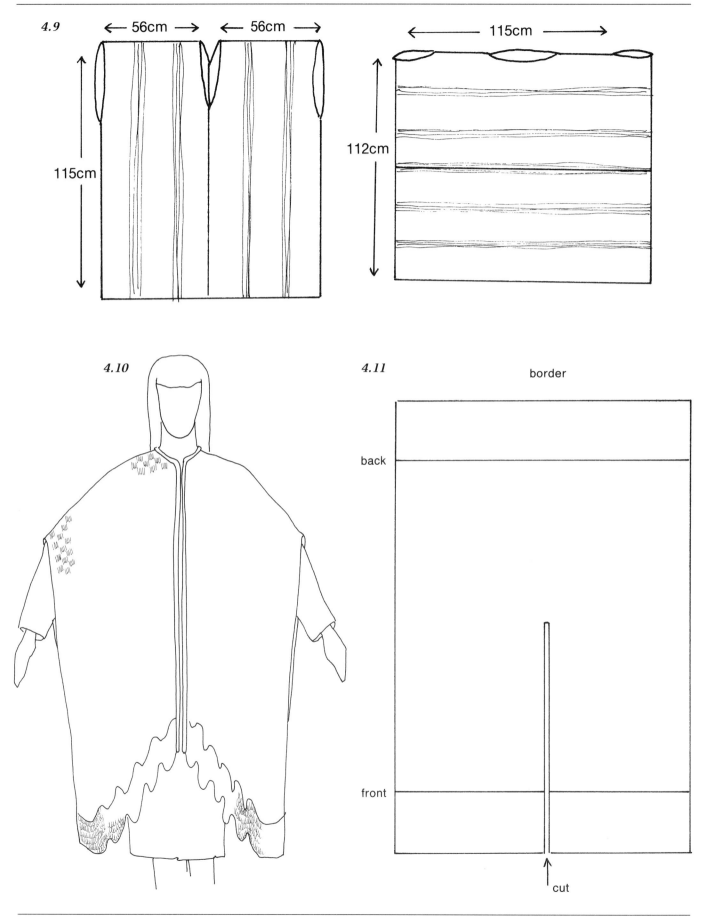

4.9

← 56cm → ← 56cm →

115cm

← 115cm →

112cm

4.10

4.11

border

back

front

cut

stitch or knitweave, can be adapted for this garment. When the garment is worn the hem is lower at the sides when the arms are dropped. This factor must be borne in mind when designing a garment of your own.

The garment illustrated was knitted on a Pfaff 6000, using two of the built-in stitch patterns. It produces a thick, warm, heavy fabric which is comfortable to wear over a coat in very cold weather, or just over a suit or dress in milder weather. The yarn used was a mixture of finer yarns. Weighing the cones of yarn both before and after commencing the work shows how much yarn was used – 585g cream bouclé, 700g fine white gimp, and 600g white brite acrylic.

The rectangle measures 100cm × 160cm. At each end of the rectangle there is a 10cm border in a different

Samples of double-bed tuck stitch

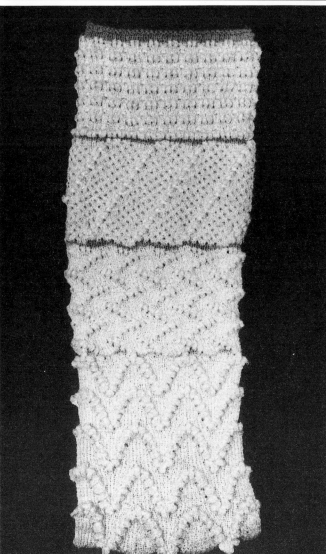

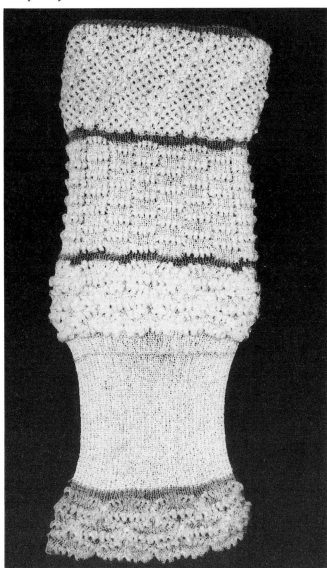

4.12

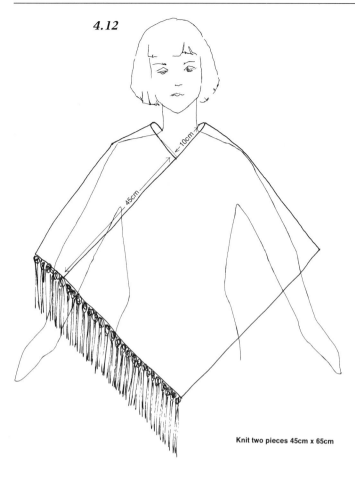

Knit two pieces 45cm x 65cm

4.13

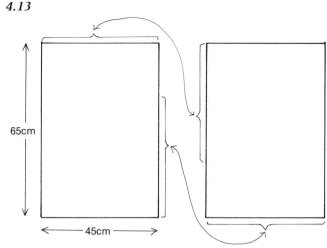

Sample swatch for green and white poncho

stitch pattern (*fig 4.11*). The border is knitted in two ends (cream bouclé and white brite acrylic). The body of the garment is knitted in three ends (the white gimp is added to the other two).

The sample swatch is programmed as follows:

1. Cast-on #3. Tension 5/5 (this is a racking cast-on).
2. Stitch Pattern A: #1011/139. Tension 3/3. Two ends of yarn. Row counter 136.
3. Stitch Pattern B: #1128/139. Tension 5/5. Three ends of yarn. Row counter 100.

When measured 1cm = 10 rows and 1.8 sts.

The garment is knitted using the whole needle bed. The borders are knitted in Stitch Pattern A for 136 rows, and the main body of the garment in Stitch Pattern B for 984 rows. Then the border is repeated. The work is taken off the machine on to waste knitting, and bound off by hand to avoid a tight cast-off. The rectangle is cut up the middle to the half-way mark. A 1 × 1 rib is knitted and sewn over the cut edge.

The second poncho (*fig 4.12*) is also based on an ethnic garment but has two seams. It is knitted as two 65cm × 45cm rectangles (*fig 4.13*). The fabric requirements for this garment are similar to the previous pattern, but, because this one wraps more closely over the body and doesn't have loose, flappy sections, it could be knitted in a Fair Isle or slip stitch pattern. The edges of the fabric are prevented from rolling by adding a fringing or edging strip. The garment illustrated was knitted on a Pfaff 6000 using two colours of yarn, and its weight is 375g. Both colours are mixtures of several ends of finer yarn. The stitch pattern chosen for the garment is #1268/193.

4.14

PONCHO   WEIGHT OF GARMENT 375 GRMS.

① PFAFF PATTERN 1268/193   TENSION 4/4

40 STS = 12.5 CM   3.2 STS IN 1 CM.
120 RWS = 7.5 CM   16 RWS IN 1 CM.

KNIT 2 PCS. 65 CM × 45 CM   144 STS., 1040 RWS.

② FRINGE
PFAFF PATTERN 104 $\frac{EX}{KX}$ TENSION $\frac{5}{5}$

a. ARRANGE NEEDLES

```
||||ooooooooo|ooooooooo||||
 |||| ooooooo|ooooooooo||||
```

ⅰ) RACKING CAST-ON T5/5   KNIT 2 RWS.
ⅱ) PUSH CENTRAL 32 NDS. TO W.P.

b. KNIT 600 RWS ON 48 NDS. $^{EX}/_{KX}$

c. CAST-OFF 8 STS AT EACH END.

d. REMOVE WORK FROM MACHINE AND UNRAVEL CENTRAL 32 STS.

The closest approximation to this on a single-bed would be a knitweave fabric.

In the tension swatch: 40 sts = 12.5cm; 1cm = 3.2 sts. 60 rws = 7.5cm; 1cm = 16 rws. Therefore each rectangle is 144 sts × 1040 rws. They are joined together end to side.

The fringe is Pfaff pattern 104 (EX/KX) Tension 5/5 (*fig 4.14*). To finish:

1.   Arrange the needles. Push 12 needles either side of 0 on both beds to WP (48 nds). Push the centre 8 nds either side of 0 on both beds back to NWP (32 nds).

2.   Do a racking cast-on T5/5.

3.   Push the centre 32 nds back up into WP and knit 600 rws EX/KX.

4.   Cast off only the 4 needles at each end on both beds (16 nds). Unravel the stitches on the centre 32 needles.

5.   Fold over the outside edge of the poncho and sew down.

After the poncho, the next development was the addition of sleeves to these garments. They could then be called all sorts of things but were still based on the width of the woven fabric as directed by the width of the loom.

The pattern for this simple shirt (*fig 4.16*), which was lengthened into a dress, was inspired by these garments. The fabric design was done with a garter carriage on a Brother Electronic, but the basic shirt could be knitted in other types of stitch patterns (using a combination of ethnic inspired patterns); single-bed tuck, double-bed tuck, slip or Fair Isle are all suitable, either using contrasting colours, or two yarns of similar colour but contrasting texture. A knitweave fabric might be too firm for a dress, but might be adapted to a coat. The patterns for the fabric were inspired by those found on Dutch fishermen's jumpers. They were

4.15

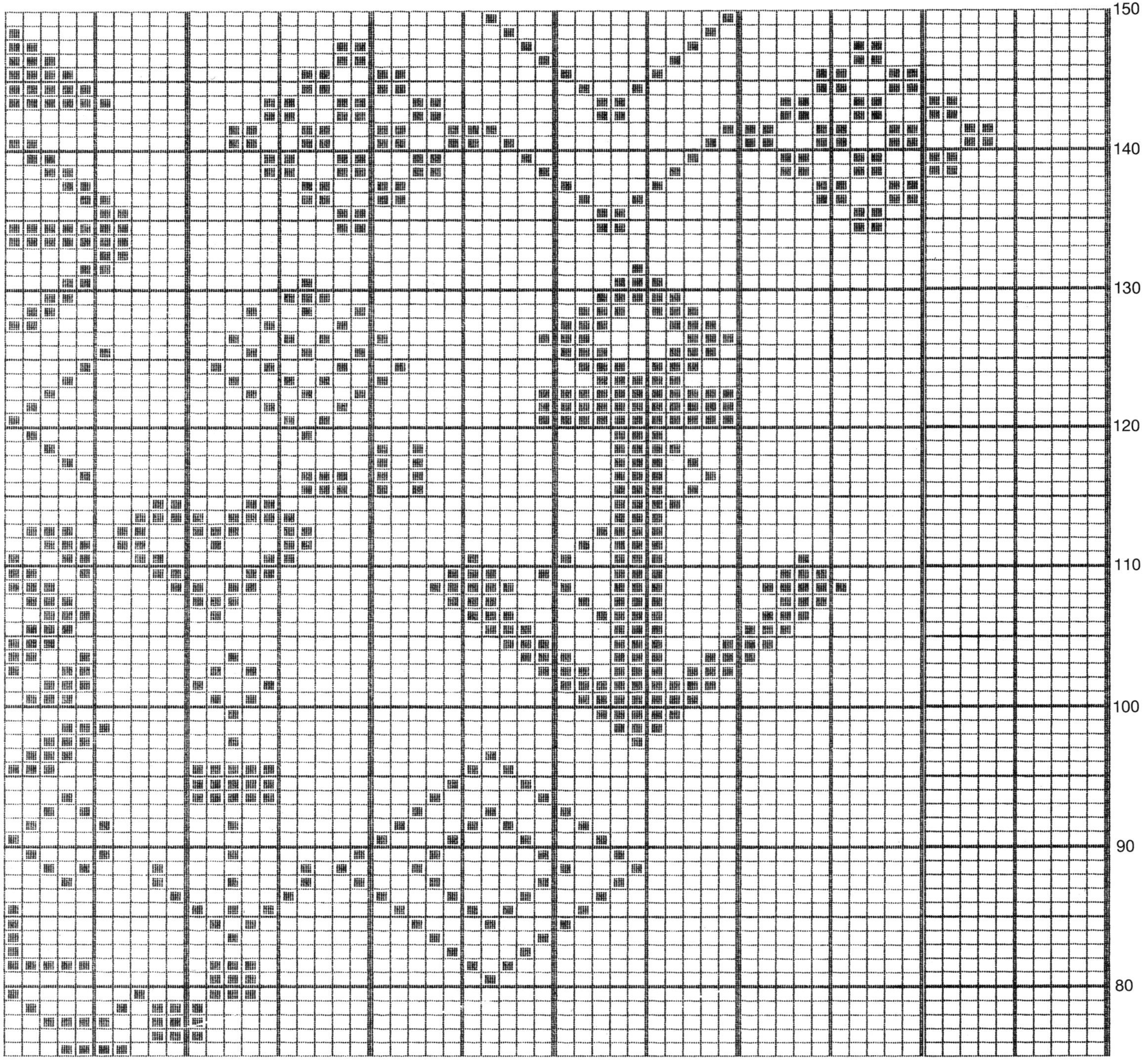

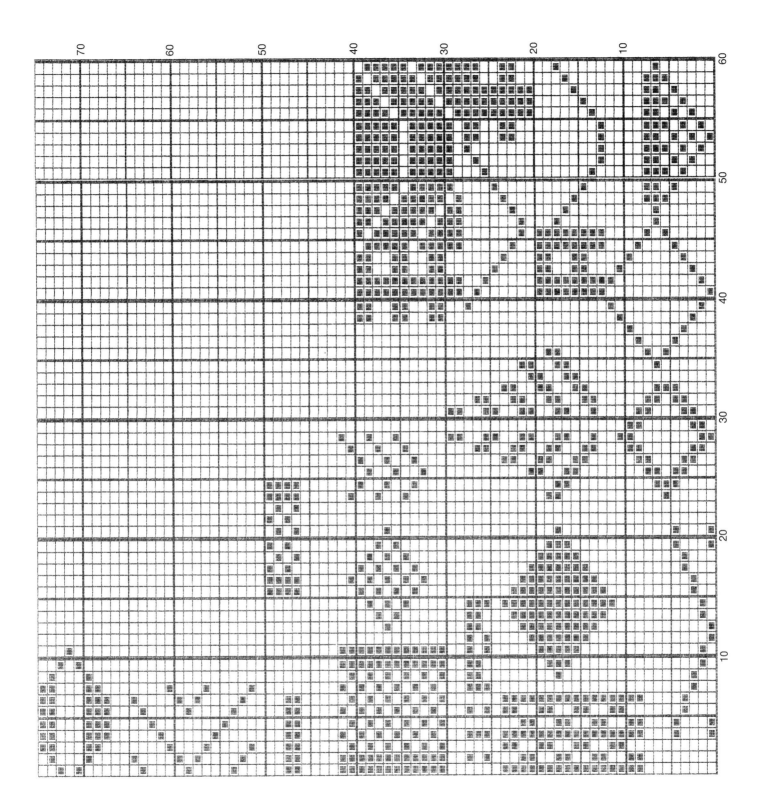

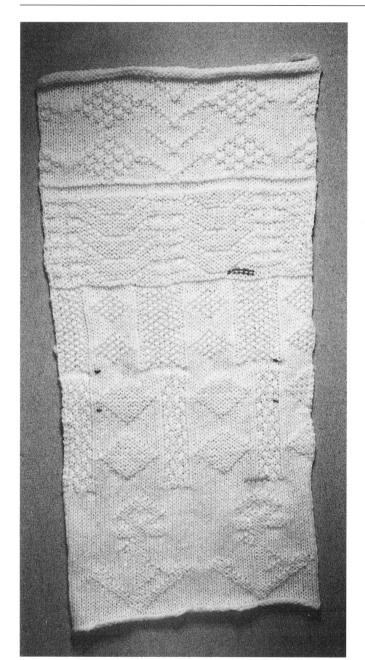

Sample swatch for dress

Tension 6. The sample starts with 4 rws of plain. There are 2 rws of plain in between each pattern.

Pattern #, co-ordinates	sts & rws	cm
1. Anchor,98,132,24,50	27sts;35rws	7.5
2. 9,24,1,22	22sts;16rws	7.5 (32rws)
3. 31,42,1,22	22sts;12rws	5.5 (24rws)
4. 29,40,39,60	22sts;12rws	6.0 (24rws)
5. 135,150,11,55	45sts;16rws	6.5 (32rws)

To design the garment (*figs 4.17, 4.18*):

1.   Draft the garment shape to scale, using your design doll to ascertain the correct proportion for your figure.
2.   Using the sample, measure each chosen pattern repeat in width and length.
3.   Fill in the garment shape with the required stitch patterns drawn to scale.

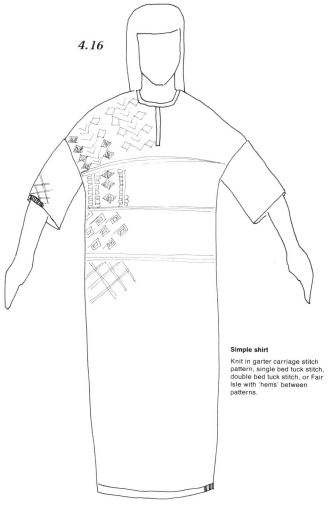

4.16

Simple shirt

Knit in garter carriage stitch pattern, single bed tuck stitch, double bed tuck stitch, or Fair Isle with 'hems' between patterns.

transcribed on to a Mylar sheet (*fig 4.15*) and samples of the patterns were knitted. The weight of the yarn before the garment was knitted was 1030g. The weight of the yarn after the knitting was finished was 500g. Knitting the garment took up 500g. If you are using a PPD with your Brother 950i, and you project the pattern on to a television screen, white on screen (equals black on sheet) represents stocking stitch; and black on screen (equals white on sheet) represents purl stitch. Some of the patterns can be seen in the sample.

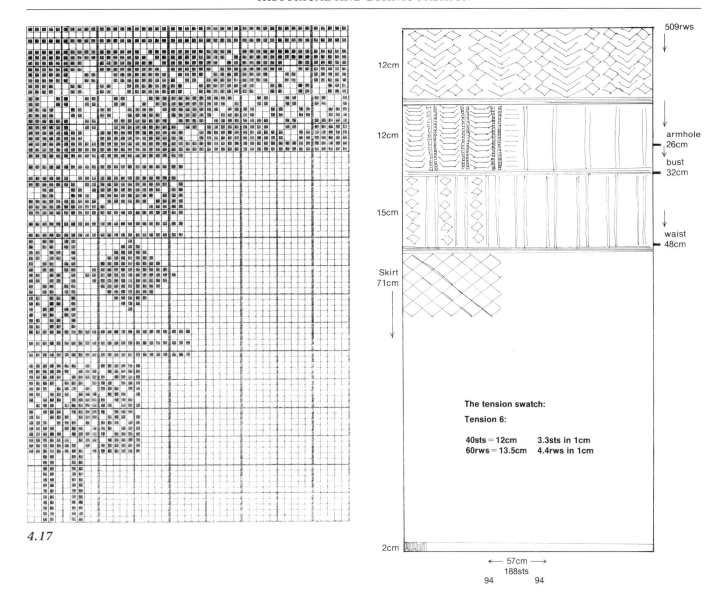

4.17

The patterns on the garment are shown in Table 1.
Body: 2 pieces, 116cm long × 57cm wide.
Sleeves: 2 pieces, 22cm long × 57cm wide.

TABLE 1

Pattern coordinates (see graph)	Cm	Rws	Row Counter
Band: 84,87,1,45.	1	4	509
D: 66,83,1,45.(45sts.18rws) × 3	12	54	505
Band: 62,65,1,22	1	4	451
C: 55,61,1,22.(22sts.7rws) × 7	12	49	447
Band: 51,55,1,22	1	5	398
B: 35,50,1,22.(22sts.16rws) × 4	15	64	393
Band: 29,34,1,22.	1	5	329
A: 13,28,1,16. (16sts.16rws)	71	312	324
Hem: 2 × 2 Rib 1,12,1,8. (#534)	2	12	12

The sleeve is knitted using the hem pattern for 12 rows and then Pattern A.

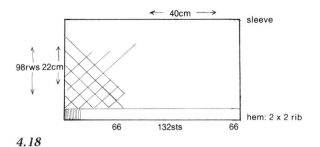

4.18

Many types of loom-width garments were made. Both the use for these garments and their length varied considerably. If the loom was very wide the sleeves could even be incorporated into the main body of the fabric. If the corners of the fabric were left unwoven, they would create areas of fringing for decorative effect.

Later, when more elaborate pattern cutting became widely practised, a section of cloth would be cut into long triangular shapes (*figs 4.19, 4.20*), and these excess 'gores' inserted into slits made in the body of the garments. While machine knitters would not necessarily cut up their knitting, this technique can be adapted very easily, by knitting slits in the fabric and inserting knitted triangular sections to alter the shape of the garment, giving it a swing and flow similar to a garment made from woven fabric. This is also an opportunity to add pieces in a different stitch pattern, or type of yarn, or colour, or weight, or to knit in a different technique or direction, thus making the design of a garment more innovative and eye-catching.

Hand knitters from the seventeenth and eighteenth centuries made garments that imitated contemporary woven garments in style. Even though there was no need to insert sections at side seams to use up fabric left over from sleeves (as would happen if the jackets were made from cloth), the hand knitters inserted sections knitted in a pattern quite different from the main body of the garment (*figs 4.21, 4.22*).

Because the garments were made from rectangular pieces of fabric with an emphasis on a minimum wastage, and because the body is not basically box shaped, people began to realize that they would have to improve on the 'fit where it hits' principle. In fact, when the wearer was active, something would have to be done to keep the garment on and to prevent it constraining necessary movement, thus leaving the body relatively unencumbered. One solution, which did not waste cloth unnecessarily by cutting out bits, was to use gathering in critical places.

Since fashion design did not exist as such, and the main idea was to use the cloth in as economical a way as possible, the size of the person inside a garment was not so important. As a result, the garment width, based on the width of the loom, was altered or made to fit by applying tucks, hems or gathers, or by inserting extra sections of fabric (*fig 4.23*). In machine knitting this can be done by using machine knitting techniques: that is, tucks can be made by picking up stitches and making 'little hems' within the fabric of the garment; or gathering can be achieved by reducing evenly across

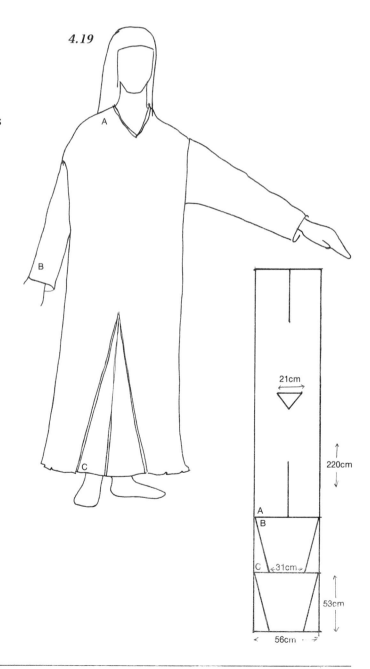

4.19

4.20

134cm

C

B

A

←40.5cm→

the row, which is done by removing the knitting (*fig 4.24*) on to waste yarn (or a garter bar) and replacing the stitches on a smaller number of needles. Since machine knitters do not feel that they have to base the width of the garment on the width of the machine, they are free to use these ideas arbitrarily in designing.

Another aspect of this 'sectional' approach to using fabric is that it inspires thinking about dividing the garment into smaller areas. The reason this is so important in designing machine knitwear is that the fabric is constructed on the machine, so that normally the pattern and colours are repeated right across the width of the needle bed used. So if you knit a front or a back in one piece, the same pattern or colour will appear with boring regularity across the whole width of the knitted section (unless you knit a single motif or use the intarsia technique). You cannot mix two different knitting techniques (e.g. tuck stitch and Fair Isle) in the same row, but if you knit a garment piece in several sections (adding wedges or gores to give the garment either fullness or shaping), each section can be in a different stitch pattern and/or colour, thus allowing you to add variety to your design.

The dimensions of the fabric can also be altered whilst knitting by using short-rowing techniques to distort a flat piece of fabric and make it curve and bubble. An example of this would be the heel of a sock or the top of a mitten. Another way of distorting the shape of the fabric you are making, so that you are not dealing with a flat plain length and width, is to

4.21

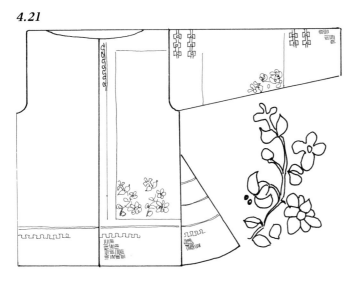

4.22

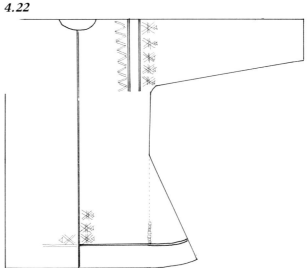

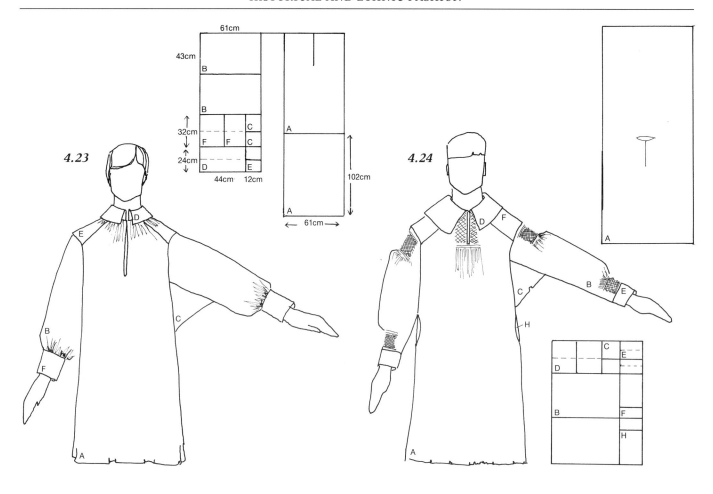

4.23

4.24

introduce some form of stitch pattern in selected parts of your knitting. For example, if you have only one side of your fabric knitting in a tuck stitch pattern, while the rest of the row is knitting in plain stocking stitch, one side will be much longer and thinner (stocking stitch) whilst the rest of the needles will produce a fabric (tuck stitch) which will be much shorter, wider and thicker. Thus, without altering the number of stitches or rows across the whole width of the knitting, you can create a fabric which is effectively gathered at one edge.

5

Traditional or folk garment knitting

Hand knitting has existed for centuries and in the fifteenth and sixteenth centuries professional guilds of handknitters were formed in England and on the Continent. The requirements for membership were that the applicant produce a carpet, ecclesiastic glove, shirt, felted beret and hose with a turned heel. Examples of these items can be seen in various museums, including the Victoria and Albert Museum, London. Knitting of gloves and hose in silk and wool was highly prized and became a thriving domestic industry. In Italy beautiful garments were produced in fine silk yarns. Charles I wore a silk shirt knitted in a damask pattern (using a combination of plain and purl stitches), now in the Museum of London, on the morning he was executed. The nobility wore silk stockings and gloves, but shepherds in Landes (south-west France) knitted woollen socks and hats while tending their sheep.

In England the Cappers Act was passed in 1571, which required everyone above the age of six (with a few exceptions) to wear a knitted cap on Sundays. Those caught bareheaded were fined three shillings and sixpence.

Silk stockings became so popular that in the fifteenth century sumptuary laws were introduced in Germany forbidding commoners to wear them. They were only permitted to wear woollen ones. Cotton-knit stockings were first introduced to England from Mantua in 1564 by William Rider, and their manufacture became a profitable home industry. In Holland knitted stockings were very expensive, but those made in the North of England and Scotland were much cheaper, and so became a major export. The Scots also depended on their thriving export of knitted hats. This led to the exploitation of the poor. In 1589 in Nottingham, the

5.1

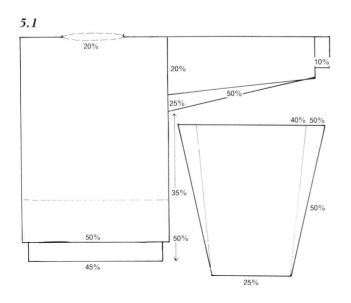

5.2

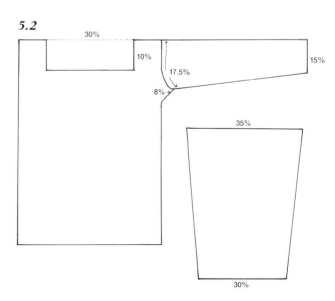

MOTIFS

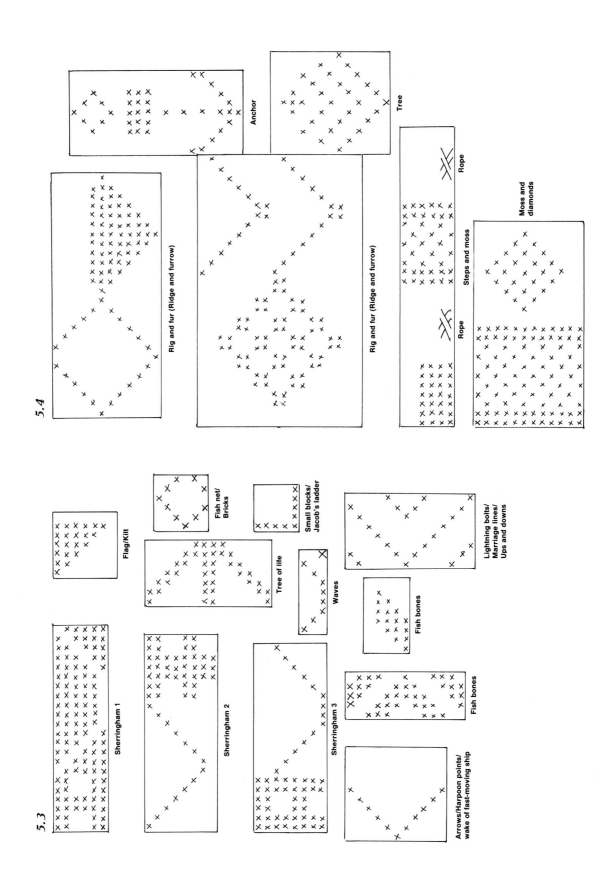

5.4

Rig and fur (Ridge and furrow)

Anchor

Tree

Rig and fur (Ridge and furrow)

Rope

Rope

Steps and moss

Moss and diamonds

5.3

Flag/Kilt

Fish net/ Bricks

Small blocks/ Jacob's ladder

Tree of life

Lightning bolts/ Marriage lines/ Ups and downs

Waves

Fish bones

Sherringham 1

Sherringham 2

Sherringham 3

Fish bones

Arrows/Harpoon points/ wake of fast-moving ship

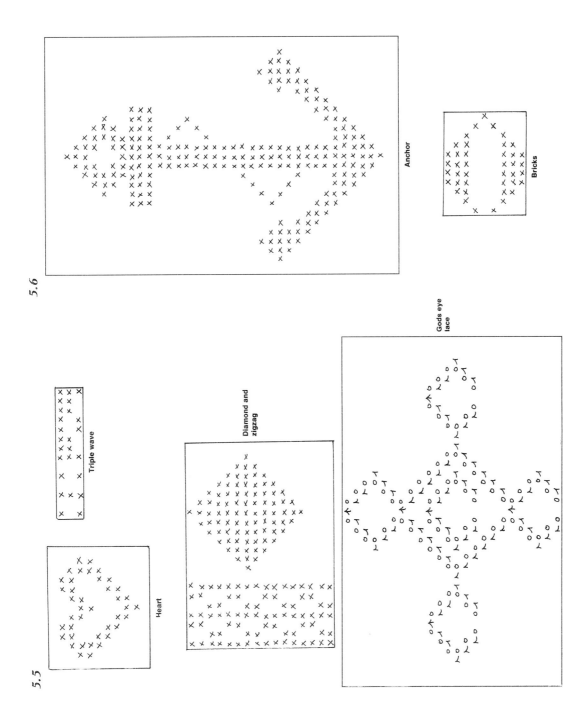

5.6

Anchor

Bricks

5.5

Triple wave

Heart

Diamond and zigzag

Gods eye lace

Reverend William Lee invented the first knitting machine. He was hoping to help the poor of his parish to knit stockings more quickly and thus to limit their exploitation. He applied to Queen Elizabeth I for a patent for his new machine, but his application failed because the knitting produced by the hand frame loom was too coarse. There was also a fear that increased automation would not help the poor, but put many of them out of work.

Traditional or folk garment shapes are simple and classic (*fig 5.1*). The measurements of the garments in the following diagrams are based on those for traditional garments. I have used a system evolved and adapted by the American hand knitter, Elizabeth Zimmerman, and used extensively by Priscilla A. Gibson-Roberts for hand knitting. She calls her system the *percentage system*. It is based on the measurement of the chest or body, plus ease. This measurement is 100 per cent, and all other measurements follow from it. In effect the system modernizes a method that may well have been used by traditional knitters. One can imagine women knitting for menfolk who were away at sea for weeks at a time, and were simply not available for constant checking of width and length. The knitter might well have used a piece of string with a knot tied in it to indicate the key measurement, and then knitted away quite happily without any need for further reference to the recipient of the garment. These simple designs can free modern knitters from bought patterns. They are quite easy to adapt to the measurements you require and you can use them whether you are a calculator freak, or wish to adapt the shapes to your patterning attachment. The basic measurements are as follows:

> Chest: 100%
> Hip rib: 80–90% for a snug band on a loose sweater
> Adult crewneck: 33–45%
> Upper sleeve on a drop shoulder garment: 50%
> Upper sleeve on a raglan garment: 33%
> Wrist band: 20%
> Hem to underarm: 35–50%
> Sleeve underarm: 50%

The earliest sweater shapes are based on rectangular woven garments, which are box-shaped with a gusset added for underarm ease. They were designed to be quite snug to take advantage of the greater stretchability of the knitted fabric as opposed to woven fabric. Craftsmen and fishermen wore linen smocks, which were later replaced by heavy knitted sweaters. The earliest folk sweaters were knitted in one colour

using textured designs. They were knitted as a tube with the armhole slashed, to allow the sleeve to be added afterwards. Possibly the earliest such garment was the Danish *natroje* (*fig 5.2*). The front and back yokes were knitted with elastic patterns, such as cables and sections with symbolic stitches.

Wool was used for these garments because it possesses particularly useful qualities:

1. It can absorb up to 30 per cent of its weight in water.

2. When wet it generates a small amount of heat, which can offset any feeling of clamminess.

3. It is highly elastic. The fibre can be stretched to more than 50 per cent of its own length.

4. It is soil resistant.

5. It has water repellant properties. (These can be encouraged by leaving the natural oils in the fibres.)

6. It has insulating properties. It can keep the heat in or out.

7. It can be 'felted' by applying heat, moisture, and pressure or agitation.

It was common practice for garments to be knitted on four needles. In fact there is a lovely photograph in the Nordiska Museum, Stockholm, of a man and a woman from Hallannd, Sweden, sitting and knitting the same garment simultaneously, one on either side! I hope one of them wasn't too much faster at knitting than the other. Can you imagine the arguments? Traditional garments were not sewn together. The body was knitted in one piece and slits left at the armholes. The stitches were then picked up at the armhole on several needles and knitted in a tube down to the cuffs.

Early folk garments were knitted in one colour, using textured patterns to add visual interest. These patterns, commonly known as damask patterns, used combinations of plain and purl stitches, and were very popular in Denmark. Later, raised stitches, such as cables, were added. Motifs were very important. The motifs on the garments knitted for fishermen in coastal settlements were often related to the sea. Motifs were usually only knitted into the tops of the garments as they used such a lot of yarn. Cables were particularly uneconomical.

Motifs were symbolic representations of things important in a fisherman's life (*figs 5.3, 5.4, 5.5, 5.6*):

ladders (rigging of a boat); cables (coils of rope); diamonds (fishnet mesh, or uneven coloured brickwork); anchors and flags; herringbone (harvest from the sea); and purl ridges (waves, or 'rig and fur' (ridge and furrow)). There were also important Christian symbols, such as: tree (ladder of life, leading towards heaven); marriage lines; trellis (man's bond with God); 'Trinity stitch'; and 'God's Eye'.

A newly affianced girl would knit her prospective husband a sweater, often including those motifs special to their village, and would work his initials on the garment either in the centre or on the hem. These motifs proved very important when it came to identifying drowned bodies. In Brittany the colours and widths of the stripes could pinpoint exactly where the victim came from.

Fishermen in the Netherlands often had two jerseys. One was worn during the week on the boats and was quite thick. The other, thinner garment was worn on Sundays. The one worn for work could be made at least twice the correct size and knitted with heavy yarn. It was then 'felted' until the size was reduced by half, which resulted in a heavy, waterproof, windproof garment. An elastic type 'lace' was used as a neckband.

Machine knitted garments were also worn by fishermen. In Volendam, authentic hand-knitted traditional patterns were called 'sweaters', while garments knitted by machine to a fashion pattern were called 'frocks'.

On stranded, multicoloured garments the shapes followed the early 'gansey' shape, which was looser (*fig 5.7*). It was really based on a modified blouse shape with a split welt hem, an equivalent of a woven smock worn by farmers. Jerseys and Guernseys were really identical in shape – essentially square and reminiscent of the short smocks worn by country or farm workers. They were cast on in double yarn for added strength at the edges, which took the hardest wear. Gussets at the underarm and side neck gave the garment shape and fit. The neck was knitted in the round on several needles after the garment was completed, and a stand-up collar, 5cm high, was made. In Scotland collars were fastened by buttons to keep out the cold wind. Knitters often worked the wearer's initials in the garment above the welt. Decorative ribbing, side vents, gussets at the neck and underarm, and set-in sleeves within cut armholes, were common features of the style.

The introduction of colour stranding technically created a double fabric thickness which produced a warmer garment with designs in contrasting colours. Colour stranding is using only *two* colours in a row in

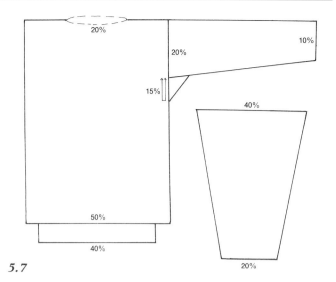

5.7

a regular repeating pattern (as opposed to 'picture knitting'). In this field, Fair Isle patterns are unique in their use of colour within the design. They use only two colours in any one row, but the background colour and the contrast colour shift within the motifs. The origins of Fair Isle patterns lie in the 1850s, when local fishermen returned from the Baltic with beautifully patterned shawls which were then adapted to knitting.

The Nordic *Luskofte* or *Lice jacket* originated in the Setesdal Valley in Norway in the 1840s. The name derived from the elaborate two-colour stitch patterns knitted into the jacket. The body of the garment consisted of a small fine pattern, while the elaborate heavy patterns were confined to the shoulder or yoke area where they could be admired. The cuff and neck openings were made of felted black woven fabric which was heavily embroidered and sewn on to the knitting. Modern jumpers are made in the round and then cut and sewn. Colourful bought woven braid is then sewn around the openings.

Knitting arrived in Sweden with Magna Brita Crassus, the wife of a newly appointed governor in the mid-seventeenth century. Coloured knitting became popular in the mid-1800s. The *Ullared Jersey* is traditionally tightly knitted in small diagonal patterns in red and black. It is worn by loggers and is warm and windproof. The centre panel of the garment often shows the initials of the wearer and the date it was made.

In the nineteenth century the men of the Halsingland area wore a *Delsbo jacket*, which was knitted in red and green on a black background. This jacket is related in shape to the Danish blouse, with half a gusset and a square neck faced in woven fabric. The Scandinavians

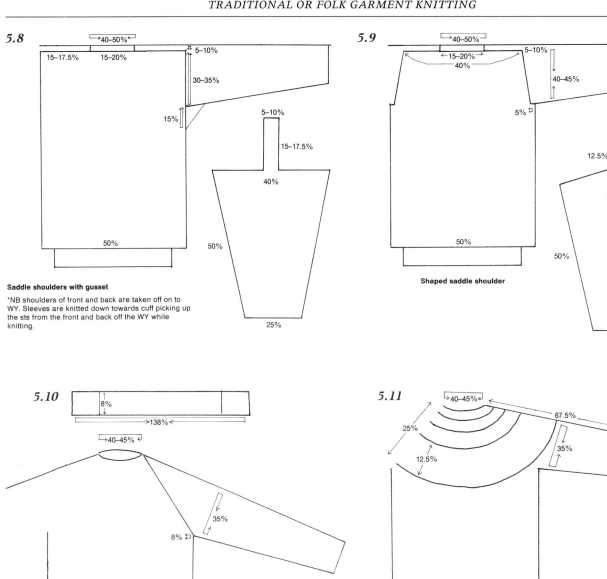

5.8

Saddle shoulders with gusset

*NB shoulders of front and back are taken off on to WY. Sleeves are knitted down towards cuff picking up the sts from the front and back off the WY while knitting.

5.9

Shaped saddle shoulder

5.10

The raglan

Originally designed to be knitted in the round

5.11

Yoke jumper

Total circumference at beginning of yoke includes front, back and two sleeves. 138%.

were not purists about combining knitting with woven fabric, and in some regions garments were made with a woven body and knitted sleeves!

As folk knitting evolved, shapes became more sophisticated and more attention was paid to fit. Greater emphasis was given to garment shaping. Dropped shoulders gave way to a more fitted sleeve and gussets were no longer needed. In Britain the *saddle shoulder*, also called a shoulder strap, developed (*fig 5.8*). This style is commonly found in Scottish

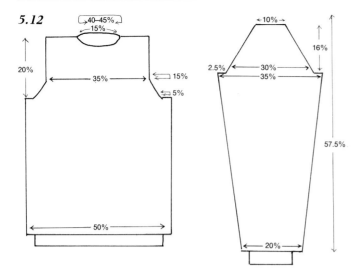

5.12

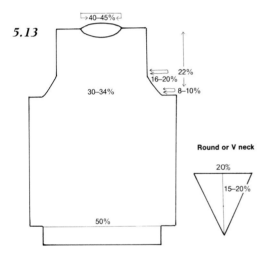

5.13

Round or V neck

and tulips predominate. Garments are often box-like, with little or no shaping, and very loose. Deep armholes are finished in a wide rib band, mitred at square corners. The neck is often in a straight boat style or has a wide crew neck line (*figs 5.12, 5.13*).

Pattern for a strap-shoulder garment using the percentage system

This garment is first drawn out on a design doll, and then transferred to a diagrammatic pattern. The use of the design doll helps in placing the stitch patterns on the garment (*figs 5.14, 5.16*). The patterns used are on the following sheet. You will see that on the large pattern sheet there are a number of patterns. Their co-ordinates are shown in Table 2 (the numbers are listed in the order– bottom, top, left, right) (*fig 5.15*).

The individual patterns which follow show the colour changing in the column on the left. The colour changing refers only to the yarn in Feeder B (the contrast colour). The yarn used is a 4-ply acrylic. The garment is knitted on tension 7.

60 rows = 18cm (1cm = 3.3 rws)
40 stitches = 12.6cm (1cm = 3.2 sts)

ganseys. Straight saddle shoulders could be modified further to reduce boxiness and create ease without excess fabric (*fig 5.9*). The *raglan* shoulder is a more recent development to increase ease without increasing boxiness in shaping (*fig 5.10*), from which the *yoke* jumper developed. The full yoke (*fig 5.11*) is one of the youngest shapes. It was originally developed by the Bohus knitting co-operative in Sweden, organized in 1939 by Emma Jacobson, which unfortunately flourished for only a short time. They excelled in making multicoloured seamless round-yoked sweaters. The first was credited to Ann-Lisa Mannheimer Lunn early in the 1940s.

In American colour-stranded knitting, stylized figures are used in bands of colours. These motifs are often copied from other folk art items. Hearts, birds

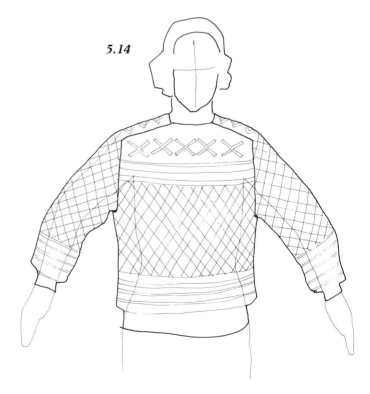

5.14

5.15

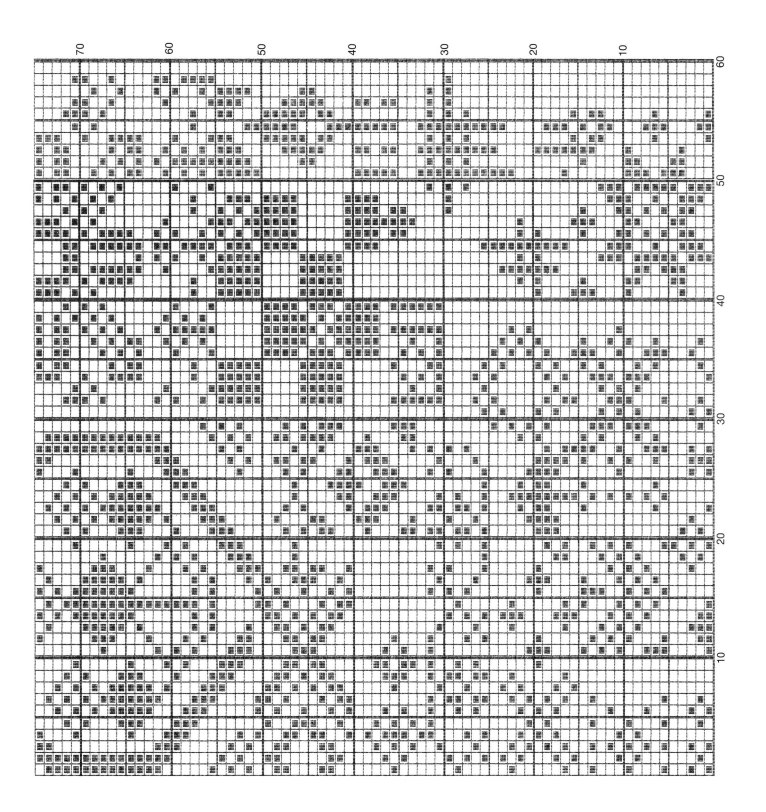

5.16

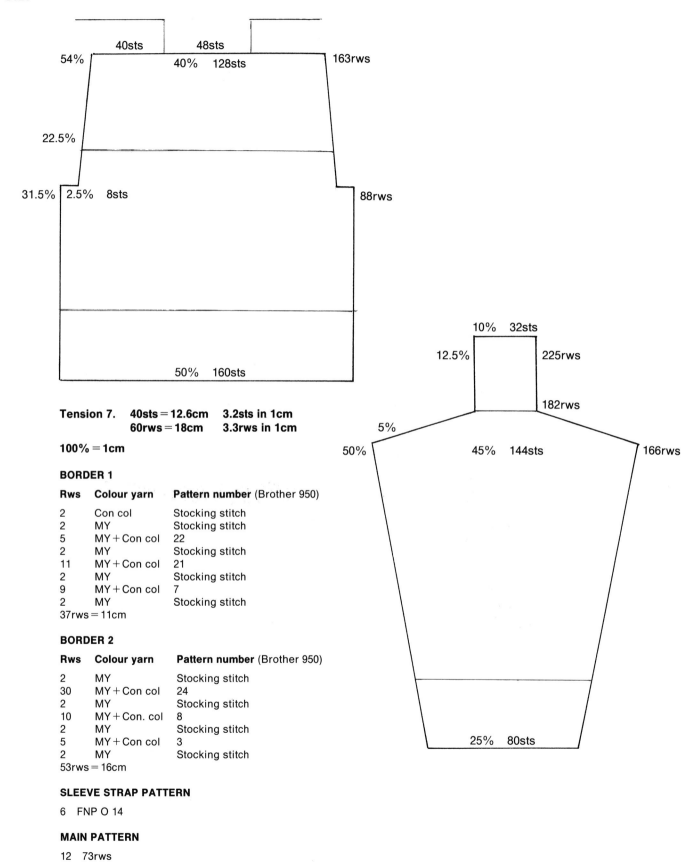

Tension 7. **40sts = 12.6cm** **3.2sts in 1cm**
60rws = 18cm **3.3rws in 1cm**

100% = 1cm

BORDER 1

Rws	Colour yarn	Pattern number (Brother 950)
2	Con col	Stocking stitch
2	MY	Stocking stitch
5	MY + Con col	22
2	MY	Stocking stitch
11	MY + Con col	21
2	MY	Stocking stitch
9	MY + Con col	7
2	MY	Stocking stitch

37rws = 11cm

BORDER 2

Rws	Colour yarn	Pattern number (Brother 950)
2	MY	Stocking stitch
30	MY + Con col	24
2	MY	Stocking stitch
10	MY + Con. col	8
2	MY	Stocking stitch
5	MY + Con col	3
2	MY	Stocking stitch

53rws = 16cm

SLEEVE STRAP PATTERN

6   FNP O 14

MAIN PATTERN

12   73rws

TABLE 2: Co-ordinates for isolating patterns on fig 5.15

1,3,1,8	1,3,11,16	1,5,18,23	1,3,25,32
1,3,34,37	1,16,41,56	6,15,1,7	6,15,11,20
6,16,23,38	16,24,1,18	17,23,19,28	17,27,29,38
17,33,41,59	26,32,1,28	31,36,31,40	33,39,1,6
34,38,8,12	34,44,21,30	38,55,32,49	36,55,51,58
41,51,1,18	45,49,19,30	52,97,1,30	56,85,32,59
86,96,31,42	86,99,43,56	98,115,1,15	98,130,16,37
100,110,53,60	111,144,39,60	33,37,46,49	116,127,1,12

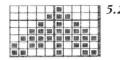

5.21

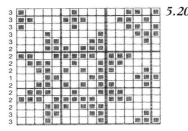

5.20

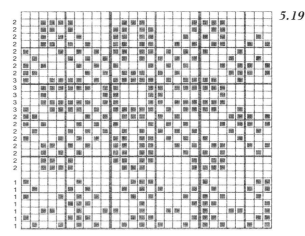

5.19

On the sample knit for the edge (pulled taut), 20 sts = 8.5cm (1cm = 2.4 sts).

Patterns for Border 1:
   45,49,19,30
   41,51,1,18
   6,15,1,7

There are two plain rows in MY in between each pattern (*fig 5.17*), thus making 37 rows in all and measuring 11cm.

Pattern for the body of the garment: 17,27,29,38 (*fig 5.18*). After calculating the number of rows for the top and bottom border there are 110 rows left, so these are knitted in the main pattern.

Patterns for Border 2 (fig 5.19):
   56,85,32,59
   6,15,11,20
   1,5,18,23

There are two plain rows in MY in between each pattern, thus making 53 rows in all and measuring 16cm.

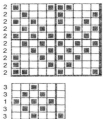

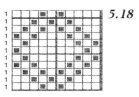

5.18

Pattern for the sleeve strap: 1,16,41,56 (*fig 5.20*). The FNP (first needle position) is Yellow 14. This means that there is room for two repeats of the pattern, side by side, rather than having one pattern in the middle with half a repeat at either side.

Pattern for the hem: 36,55,51,58 (*fig 5.21*). The garment is knitted beginning and ending with WY and the edges and hems are added afterwards. The stitches are picked up from the WY, decreasing evenly across the row.

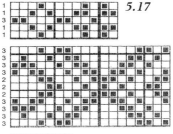

5.17

Tension 6. Pick up the required stitches. Knit as follows:

1 row Col.3
(Push alternate needles to HP and set carriage to HP)

2 rows Col.2 (Cancel carriage setting to HP)
1 row Col.3
(Pick up loops of 1st row in Col.3. Set carriage to select
    nds for pattern knitting)
1 row MY
7 rows Fair Isle Pattern MY in Feeder A, and Col. 2 in
    Feeder B
(Cancel pattern knitting)
1 row MY
1 row Col.3
(Push alternate needles to HP and set carriage to HP)
2 rows Col.2 (Cancel carriage setting to HP)
1 row Col.3
(Pick up loops of last row in Col.3)
9 rows MY
Pick up the first row of the hem. Knit 1 row and cast
    off

The sleeve cuff is reduced from 80 stitches to 48
stitches.
The neckband is reduced from 160 stitches to 128
stitches.
The hem is reduced from 160 stitches to 128 stitches.
On the hem the pattern is knitted twice, but the second
time the pattern is turned upside-down. The back of
the hem requires 15 rows. The rest of the relevant
information is written on the diagram.

Now that you have seen how a pattern is created, you
can make one for yourself by using your own
measurements.

Yoke jumper using the percentage system

Although drafting this jumper may seem a little
complicated, it is, in fact, very easy. It had to be done
by women with no access to calculators, large sheets of
paper or other mod cons. It only seems complicated
when it is translated into diagrams.

STEPS IN DRAFTING

The key measurement is the chest circumference plus
ease, which equals 100 per cent.

1.   Draft the body length (75%) and width (50%).
Draft the neck (15%) (*fig. 5.22*).

2.   Draft the yoke depth (25%). Draft the yoke width

less 4% at each side for the underarm shaping (*fig
5.23*).

3.   *The sleeve:* from the SNP draw a line equal to
67.5% of the key measurement (*fig 5.24*). This is the
shoulder/top of the sleeve line. The distance between
this line and the point 4% in from the underarm point
is 13.5%. The measurement of the whole width of the
sleeve is 35%. The distance between the UP on the
sleeve and the wrist is 42.5%. The width of the cuff is
20%.

4.   These two diagrams give you the shaping for the
bottom of the body (front and back) and the sleeves up
to the base of the yoke (*fig 5.25*).

5.   The yoke decreases can be divided into three
sections. At each point the stitches are reduced evenly
across the row. The first shaping occurs after 50% of
the yoke has been knitted. (Alternatively, the yoke can
be divided into more sections (*fig 5.26*) which makes
each decrease less drastic.)

(*a*) If you are dividing the yoke into three sections,
decrease each section as illustrated (*fig 5.27*). Calculate
the decreasings using either the percentage system or
the easier mathematical system.

(*b*) You can decrease the yoke in five sections (*fig 5.28*),
which will result in a more gradual shaping. The
decreasing still commences after half the yoke has been
knitted, but continues in smaller steps.

6.   *Construction:* The best way to knit a yoke jumper
is to begin on WY and knit the four yoke sections.
Then turn these upside-down and begin the body and
sleeve sections, working towards the hem edge or the
cuff (*fig 5.29*).
    Because the distance between the top of the back
neck and the hem is greater than the distance between
the front neck and the hem, the garment will fit better
if you make the back half longer. You cannot alter the
depth of the yoke, so you must introduce some short-
row shaping at the back and at the back of each sleeve.
You can do this on both the three-step or five-step
yoke.

Pattern repeats on yokes

The following shows how to calculate the programming
for an electronic machine when knitting a percentage-

Steps in drafting a yoke jumper using the % system

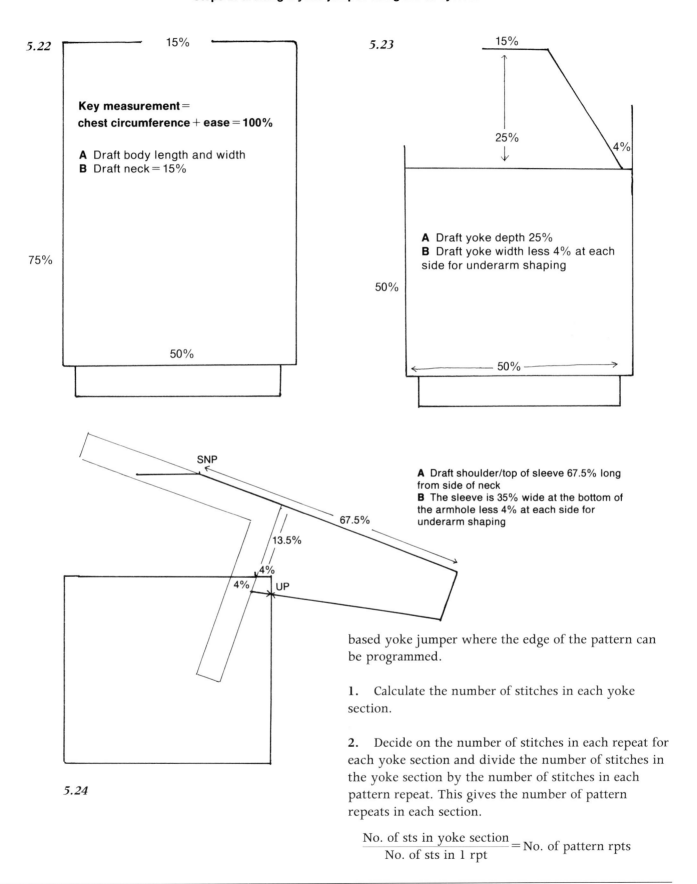

5.22

15%

**Key measurement =
chest circumference + ease = 100%**

A Draft body length and width
B Draft neck = 15%

75%

50%

5.23

15%

25%

4%

50%

A Draft yoke depth 25%
B Draft yoke width less 4% at each
side for underarm shaping

50%

SNP

67.5%

13.5%

4%

4%

UP

A Draft shoulder/top of sleeve 67.5% long
from side of neck
B The sleeve is 35% wide at the bottom of
the armhole less 4% at each side for
underarm shaping

5.24

based yoke jumper where the edge of the pattern can
be programmed.

1. Calculate the number of stitches in each yoke
section.

2. Decide on the number of stitches in each repeat for
each yoke section and divide the number of stitches in
the yoke section by the number of stitches in each
pattern repeat. This gives the number of pattern
repeats in each section.

$$\frac{\text{No. of sts in yoke section}}{\text{No. of sts in 1 rpt}} = \text{No. of pattern rpts}$$

The body and sleeve

5.25

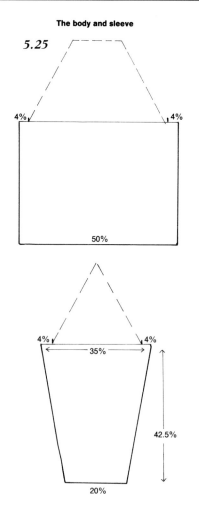

5.26

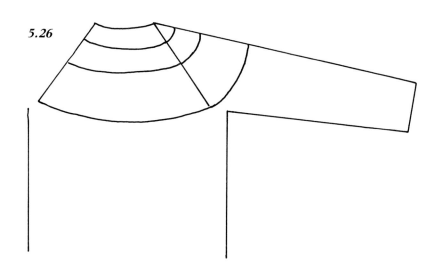

A The yoke decreases can be divided into 3 sections
B The knitting is decreased evenly across the row each time
C The first shaping occurs after 50% of the yoke has been knitted

5.27 **Yoke jumper**

Yoke detail divided into 3 sections

Calculate by percentage

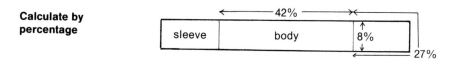

Percentage as decreasing in the row

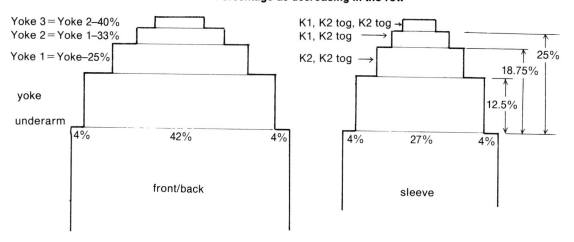

Yoke 3 = Yoke 2–40%
Yoke 2 = Yoke 1–33%
Yoke 1 = Yoke–25%

yoke
underarm

front/back

K1, K2 tog, K2 tog →
K1, K2 tog →
K2, K2 tog →

sleeve

5.28   **Yoke divided into 5 sections**

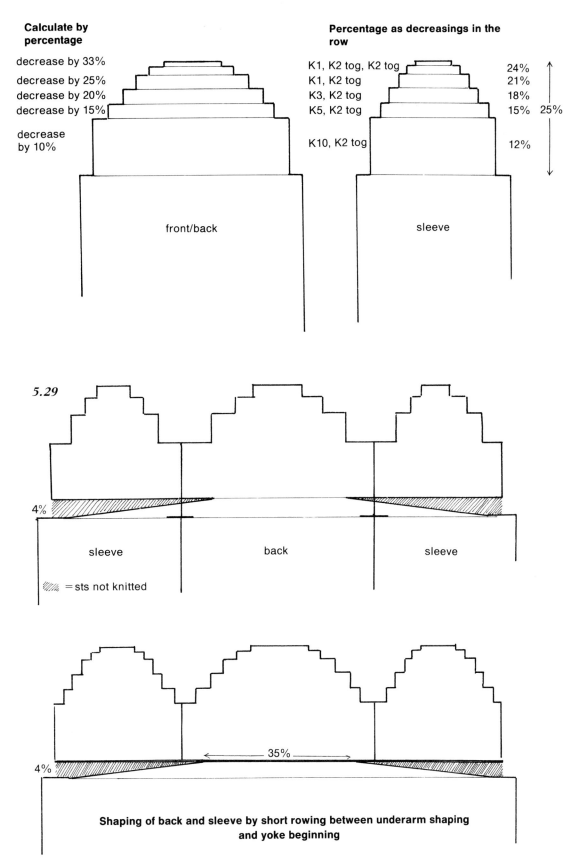

Calculate by percentage

decrease by 33%

decrease by 25%

decrease by 20%

decrease by 15%

decrease by 10%

front/back

Percentage as decreasings in the row

K1, K2 tog, K2 tog   24%

K1, K2 tog   21%

K3, K2 tog   18%

K5, K2 tog   15%   25%

K10, K2 tog   12%

sleeve

5.29

4%

sleeve   back   sleeve

////// = sts not knitted

4%   ←————— 35% —————→

Shaping of back and sleeve by short rowing between underarm shaping and yoke beginning

3. The number of pattern repeats is either odd or even.

(*a*) *For even repeats:* start with the FNP at one edge of one garment section (e.g. the back). Divide the number of stitches in this section by the number of stitches in the repeat. This equals the number of pattern repeats in the back section, *plus* the number of stitches left over from the last repeat. These stitches must be subtracted from the next garment section before you can start deciding how many repeats you will have in that section.

$$\frac{\text{No. of sts in back}}{\text{No. of sts in rpt}} = \text{No. of rpts} + \text{no. of sts 'over'}$$

e.g. $\frac{68}{12} = 5(+r)$ $5 \times 12 = 60$ $r = 8$

For the adjacent garment section (i.e. sleeve) the first eight stitches must complete the end of the pattern from the back section. So the FNP of the pattern must be the ninth stitch in from the edge of the knitting. You will find that the front will have the FNP at the edge of the knitting the same way as the back.

(*b*) *For odd repeats:* to match up an odd number of repeats on several garment pieces of knitting, e.g. a round yoke, determine A (number of stitches in the yoke section) and B (number of stitches in each pattern repeat).

Example:

1. Start at the LH edge of the one garment section (e.g. back).

FNP is the same as the LH edge needle
There are 55 sts in the back in WP Y28–G27
FNP is Y28
There are 55 sts and each repeat is 12 sts
$\frac{55}{12} = 4$ r.7 $12 - 7 = 5$

You will have four whole repeats plus 7 sts from the last pattern repeat, leaving 5 sts from that repeat to be carried over to the next garment section (the sleeve).

2. there are 35 sts in the sleeve.
The first 5 nds at the left-hand edge are needed to complete the pattern left over from the back.

Nds in WP are Y18–G17
FNP (leaving 5 sts at LH edge) is Y13

You have $13 + 17 = 30$ nds remaining to knit your
    pattern rpts
$\frac{30}{12} = 2$ r.6 $12 - 6 = 6$

You will have two whole repeats of the pattern (after 5 nds at the LH edge have completed the pattern rpt from the previous garment section) *plus* 6 sts, leaving 6 sts from the repeat at the RH edge to be carried over to the next garment section (the front).

3. The next garment section has 55 sts.
The first 6 nds at the LH edge are needed to complete the pattern repeat 'left over' from the previous section

Nds in WP are Y28–G27
FNP (6 in from LH edge) Y22
You have $22 + 27 = 49$ nds remaining to knit your
    pattern rpts
$\frac{49}{12} = 4$ r.1 $12 - 1 = 11$

You will have four whole rpts plus 1 st from the last pattern repeat, leaving 11 sts from that rpt to be carried over to the (last) garment section.

4. The last sleeve, which uses 35 sts.
The first 11 nds at the LH edge are required to complete the pattern left over from the front

Nds in WP are Y18–G17
FNP (11 in from LH edge) Y7
$7 + 17 = 24$ nds remaining to knit your pattern rpts
$\frac{24}{12} = 2$

Two yoke patterns using the percentage system

The first step is always to draw out the design doll and then 'dress' it. This pattern was based on a bust measurement of 94cm ($37\frac{1}{2}$in) plus 16% ease – a key measurement of 112cm ($44\frac{1}{2}$in). This would make a very roomy jumper (*fig 5.30*)!

1. The yoke is divided into 5 sections and the measurement of each section is calculated from the key measurement (*fig 5.31*).

A yoke garment made on the knitting machine using the percentage system

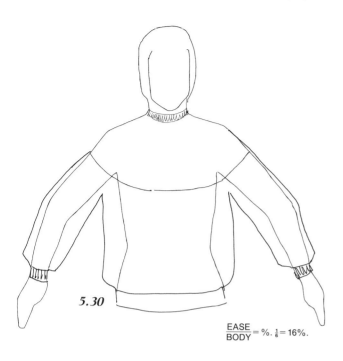

5.30

$$\frac{EASE}{BODY} = \%. \frac{1}{6} = 16\%.$$

94cm bust + 16% = 112cm = key measurement

2. The body and sleeves of the garment are then drafted upside-down with the short row shaping included (*fig 5.32*).

3. Once the measurements are obtained, the tension swatch is knitted:

40 sts = 11.8cm (3.4 sts in 1cm)
60 rws = 18.2cm (3.3 rws in 1cm)

Each section is allocated the appropriate number of stitches and rows (*fig 5.33*). The stitch patterns for each section must be the right number of rows, and the stitches must divide evenly into the number of stitches required for that section. It is a complicated business, and sometimes the number of stitches in any one section may have to be altered slightly in order to make the pattern repeat even. The patterns used, shown in Table 3, are *parts* of patterns built into the Brother KH 950i (*fig 5.34*).

Once you have finished knitting the yoke sections you can replace the stitches from the bottom of each section and knit the rest of the garment (*fig 5.35*):

Yoke jumper body
Left Sleeve:
Replace 100 sts from the bottom of the sleeve yoke on to 96 needles decreasing evenly across the row. COL. RC000
Push 16 needles on right to HP K1 rw, (wrap yarn) K1 rw. Repeat from * to * six times. RC12
RC000
Increase 14 sts at the beginning of the next 2 rws.

5.31 **Yoke measurement diagrams**

112cm = key measurement = chest + ease

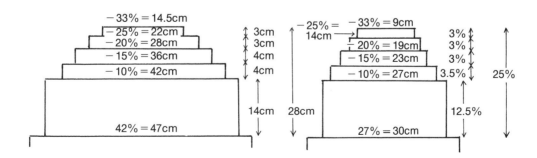

e.g. on a calculator
47cm × 10% = 4.7cm
47cm − 4.7cm = 42.3cm(42cm)
42.3cm × 15% = 6.345cm
42.3cm − 6.345cm = 35.955cm (36cm)

TABLE 3

Yoke sections   *O = Orange   G = Green*

		Patt/No. & co-ordinates	Sleeve	Back	Sleeve	Front
I.	520sts/42rws Patt 26sts/34rws	#75 1,34,4,29	100sts	160sts	100sts	160sts
	or Patt 26sts/38rws (Start CF11 Knit to R4) 20 repeats of the pattern	#81 1,44,1,26	FNP = G1			
II.	474sts/14rws Patt 6sts/12rws 79 repeats of the pattern	#68 9,20,5,10	90sts 45/45 FNP = O.45	147sts 74/73 O.74	90sts 45/45 O.42	147sts 73/74 O.70
III.	400 sts/14rws Patt 20sts/14rws 20 repeats of the pattern	#71 1,14,1,20	76sts FNP = G1	124sts	76sts	
IV.	324sts/10rws Patt 9sts/8rws 36 repeats of the pattern	#44 1,8,1,9	62sts FNP = G1	100sts	62sts	
V.	210sts/10rws Patt 14sts/8rws 15 repeats of the pattern	#54 21,28,5,18	40sts 20/20 FNP = O.8	65sts 33/32 O.33	40sts 20/20 O.1	65sts 33/32 O.12

Number of sts to lose:

Back:	I–II	II–III	III–IV	IV–V	V–VI (neckband)
	160–147	147–124	124–100	100–65	65–38
	−13	−23	−24	−35	−27

Sleeve:	I–II	II–III	III–IV	IV–V	V–VI (neckband)
	100–90	90–76	76–62	62–40	40–24
	−10	−14	−14	−22	−16
	K10,K2tog	K5,K2tog	K3,K2tog	K1,K2tog	K1,K2tog K2tog

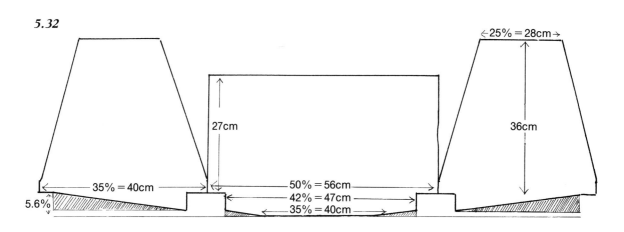

5.32

25% = 28cm

27cm

36cm

35% = 40cm

5.6%

50% = 56cm

42% = 47cm

35% = 40cm

Chest + 16% ease = key measurement = 112cm
Side neck to wrist = 64cm Sleeve = 36cm
CB to 'hem' = 52cm Body = 27cm Dart = 3.5cm

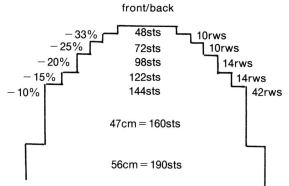

front/back

Calculating the yoke using stitches as a basis

1. 160 × 10% = 16
    160 − 16 = 144sts
2. 144 × 15% = 21.6
    144 − 21.6 = 122.4
3. 122 × 20% = 24.4
    122 − 24.4 = 97.6 etc.

Pattern programs for the Brother electronic knitting machine

Pattern number		Co-ordinates
I	71	14,51,1,40
II	68	21,32,1,10
III	71	1,14,1,40
IV	24	3,12,1,12
V	67	1,10,1,8

Fair Isle tension swatch   Tension 6

40sts = 11.8cm   3.4sts in 1cm
60rws = 18.2cm   3.3rws in 1cm
100% = 380sts

Calculating the yoke using a regular progression of decreasings as a basis

Total number of sts in yoke

Front/back/sleeves = total
76 + 48 = 124
130 + 80 = 210
200 + 124 = 324
248 + 152 = 400
294 + 180 = 474
320 + 200 = 520

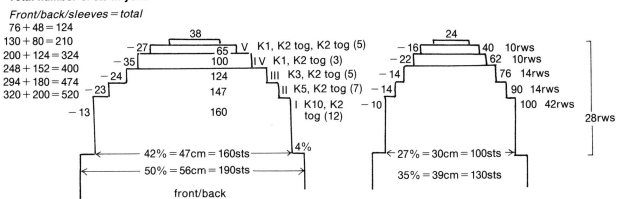

Stitch pattern repeat possibilities for each section

	Total number of sts in yoke		*Number of rows*
I	520	2,4,5,8,13,26	42
II	474	6,79	14
III	400	4,5,10,20,40	14
IV	324	3,4,9,12,36	10
V	210	2,3,6,7,14,15,30,35	10

5.33

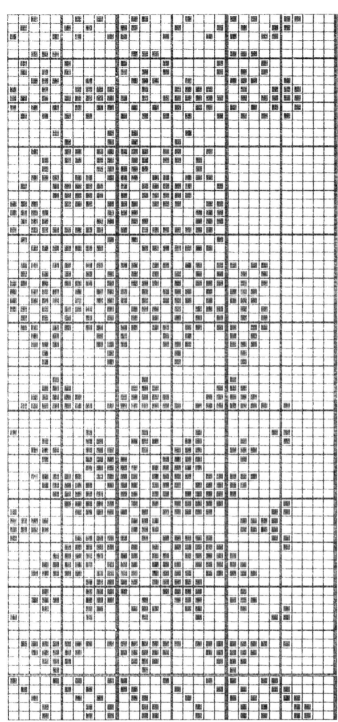

5.34

Decrease 1 st at each end of the next and every following 7th rw 17 times (90 sts). Knit to RC122 in MY

RC000

Knit:

2 rws Con Col

2 rws MY

8 rws Fair Isle pattern (#54,21,28,5,18. 14 sts, 8 rws)

2 rws MY

2 rws Con Col

2 rws MY RC 18

Remove the work on to WY

Cuff:

RC000

Replace the sts on to the needles decreasing even across the rw putting 2 sts on every needle.

Transfer the sts for a 1 × 1 rib. Tension 1/1 knit 24 rws.

Cast-off.

Repeat reversing the shapings for the *Right Sleeve*.

Back:

Replace 160 sts from the bottom of the back yoke onto 148 needles decreasing evenly across the row, COR.

RC000

Push needles 45–74 on L to HP. K1 rw COL (wrap yarn)

Push needles 45–74 on R to HP. K1 rw COR (wrap yarn)

Push needles 45–60 on L to UWP. K1 rw COL (wrap yarn)

Push needles 45–60 on R to UWP. K1 rw COR (wrap yarn)

Push needles 61–70 on L to UWP. K1 rw COL (wrap yarn)

Push needles 61–70 on R to UWP. K1 rw COR (wrap yarn)

Push all remaining needles on L to UWP. K1 rw COL

Push all remaining needles on R to UWP. K1 rw COR.

RC18

* RC000

Increase 14 sts at the beginning of the next 2 rws

Knit 90 rws MY

Knit:

2 rws Con Col

2 rws MY

8 rws Fair Isle pattern # 54 (21,28,5,18. 14 sts, 8 rws)

2 rws MY

2 rws Con Col

2 rws MY RC18

Remove the work on to WY

Band:

Replace the sts on to the needles decreasing evenly across the rw by placing 2 sts on every alternative needle.

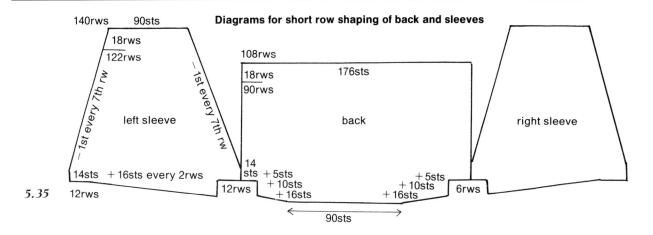

Diagrams for short row shaping of back and sleeves

5.35

Transfer the sts for a 1 × 1 rib. Tension 1/1 knit 24 rws.
Cast-off.*
For the *Front*: Pick-up 160 sts from the bottom of the
front yoke on to 148 needles decreasing evenly across
the rw COR.
Knit as for back from * to *.
Neckband:
Replace all sts from the yoke pieces on to needles purl
side facing you. Transfer for a 1 × 1 rib.
Knit 18 rws tension 1/1
Knit 1 rw on Main Bed only
Knit 18 rws tension 1/1.
Remove the work onto WY and catch-stitch the last
row of MY sts from the band onto the inside of the
garment.
Three yoke seams can be joined before commencing the
neckband.

The next garment, a red, white and blue yoke
jumper with a 5-section yoke, was also based on the
percentage system. However, the amount of ease was
reduced, so that the key measurement was only 100cm
(40in). The pattern was drawn out on the Mylar sheet,
and the changes in contrast colour are indicated in the
column on the left-hand side. Contrast colour 2 is
indicated by an x (*fig 5.36*). See over for figs. 5.37 and
5.38.

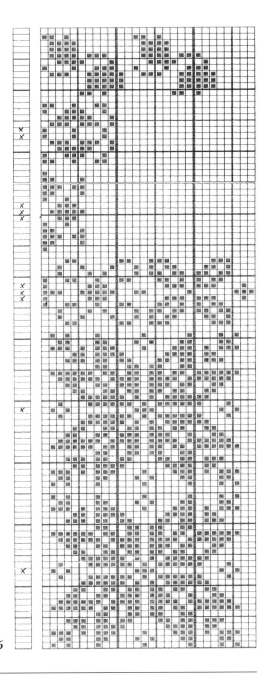

5.36

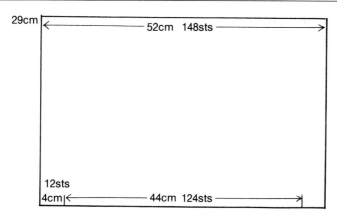

To knit body: pick-up sts from bottom of yoke sections and knit downwards.

FRONT
Decrease evenly across the row front and back 132sts to 124nds. Lose 8sts.
Sleeves: pick-up sts from bottom of yoke section and knit downwards.
Decrease evenly across the row 84sts to 76nds. Lose 8sts.

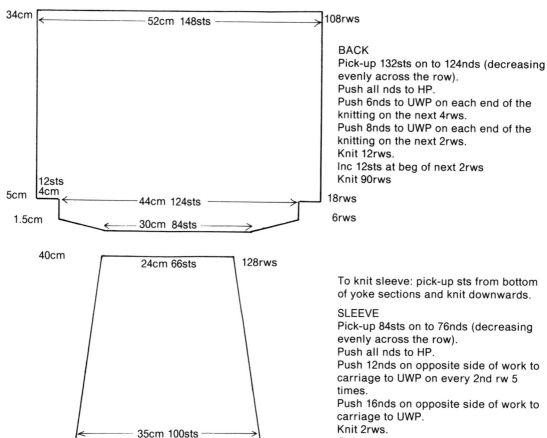

BACK
Pick-up 132sts on to 124nds (decreasing evenly across the row).
Push all nds to HP.
Push 6nds to UWP on each end of the knitting on the next 4rws.
Push 8nds to UWP on each end of the knitting on the next 2rws.
Knit 12rws.
Inc 12sts at beg of next 2rws
Knit 90rws

To knit sleeve: pick-up sts from bottom of yoke sections and knit downwards.

SLEEVE
Pick-up 84sts on to 76nds (decreasing evenly across the row).
Push all nds to HP.
Push 12nds on opposite side of work to carriage to UWP on every 2nd rw 5 times.
Push 16nds on opposite side of work to carriage to UWP.
Knit 2rws.
Cast-on 12sts at beg of next 2 rws.
Dec 1st each end of next and every 6rws 5 x's and every 7rws 12 x's.
Knit to RC 128.

5.37

Red, white and blue yoke jumper (with a 5-section yoke)

4 ply yarn: red 100g, white 245g, blue 15g

Tension 7	Fair Isle	Stocking stitch
40sts	13cm	14.2cm
60rws	15.4cm	16cm
100% = 100cm (chest + ease) in Fair Isle this is 310 sts.		

TABLE 3A

| | | Patt/No. co-ordinates | Stitches and FNP | | | |
			Back	Sleeve	Front	Sleeve
I.	432sts	1,51,1,27	132	84	132	84
	51rws		66/66	42/42	66/66	42/42
	16rpts of the pattern		O.66	O.39	O.66	O.39
II.	392sts	53,63,1,28	119	77	119	77
	28sts		60/59	39/38	60/59	39/38
	11rws		O.60	O.18	O.60	O.18
	14rpts of the pattern					
III.	336sts	65,77,1,6	102	66	102	66
	6sts		51/51	33/33	51/51	33/33
	13rws		O.51	O.33	O.51	O.33
	56rpts of the pattern					
IV.	270sts	79,88,1,10	82	53	82	53
	10sts		41/41	27/26	41/41	27/26
	10rws		O.41	O.19	O.36	O.24
	27rpts of the pattern					
V.	180sts	90,99,1,24	55	35	55	35
	12sts		28/27	18/17	28/27	18/17
	10rws		O.28	O.13	O.22	O.7
	15rpts of the pattern					

Number of sts to lose:

Back:	I–II	II–III	III–IV	IV–V	V–VI (neckband)
	132–119	119–102	102–82	82–55	55–33
	−13	−17	−20	−27	−22
Sleeve:	I–II	II–III	III–IV	IV–V	V–VI (neckband)
	84–77	77–66	66–53	53–35	35–21
	−7	−11	−13	−18	−14

Neckband

Pick-up the neckband sts from all four sections of the body right side facing you.

Pick-up the 55sts from the front and back sections on to 33 needles reducing evenly across the row.

Pick-up the 35sts from the sleeve sections on to 21 needles reducing evenly across the row.

Knit 1rw on the main bed, tension 7

Transfer the sts for a 1 × 1 rib

Knit 16rws tension 2/2 Red

Knit 1rw tension 3 blue (on ribber bed only)

Knit 1rw tension 2/2 blue

Knit 16rws tension 2/2 red. Remove the work on to WY and catch-stitch down the last row in red on to the inside of the garment.

Hems on body and sleeve

After knitting the body and sleeve upside down from the finished yoke:

Knit 1rw Main bed tension 7 blue

Transfer sts for a 1 × 1 rib

Knit 17rws tension 2/2 red

Knit 2rws tension 2/2 blue

Cast-off or bind off with a needle and yarn.

6

Introduction to pattern drafting

Once you have mastered the basic techniques of the knitting machine and feel that you can knit garments in various colours using a range of different techniques, you may want to branch out a bit. There are two possibilities that you may wish to explore:

1. You may want to knit fairly standard garments of the type that one expects to see knitted, such as jumpers or cardigans. With modern machines, however, it is easy to customize these garments in various ways. You can use the pattern shaping attachment to make your own pattern shape, allowing for figure variations. Therefore, you do not have to leaf through dozens of magazines and books looking for a pattern to knit, then compromise on the type of yarn, shape or stitch pattern. You may need a garment with longer than usual sleeves, or you may prefer a longer body length. You know that you cannot measure your knitting on the machine as you go along, because it is only when you remove the knitting from the machine that it can 'relax' and assume its proper shape. So you must plan the garment shape before you begin knitting, to ensure that it will ultimately turn out to be what you want.

2. We have been used to accepting, over the years, that certain garments are always knitted, and conversely that other garments are *never* knitted! Today, it is possible to break away from the mould. Of course, jumpers are by definition knitted, but now all sorts of fashion garments can be made from fabric which is produced on a knitting machine, as well as that produced on a loom. With increased mechanization in the industrial fabric-producing process, we have come to accept all sorts of 'fashion fabric', such as jerseys, tricot fabrics, laces, etc. In fact,

on the normal domestic knitting machine, it is possible to produce a kind of woven fabric that includes some of the characteristics of the kind produced on a loom.

So now you can produce a whole range of garments which you might never have attempted if you had confined yourself to ordinary knitting, for example coats, suits, dresses, skirts, and trousers. They can be worn in all sorts of circumstances, from the dressiest of evening occasions, to weddings; from sports like jogging, to just sunning yourself on a hot beach. Knitting is no longer confined to one season of the year. Lace knitting in linen yarn produces a garment which is as cool and easy to care for as any other summer wear.

If you have never done any dressmaking or pattern drafting before, making your own garment pattern can be a bit daunting, but it is really very simple if you follow the procedures logically, step by step.

There are certain basic principles you must remember. You must measure the following accurately:

1. The body: to make the basic pattern or *body block*. All pattern variations are added on and adjustments made to this, so it *must* be correct. Remember that you cannot fit and alter your garment after it is made as easily as when dressmaking with woven fabric. You cannot cut your knitting up as easily as you can cloth. (Although you can use a technique called cut and sew, which can be a life-saver in some situations and hide a multitude of evils. It is really better to plan in advance to use this technique rather than to fall back on it in desperation.) You may be able to make some small adjustments by blocking your garment carefully, but, basically, if you make a disastrous mistake the only solution may be to unravel the piece and start again.

2. The *tension swatch:* this includes the fabric for your garment plus all the samples for such things as hems, edges, etc. These are essential to be able to calculate *accurately* how many stitches and rows you will have to knit to make the garment look the way you want it to.

Design decisions

1. *Shape assessment.* Often people will say, 'I know whether something suits me when I try it on.' But as we have already seen, you cannot always do that with knitting. You cannot take a half-knitted sleeve off the machine and hold it up against you to discover if it is long or wide enough. You must often finish the whole garment, put it together and wash it before you know whether it will suit you or not. People often have unrealistic expectations and a completely idealized mental picture of what they look like. They retain, in their mind's eye, a picture of how they think they would *like* to look, which is not always true or even almost true. Some of my students who are in their mid-forties and weigh fourteen stone admitted that they see themselves (albeit wishfully) as sixteen years old and nine stone! So they measure themselves, and if the figures appear uncomplimentary, they may 'adjust' them. They are then horrified when the finished garment fails to suit or, even worse, to fit them.

2. *Colour assessment.* People tend to choose the colours they like rather than those that like them. By this I mean that people often choose a colour from a shelf or draped on a hanger. Once this coloured garment is put on, the shade might prove totally unattractive, making them look pale and washed out. So, before making a final decision, always try out selected shades, using a mirror for accurate assessment.

3. *Fashion influence.* The other insidious factor is fashion. We have all seen how, each season, in order to sell new clothes, colours and shapes are manipulated and altered by the fashion arbiters. Some people follow the trends regardless of suitability, and can look either fantastically good or fantastically freakish; on the other hand there are those who *never* follow fashion and can often look like misfits from another age.

In all of this, of course, the important thing is to learn to assess your own appearance realistically, not as you wish you were. This is not a difficult skill to acquire and, like all skills, it comes with patience and improves with practice. You should not feel that if you do not have a gift naturally you cannot learn it: you can if you really want to.

4. *The practical.* This can seem rather daunting, especially if you have never done anything like this before, but if taken step by step, it is very simple. You may have read about body shapes and body types – big bones, small bones, and so on. But how can you tell what is right for your figure? It is difficult to make value judgements if you are not used to doing so. You may have been to a hairdresser who does your hair up in a high-fashion style so that you can't wait to get home and wash it all out! Her vision of you is not your vision of yourself. Conversely, there is the mousey little girl who is taken in hand by the fashion magazine and her make-up, hairstyle and outfit are totally re-done so that she emerges as a completely convincing *femme fatale*. Why couldn't that happen to us? Because we haven't the courage, the experience or the vision to alter our image of ourselves; perhaps we are afraid of making a mistake and being laughed at. Or perhaps we simply do not think that it is important enough to be bothered or simply do not know where to begin.

In order to design garments, you must be fully aware of the way they will cover the body beneath. You must study and analyse the underlying structure that the garment will be required to cover. You must not only measure every lump and bump carefully, but must see where everything is relative to everything else.

This means you must make a very accurate body block which will be the foundation stone of all your fashion garments and design efforts, regardless of whether the final result is to be a second skin or just an over-large brown paper-bag. It is only when you know the structure underlying your garments that you can add and subtract fashion lines and features to constantly modernize your designing and enable you to make a new, witty and clever fashion statement.

Here is where use of the 'doll' will help determine the dimensions of simple garments based on ethnic and/or historical sources. The doll will help you to decide how wide and how long to make your garments, as you are not restricted by the size of your loom (only by the width of your machine). When you come to design more sophisticated garments, the doll will be of even more use.

First, the doll can help to determine and assess your figure type (*fig 6.2*). Are your shoulders wider or narrower than your hips? Is your body square or curved? Is your waist high or low?

6.1

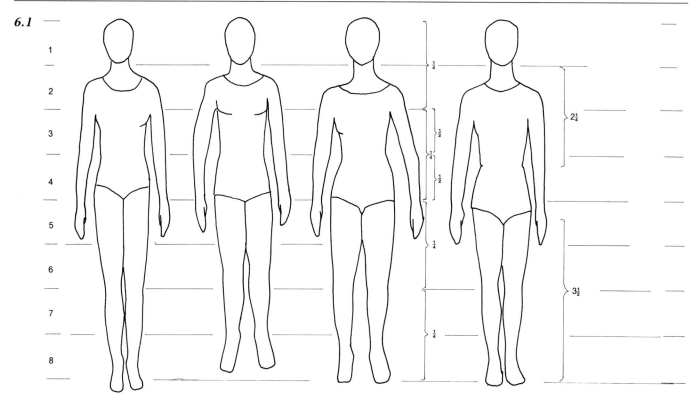

Some examples of 'perfect proportion'

6.2

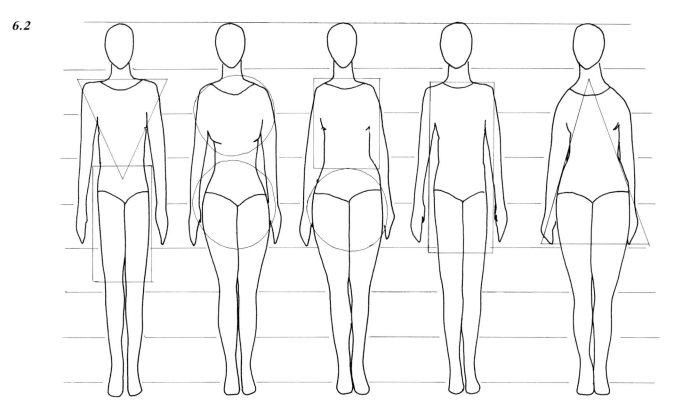

Assess your figure
Are you round, rectangular, pear-shaped, or a combination?

6.3

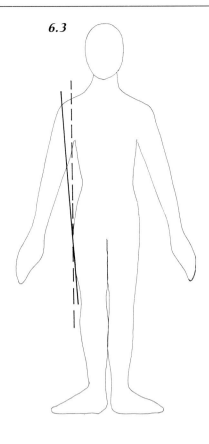

6.4

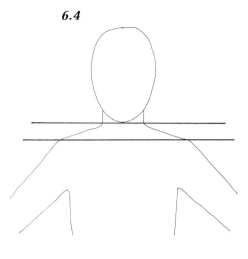

6.5

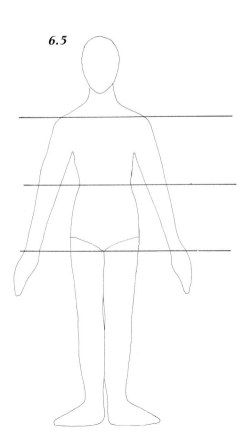

To assess your figure, use your newly-drawn doll, which is really you drawn in one-fifth scale. Draw your doll on squared graph paper.

1. Draw a straight line from your widest point (hips thighs, etc.) to your shoulder point (*fig 6.3*). Is this line parallel to the graph lines? If it deviates from the vertical, does it slope inward to your shoulder or outward from your hips? Does your waist curve in markedly from this straight line? Are your body lines curved or sharp?

This will help to determine your figure type. Now look at your figure proportion.

2. Draw a horizontal line at your neck base and your shoulder point (*fig 6.4*). Calculate the actual measurement difference (the number on the doll divided by two and the decimal point moved one place to the right).

If the difference is:	your shoulders are:
less than 2.5cm	very straight
less than 4cm	straight
about 5cm	slightly tapered
more than 6cm	sloping

3. Draw horizontal lines at your shoulder point, waist and crotch (*fig 6.5*). Is your waistline half-way between your shoulder and your crotch, or are you long-waisted/short-waisted (*fig 6.6*)?

4. Draw horizontal lines at the top of your head, leg break, and floor (*fig 6.7*). Is your leg break half-way between the top of your head and the floor, or are you long-legged/short-legged (*fig 6.8*)?

6.6

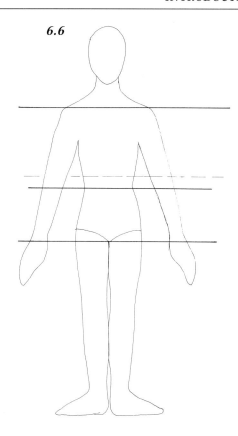

6.7

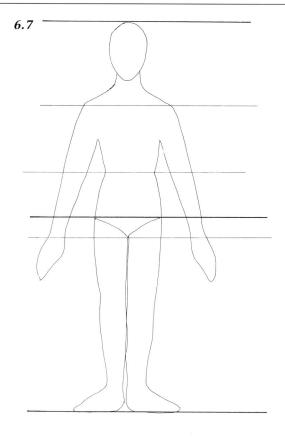

6.8

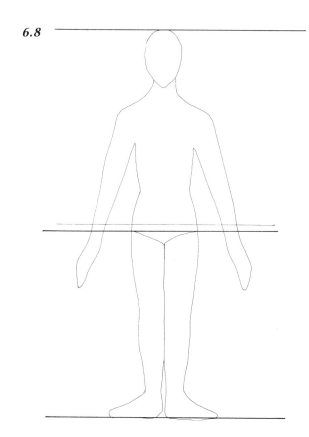

6.9

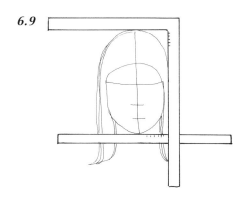

This way of assessing your figure is done easily against a sheet of squared graph paper and will leave you in no doubt exactly how your body fits together. You can get quite a good idea of which features you wish to emphasize and which to minimize!

Another aid to helping you with proportion assessing is:

1. Measure your head with the help of a right-angle rule and a straight rule (*fig 6.9*).

6.10

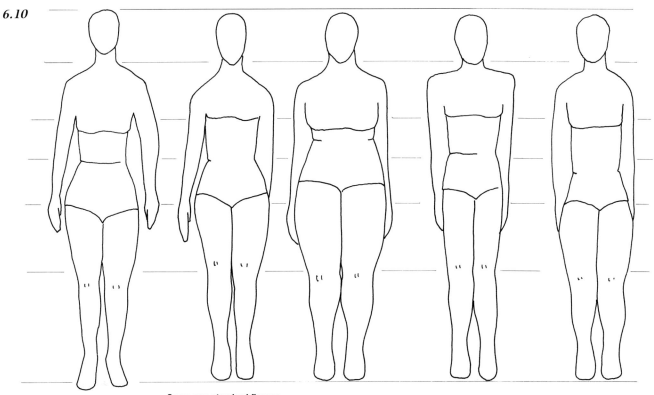

Some non-standard figures
Notice the difference in distance between the shoulders, bust, waist, hip and knees.

6.11

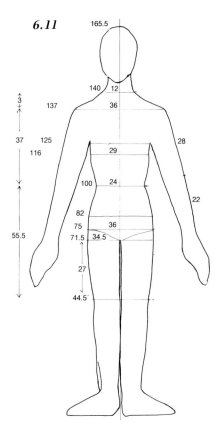

2. Use your 'head height' to help assess your own figure proportion. The figure is normally 7.5–8 heads high (*fig 6.10*).

(*a*) Bust level (chin to bust) = 1 head

(*b*) Waist level (chin to waist) = 2–2.25 heads

(*c*) Crotch level (chin to crotch) = 3 heads

(*d*) Knee level (chin to mid-knee) = 4.5 heads

However you wish to do it, you will find your 'doll' a great aid to designing attractive and becoming outfits (*fig 6.11*).

Pattern drafting

We all know what we look like in silhouette because we've seen ourselves in the mirror and in photos, but when it comes to taking a piece of flat fabric and moulding it around all our lumps and bumps not only to cover and keep us warm but also to make us look attractive and appealing, things can be very difficult indeed.

Pattern drafting for dressmaking is a highly refined art, and its basic principles apply to machine knitting as well as to hand knitting and crochet. We are doing exactly what dressmakers do but have gone one step further back in the chain of production in that we are making the fabric to make the garment, rather than buying it by the yard or metre. What we have to bear in mind is that our fabric is often much more elastic and stretchy than woven fabric, and that we have more control over the production of the fabric, therefore we can change its nature while producing it by altering the type of stitch, type of yarn, etc.

However, unless you are just going to produce 'yardage,' that is, knitting a great length of fabric, placing a pattern on it, cutting the fabric out and sewing it up on a sewing machine as if you were dressmaking, you have to decide *before you begin* just what the dimensions of your pattern shapes must be in order to create the garment you have designed.

When you draft your basic block, whether it is simple or fitted, it is very important that you draft the body without allowances. This is because the block is not really a guide to a 'wearing out' garment, but a basic guide to the body the garment will cover. You will then be able to add the ease you require to any pattern drafted using the basic block. Each time you knit a garment the amount of ease you require will be different, so you must always begin with the basic block.

You will also find instructions for drafting sleeves in a number of different ways: use the one that you find the most sympathetic. Some people have a more 'casual' approach than others. Fortunately knitwear is a very pliable and agreeable fabric to work with when joining together the components of a garment. *All sleeve drafting is based on the size of the armhole.* As the size of the armhole changes from pattern to pattern according to style and amount of ease added, the sleeve must be drafted from scratch. The one measurement that remains constant on a sleeve is the length, unless you alter the width of the shoulder, e.g. to allow room for shoulder pads or to accommodate clothing when drafting jackets or coats.

On the fitted basic block, the armhole is drafted for a neat fitted garment: the measurement of the pattern armhole should be equal to the armscye plus 5cm. (The armscye is the *neat* measurement around the arm, through the armpit and up over the shoulder point.) For a sleeveless garment, the underarm line should be raised by 1.5cm. This will decrease the pattern armhole measurement. If you are drafting a jumper, cardigan or

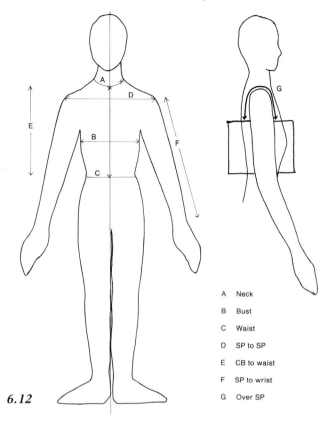

Measurements for a simple block

6.12

A	Neck
B	Bust
C	Waist
D	SP to SP
E	CB to waist
F	SP to wrist
G	Over SP

light jacket, lower the underarm line by 1.5cm (½in) thus increasing the pattern armhole measurement so that it is equal to the armscye measurement plus 8cm.

There are other little 'guides' we can borrow from dressmakers and earlier knitters. Here are some tips that have been used in the past.

Passap

Width of neck = SP to SP (shoulder point) divided by 3 (plus). The two shoulders are slightly shorter.
Shoulder drop: Ladies = 4   Children = 3   Babies = 2
Front length = from above the collarbone, over the bust to the waist
Armhole depth = front length minus shoulder drop divided by 2.

Others

Armhole depth = depth of armscye divided by 2, minus 1.9–3.2cm
Sleeve cap = $\frac{2}{3}$ armhole depth
Sleeve cap = approx. $\frac{1}{3}$ X–back
Neck width = SP to SP divided by 3 (back neck plus 1cm) or = X–back divided by 2 minus 1.5cm

Armhole: Before drafting the sleeve for a full bust *raise the armhole depth.*

Ease

CB to W = plus 1.5cm

X–back = plus 1cm

Armhole depth = plus 1.5cm

Sleeve cap should be 3–4.5cm larger than the armhole

SP to SP – Measure from the outside edge point of the shoulder, across the top of the shoulder (across the top of the back) to the outside edge of the opposite shoulder. Then subtract 2cm to allow for stretchability of the fabric.

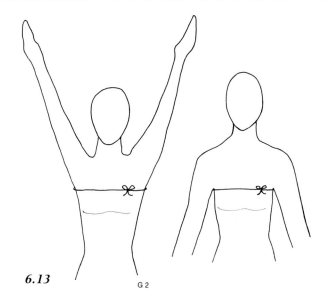

6.13

G 2

Taking personal measurements

All measurements must be taken neat (not with ease).

Personal measurements for the simple block (*fig 6.12*).

A = Neck base (jewel line)

B = Bust (or chest)

C = Waist

D = SP to SP (shoulder point to shoulder point)

E = CB (centre back, the bone at the top of the spine) to waist

F = SP to wrist

G = Over SP. To determine your underarm level, use one of these methods:

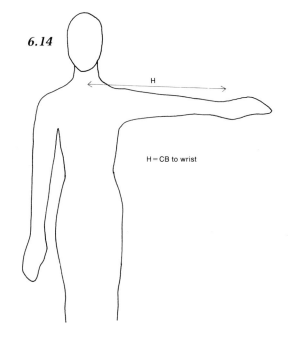

6.14

H = CB to wrist

1. Hold a book tucked neatly up under your armpit and level with the floor. Measure from the edge of the book in front of your arm, up over your shoulder point and down to the edge of the book behind your arm.

2. Lift your arms up and hold them straight above your head. Get a friend to tie a piece of string around your body at armpit level – above the bust. Drop your arms. The string should lie straight across your front and back and not sag. When you drop your arms the string will roll into the correct position marking your underarm level (*fig 6.13*).

H = CB to wrist (*fig 6.14*). (If you have trouble measuring yourself, tuck the tape measure under your watch strap.)

7

The simple block

Basic front and back block

1. Take a large piece of paper. It should be larger than half your bust measurement (B) by CB to waist measurement (E). Fold it in half. The fold line is the centre front/back line of your block. Mark the CB and waist point on the fold line.

(*a*) With the fold on your left, draw a horizontal guideline at the CB point.

(*b*) Draw a horizontal guideline at the waist point (*fig 7.1*).

2. On the guideline at the top of your block:

(*a*) Mark half the SP to SP (D).

(*b*) Mark half back neck width (7–10cm) or $\frac{A}{6}+0.5\text{cm}$ (*fig 7.2*).

3. Draw a vertical guideline through the SP mark.

(*a*) Mark the shoulder drop on this line (2–4cm).

(*b*) Mark the armhole drop on this line ($\frac{G}{2}$).

(*c*) Draw a line from the shoulder drop point to the side neck point (*fig 7.3*).

4. Draw a horizontal guideline from the centre back fold line through the armhole drop point (UP, underarm point) and mark it equal to bust measurement divided by 4 ($\frac{B}{4}$) (*fig 7.4*).

5. Draw a vertical line from the UP down to horizontal guideline at the waist (*fig 7.5*).

6. Now you may cut out your block. It is useful to make two blocks, one for the front and one for the back. You can put your crew neckline on your blocks, which will be helpful when altering your basic simple block (see point 10 – front neck curve, in the instructions on the basic fitted front, page 84).

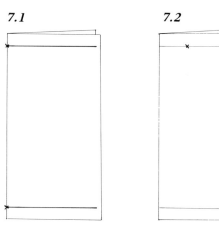

7.1   7.2

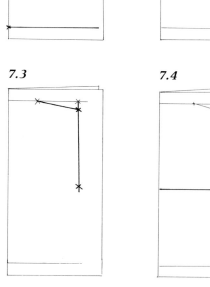

7.3   7.4

7.5

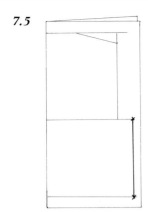

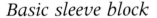

7.6

7.7

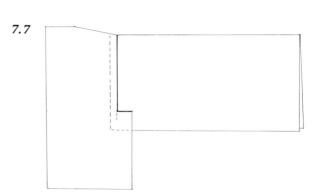

Ease is usually added to the body length and width, but the shoulder width remains constant (unless, of course, fashion dictates alterations such as broad shoulder pads, etc.).

Basic sleeve block

7.8

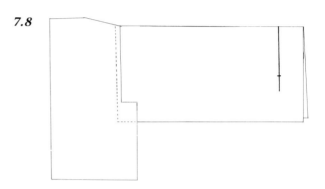

1. Take a large piece of paper, larger than your over-shoulder measurement (G) by SP to wrist (F). Fold it in half. The fold line is the centre of the sleeve. Place the paper with the fold line on the top.

2. Draw a vertical guideline at the left-hand edge of your folded paper (*fig 7.6*).

3. Place the armhole of your cut-out body block over the paper so that the fold comes at the SP and the vertical line of your armhole drop lines up with the guideline you have just drawn. Don't worry if the fold line does not form a straight line with your shoulder line on the block: this is because of the angle of the shoulder slope on the body block (*fig 7.7*).

7.9

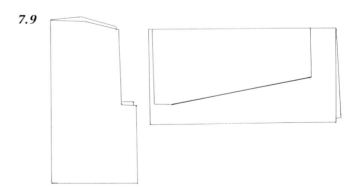

4. Measure from the centre line of your body block along the shoulder slope line and down the sleeve fold line. Mark your sleeve at a point equal to your CB to wrist measurement (H). This is the cuff point.

5. At your cuff point, drop a vertical guideline and mark it equal to half the closed fist measurement (*fig 7.8*). (This measurement can be varied, but remember you must be able to get your sleeve on over your hand.)

6. Draw a line to connect the cuff to the underarm point (*fig 7.9*).

7. Now you may cut out your sleeve block. Simple pattern variations can be done using the blocks you have just made, but remember that if you alter your basic body block in any way (such as adding ease across the bust) you will be altering your armhole, in which case you may have to draft a new sleeve altogether rather than work from the block you have

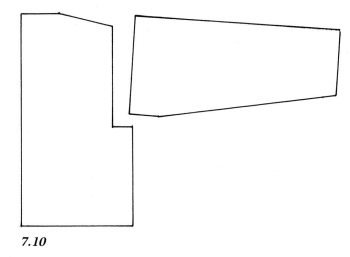

7.10

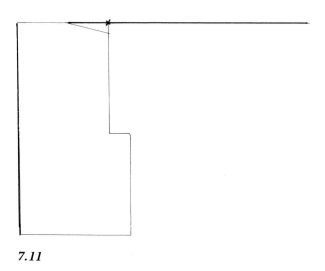

7.11

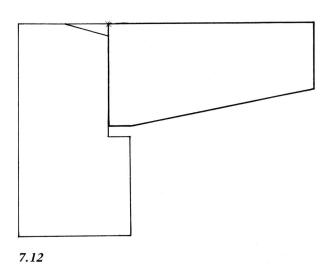

7.12

just made. You will not have wasted your time, however, because this measuring and marking will have given you valuable practice.

Variations for the simple block

Some patterns are best drafted from the simple block either because the patterns themselves are less fitted or because the fitting involved in the more sophisticated block is not necessary and therefore confuses the issue. With most of the variations you will have to add the required ease to the block before you alter it. The only exception is the batwing or dolman block. This is because ease is introduced as an integral part of the pattern.

DOLMAN OR BATWING PATTERN

Both the body and sleeve block are used for this pattern (*fig 7.10*). The neckline will be added later. There are three versions of sleeve for this pattern. In these versions, the block is based on the bust measurement so that there will be a degree of fullness at the waist. You should bear this in mind, as if you wish the garment to be fitted at the waist you will have to narrow the garment at the hem. As the design of the underarm shaping line gives additional fullness at the bust point, you may alter the hemline to give a more fitted garment using either the waist measurement or the top of the hip measurement (depending on the length of the garment) as a guideline.

1. For a simple sleeve:

(*a*) Draft the body block and extend the horizontal line at the top of the back neck. Draw a vertical line up from the armhole and mark the point where it crosses the horizontal line (*fig 7.11*).

(*b*) Draft the simple sleeve so that the top of the sleeve meets the point marked on the horizontal line (*fig 7.12*).

(*c*) Draft in the underarm and neckline shaping you require (*fig 7.13*).

2. For sloped sleeve line with shaping:

(*a*) Draft the body block and extend the diagonal line at the top of the shoulder (*fig 7.14*).

(*b*) Draft the simple sleeve so that the top of the sleeve

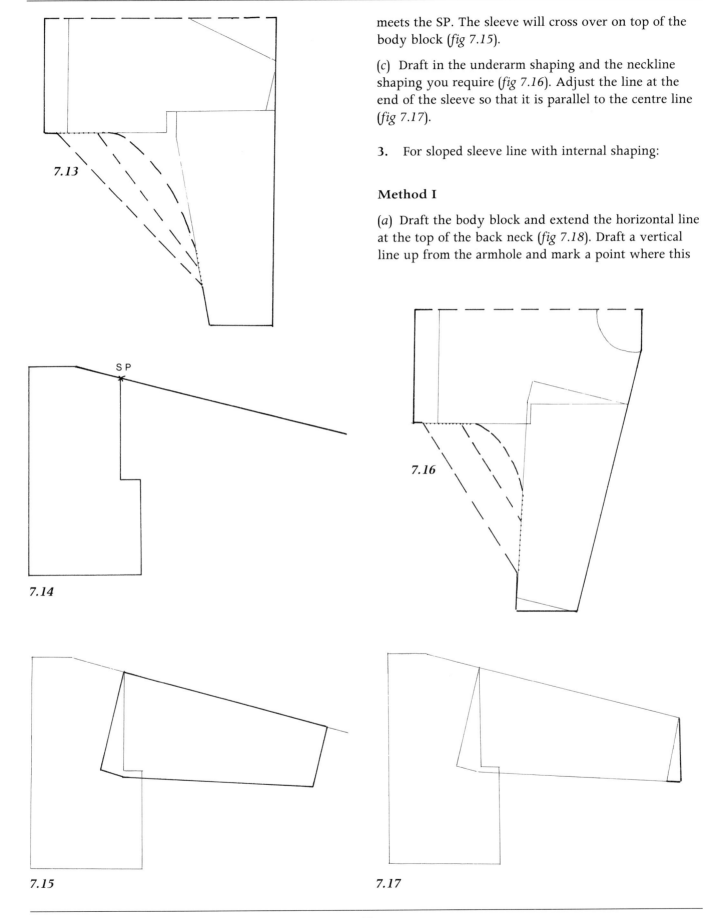

7.13

S P

7.14

7.15

meets the SP. The sleeve will cross over on top of the body block (*fig 7.15*).

(*c*) Draft in the underarm shaping and the neckline shaping you require (*fig 7.16*). Adjust the line at the end of the sleeve so that it is parallel to the centre line (*fig 7.17*).

3. For sloped sleeve line with internal shaping:

Method I

(*a*) Draft the body block and extend the horizontal line at the top of the back neck (*fig 7.18*). Draft a vertical line up from the armhole and mark a point where this

7.16

7.17

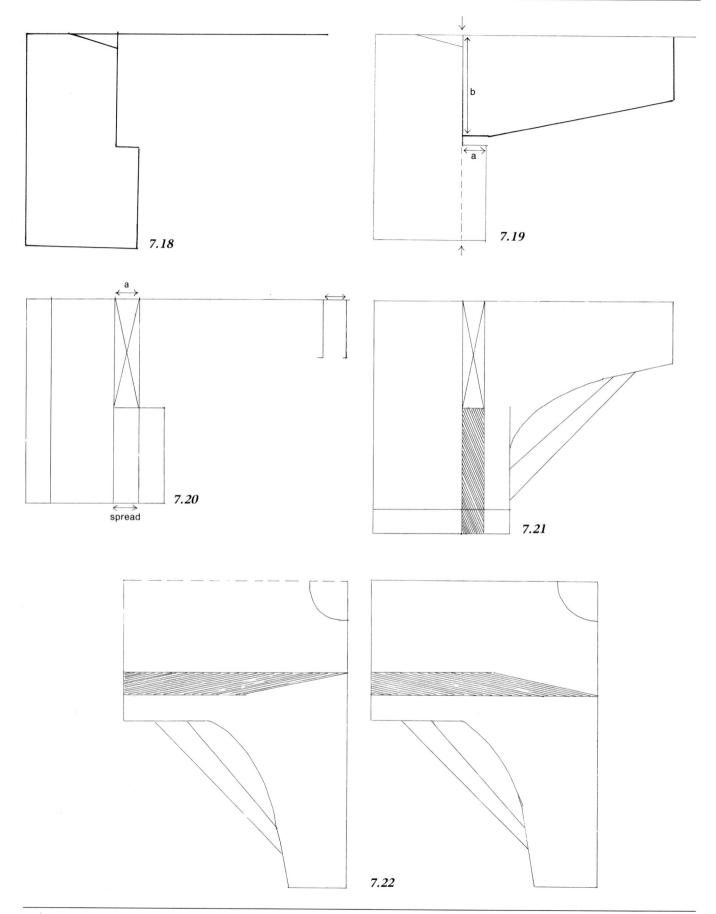

7.18

7.19

7.20

spread

7.21

7.22

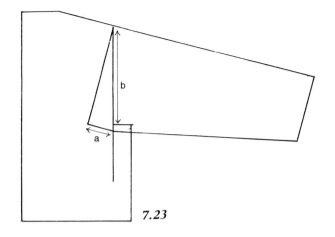

7.23

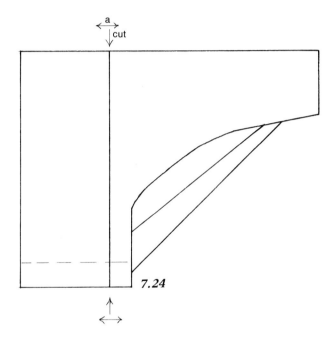

7.24

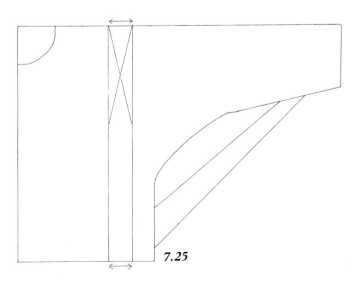

7.25

line crosses the horizontal line. Measure the underarm line (a) (*fig 7.19*). Place the simple sleeve next to the body block so that the top of the sleeve lines up with the mark. Draw a vertical line down from this point and cut this pattern piece in two.

(*b*) Move these two sections apart equal to the underarm distance (a) (*fig 7.20*).

(*c*) Draw in your chosen underarm line and neckline (*fig 7.21*). The shaded area represents needles which will be in HP when you knit the garment sideways (short rowing). This will give you an internal dart which will give your sleeve an angled position relative to the body block (*fig 7.22*).

Method II

(*a*) Take the body block and place the sleeve block into the armhole so that the top of the sleeve corresponds to the top of the armhole. Measure the distance between the bottom of the sleeve and the bottom of the armhole (a). This will be the width of your dart. The depth of the dart equals the armhole depth (b) (*fig 7.23*).

(*b*) Draft the batwing for a straight sleeve and cut it at the shoulder point. Spread the two sections apart equal to the distance you measured above (b) (*fig 7.24*).

(*c*) Continue to draft the underarm line and neckline (*fig 7.25*).

The pattern (*fig 7.26*) shows how a simple batwing style can be modified. This garment has been drawn out on the design doll. The distance between the waist and the bottom of the garment has been measured and this information transferred to the shaped sleeve block.

7.26

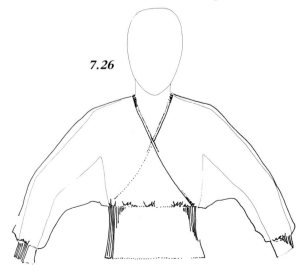

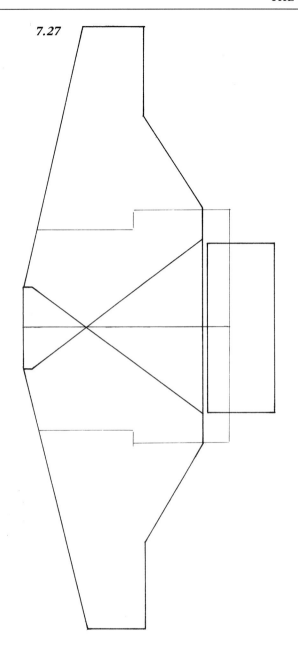

7.27

2. On the underarm line, measure in from the underarm point 2–3cm. Mark a point on the underarm line (*fig 7.29*).

3. Measure down from the SP 4–6cm. Mark this point on the armhole drop line. Join the two points (*fig 7.30*). This is your new armhole.

SLEEVE

1. Draw a vertical line. At the top draw a horizontal line (*fig 7.31*). Mark a point on this line equal to three times the distance on the body block between the SP and the point marked on the armhole drop line where the vertical line becomes a diagonal line (*fig 7.32*).

2. Place your body block over the sleeve draft with the point marked on the armhole on top of the point on the horizontal line at the top of your sleeve (*fig 7.33*). (*Optional:* you can angle your body block to give you a wider or narrower sleeve.) Draw in the sleeve cap.

3. Adjust the underarm line so that it is horizontal. Measure down from the top of the sleeve cap and mark a point on the vertical line equal to the measurement of

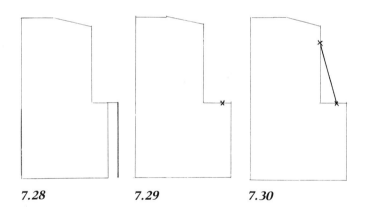

7.28   *7.29*   *7.30*

Then the crossover lines have been drawn out on the block. The waist section was measured on the doll and has been drafted out separately (*fig 7.27*).

High shaped armhole with puffed sleeve

BODY

1. Trace out the simple body block. Add the ease required to the bust. Extend the underarm line to the new side line (*fig 7.28*).

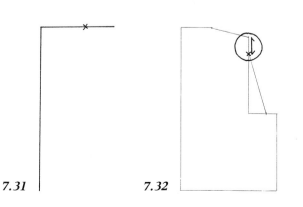

7.31   *7.32*

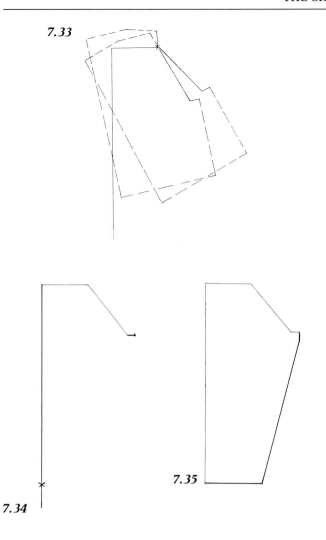

7.33

7.34

7.35

new SP is where this line crosses the new vertical side line. Draft a new shoulder slope line from the new SP to your SNP (side neck point) (*fig 7.37*).

SLEEVE

Variation I

1. Trace out the simple sleeve block (from the centre line).

2. Place the new body block on the sleeve, fitting the sleeve head into the old armhole. Mark a new UP (underarm point) on your sleeve at the new underarm point on the body block (*fig 7.38*). Draw a new horizontal line straight across the sleeve top at this point. This is your new sleeve length.

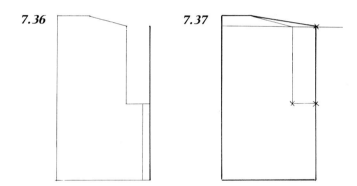

7.36   *7.37*

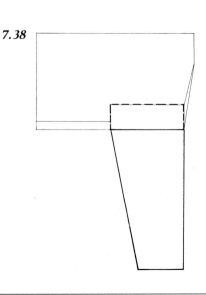

7.38

your SP to wrist *plus* 2–3cm allowance for the height of the 'puff' at the sleeve head (*fig 7.34*).

4. Draw a vertical line at this point and mark it equal to half the required measurement for the bottom of the sleeve. This measurement is optional. Join this point to the underarm point (*fig 7.35*).

Dropped shoulder with sleeve variation

BODY

1. Trace out the simple body block and add the required ease to the bust. Draw a new vertical line (*fig 7.36*).

2. Extend the underarm line, bottom line and draft a horizontal line out from the SP (shoulder point). Your

Variation II

1. Trace out the entire simple sleeve block (*fig 7.39*). (Trace both halves out from the centre line.)

2. Place the body block on the sleeve, fitting the sleeve head into the old armhole. Mark the new underarm point (*fig 7.40*).

3. Draft a new sleeve head. Raise the centre 4–6cm and draft a gentle curve from the underarm point to underarm point with the centre 8–10cm straight (horizontal) (*fig 7.41*).

Shorten the sleeve length by the same amount you raised the sleeve head.

Remember to draft your chosen neckline and adjust the length of the body block before you knit the garment.

7.41

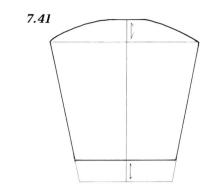

7.39

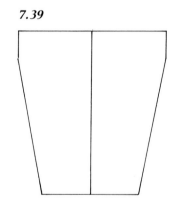

7.40

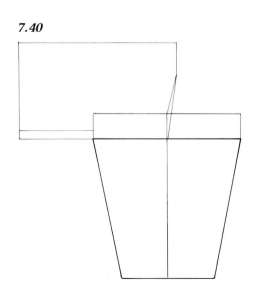

7.42   **7.43**

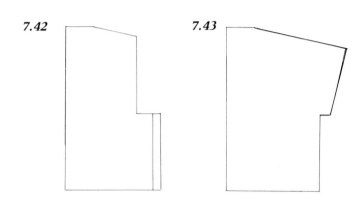

Cap sleeve variations

Cap sleeve tops are very comfortable in warm weather. They are also useful for wearing under suit jackets or cardigans where a long sleeve would be awkward. They can be drafted in two ways. In the second, the cap sleeve may be prevented from sticking out a little.

Method I

1. Trace out the simple body block and add the required ease to the bust (*fig 7.42*).

2. Extend the shoulder slope line. The length of this is optional, but is usually limited by the width of the needle bed, so you may have to do a tension swatch before drafting out your pattern.

Increase 2cm or more at the UP then join the new UP to the new end of the shoulder slope line (*fig 7.43*).

You will find that even if you do not increase the length of the shoulder slope line and continue to knit straight up to the SP, you will have a cap sleeve garment.

7.44

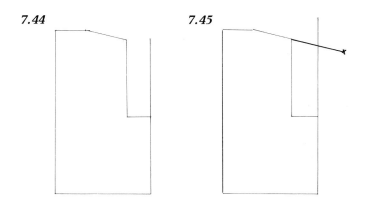

7.45

Method II

1.   Trace out the simple body block and add the required ease at the bust. Extend the vertical side line up past the shoulder line (*fig 7.44*).

2.   Extend the shoulder slope line 7cm beyond the vertical side line (*fig 7.45*).

3.   Mark a new UP 4cm below the one on the block. Join this point to the new end of the shoulder slope line (*fig 7.46*).

4.   Mark a new point 3cm below the end of the sleeve cap (end of the shoulder slope line). Join this new point to the SP on the block (*fig 7.47*).
After drafting your new pattern do not forget to draft the neckline and alter the hemline.

7.46

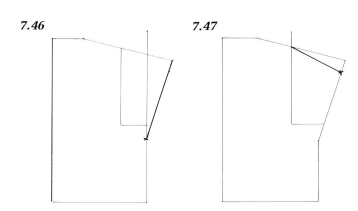

7.47

Simple set-in sleeve

In some cases where the difference between the measurements of the bust/chest and the shoulders is quite large this can result in an awkward point where the sleeve joins the body. To minimize this, redraft the block as follows:

1.   Trace out the body block and add the required ease at the bust (*fig 7.48*). Set the sleeve block into the armhole and trace it out.

2.   On the body block mark a point on the underarm line 2cm in from the underarm point (*fig 7.49*).

3.   On the armhole drop line mark a point one-third of the way up from the underarm line. Draw a line between these two points (*fig 7.50*).

7.48

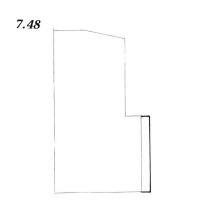

7.49

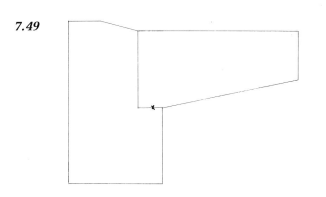

7.50

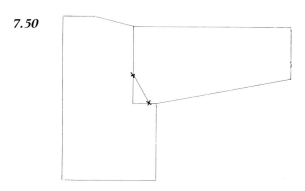

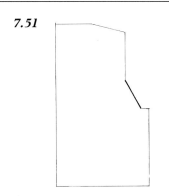

7.51

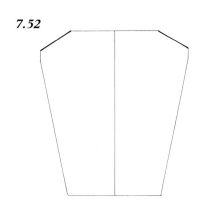

7.52

2. Trace out the simple sleeve upside down, so that the sleeve top is at the bottom of the pattern. Draw a vertical line upwards at the end of the sleeve top line. Extend the sleeve top line at the outside edge by an amount equal to the measurement of the underarm line of the armhole on the body block. Draw another vertical line upwards from this point (*fig 7.54*). (When knitting the garment, the front and back will be knitted first. The shoulders will be joined and then the sleeve may be picked up from the armhole edge with the shoulder join at the centre of the needle bed.)

3. Mark a point on the sleeve top line 4cm from the centre (*fig 7.55*). Draw a bias line from this point. To draw a bias line:

(*a*) Mark a point on the sleeve top line equal to a measurement of 10 stitches (on your tension swatch) away from the 4cm point. Draw a vertical line at this point (*fig 7.56*).

(*b*) Mark a point on this vertical line equal to a measurement of 10 rows (on your tension swatch) away from the sleeve top line.

4. Take the triangle formed by this line off the top of the sleeve and add it to the body block (*fig 7.51*). This will be your new shaping for both the sleeve and the body block (*fig 7.52*).

Upside-down shaped knitted sleeve

This pattern is quite complicated to draft and should not be attempted by an inexperienced knitter. The sleeve head is knitted in imitation of a sock heel; that is, you will use HP to shape the sleeve head. The shaped area of this pattern is most successful in stocking stitch, but this does not prevent you from using other stitch patterns in other areas of the garment.

NB: The pattern cannot be drafted accurately until a tension swatch is made.

1. Trace out the body block and add ease required at the bust (*fig 7.53*). (When knitting the garment the underarm stitches are removed to WY and not cast off.)

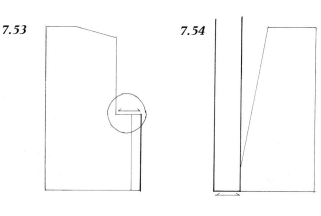

7.53   *7.54*

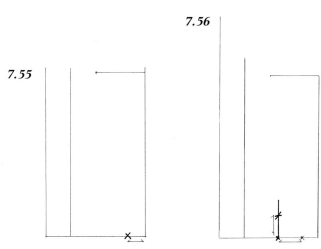

7.55   *7.56*

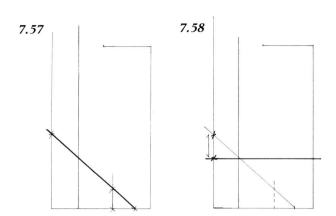

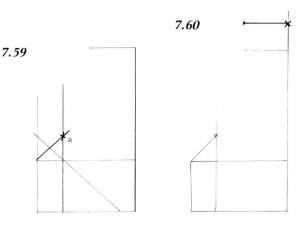

(*c*) Draw a line between this point and the 4cm point on the sleeve top line (*fig 7.57*). This is your bias line and indicates the shaping you will achieve if you increase one stitch every row. Extend this line until it crosses the vertical line drawn up from the end of the picked-up sleeve top line.

4.   Measure down from this point by the measurement of the underarm line at the bottom of the armhole. Draw a horizontal line at this point (*fig 7.58*). This will indicate the end of the short row shaping and all needles should now be in WP.

5.   Draw another bias line from the end of the horizontal line you have just drawn. Extend it to cross the vertical line drawn up from the original end of the sleeve top line. Mark this point (a) (*fig 7.59*).

6.   Measure along the centre line from the top of the sleeve and mark a point equal to the measurement of SP to wrist. Draw a horizontal line from this point equal to half the cuff measurement (optional). This is your new cuff (*fig 7.60*).

7.   Draw a line from point (a) to the new cuff line (*fig 7.61*).

8

The fitted block

Personal measurements for the fitted block (fig 8.1)

A = Neck base (jewel line)

B = SP to SP (shoulder point to shoulder point)

C = X-front (cross front half-way up the armhole from sleeve seam, where the arm joins the body, to sleeve seam)

D = X-back (as for X-front)

E = Bust (chest)

F = BP to BP (bust point to bust point)

G = Waist

H = Hips

I = Armscye (the *neat* measurement around the arm through the armpit and up over the shoulder point)

J = UA (upper arm)

K = Wrist

L = Fist (around the closed fist)

M = CB (centre back) to waist

N = Waist to hem (this is an optional measurement determined by personal choice/fashion trends)

O = SNP (side neck point) to SP (shoulder point)

P = CB to wrist

Q = SNP to wrist

R = SP to wrist

S = Head circumference (at widest point)

T = SNP to BP

U = Two additional measurements for the fuller figure are highly recommended. SNP to waist *both front and back* (fig 8.2). If you find a discrepancy

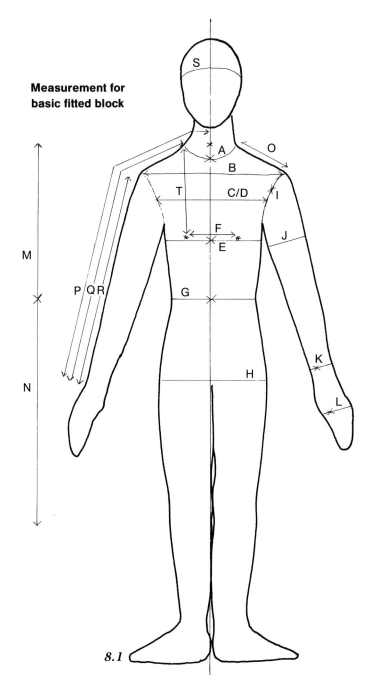

Measurement for basic fitted block

8.1

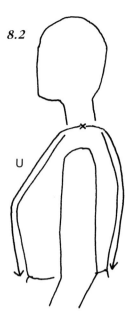

8.2

2. Draw a horizontal guideline from the CB line at the point marking the top of the shoulder. Mark a point on this line equal to $\frac{1}{2}$ SP to SP measurement less 1.5cm (*fig 8.4*). This indicates the shoulder width.

3. Mark half back neck width.

(*a*) Divide the neck base measurement by 6. Add 0.5cm. If this measurement is not exact, round the number up.

(*b*) Mark this point on the top shoulder line. This is the SNP (side neck point) (*fig 8.5*).

4. Draw a vertical guideline down from the shoulder width point.

(*a*) Mark a point on this line 2–4cm down from the top of the shoulder line, or use the measurement from your design doll. Note the difference in height between the CBNP and the SP on the doll. Divide the difference by 2 and use this measurement to give you your shoulder drop. This is the SP.

between the two measurements, you will have to add the difference between the two measurements to 'M'.

When drafting the pattern for a fitted garment for this type of figure, you may add the length at the front of the garment and insert a dart under the armhole at the side front. This can be accomplished by short-rowing when knitting a garment horizontally.

The following instructions show several different methods of drafting fitted patterns. Some of these are drawn largely from dressmaking techniques. In pattern drafting for dressmaking the starting point is the bust or chest measurement while pattern drafting for knitwear is based on the garment hanging from the shoulders. There are several different 'styles' of drafting; some are dressmaking orientated, some are American in origin and some come from Japan. You must choose the one that suits you (and your customer) best.

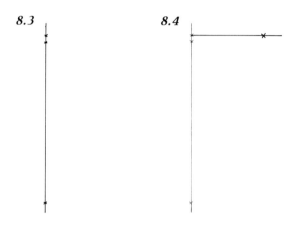

8.3

8.4

Basic fitted block

BACK

1. Draw a vertical guideline. This will be your CB (centre back) line. Mark the WP (waist point) and CBNP (centre back neck point) on this line.
Mark another point on this line 1.5cm above the CBNP. This will indicate the top of the shoulder (*fig 8.3*).

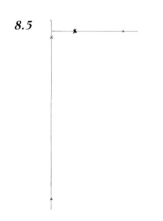

8.5

(*b*) Draw a line from the SP to the NP. This is the shoulder line and can be checked against your own measurement (-1.5cm) (*fig 8.6*).

5. On this vertical guideline measure down from the SP. Mark a point equal to half the measurement of the armscye snug. This is the armhole drop. (For bust sizes over 102cm subtract 1cm) (*fig 8.7*). (If, when measuring the circumference of the armhole, the total of the back and front measurement is greater than the armscye snug plus 5cm, you may find you will have to raise the underarm point by 1.5cm.)

6. Draw a horizontal guideline from the CB line through this point. Mark a point on this line equal to one quarter of the bust measurement plus 1cm (*fig 8.8*). This is the UP (underarm point).

7. Draw a horizontal guideline from the CB point at the waist. Mark a point on this line at one quarter of the waist measurement. Draw a line from this point to the UP (*fig 8.9*).

8.10

8.11

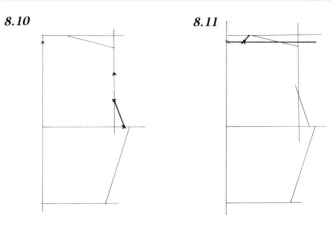

8.12

8.13

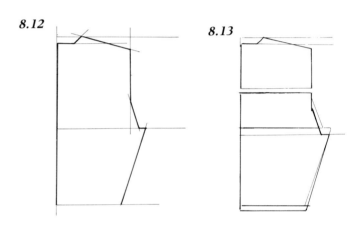

8. Armhole curve:

(*a*) Divide the armhole into thirds and mark it.

(*b*) Mark a point on the bust line 2cm in from the UP. (For bust sizes over 102cm, mark the point 3cm in from the UP.)

(*c*) Draw a line from this point to the lower mark on the armhole line (*fig 8.10*).

9. Back neck curve:

(*a*) Draw a horizontal guideline from the CB line at the CBNP.

(*b*) Mark a point on this line two-thirds of the measurement between CB and SNP (*fig 8.11*).

(*c*) Draw a line between this point and the SNP (side neck point) (*fig 8.12*).

10. If you have very rounded shoulders, you may want to slash the back horizontally at the mid-armhole point and spread the pattern lengthwise by 1cm (*fig 8.13*).

8.6

8.7

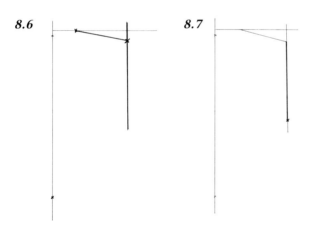

8.8

8.9

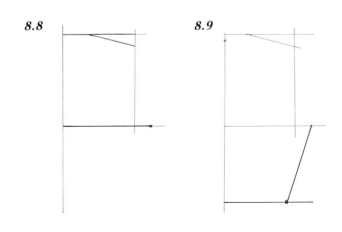

FRONT

1. Draw a vertical guideline. This will be your CF line. Mark the WP and CBNP on this line. Mark another point on this line 1.5cm above the CBNP. This will indicate the top of the shoulder (*fig 8.14*).

2. Draw a horizontal guideline from the CF line at the point marking the top of the shoulder. Mark a point on this line equal to half SP to SP measurement less 1.5cm (*fig 8.15*). This indicates the shoulder width.

3. Mark half back neck width.

(*a*) Divide the neck base measurement by 6. Add 0.5cm. If this measurement is not exact, round the number up to the nearest 0.5cm.

(*b*) Mark this point on the top shoulder line. This is the NP (*fig 8.16*).

4. Draw a vertical guideline down from the shoulder width point.

(*a*) Mark a point on this line 2–4cm down from the top of the shoulder line or use half the difference of the vertical measurement between the BNP and the SP on the design doll (*fig 8.17*). The allowance is for the shoulder drop. This is the SP.

(*b*) Draw a line from the SP to the NP. This is the shoulder line and can be checked against your own measurement, but you must remember that you subtracted 1.5cm from your SP to SP measurement.

5. On this vertical guideline measure down from the SP. Mark a point half the measurement of the armscye snug (*fig 8.18*). This is the armhole drop. (For bust sizes over 102cm subtract 1cm.)

8.16

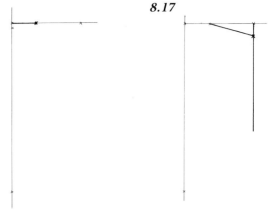
8.17

8.18   **8.19**
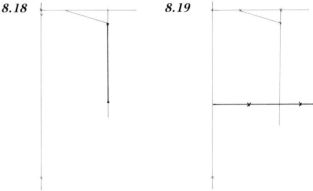

6. Draw a horizontal guideline from the CF through this point. Mark a point on this line one quarter bust measurement plus 1cm. This is the UP. Make another mark on this line equal to half the distance from BP to BP (*fig 8.19*)

7. Draw a vertical guideline through the BP. Measure from the NP (the side neck point at the top of the shoulder line) and mark the BP on this line (*fig 8.20*).

8. Draw a horizontal guideline from the CF point at the waist. Mark a point on this line at one quarter waist measurement. Draw a line from this point to the UP (*fig 8.21*).

9. Armhole curve:

(*a*) Divide the armhole into thirds and mark it.

(*b*) Draw a horizontal guideline from the CF line through the top third point.

8.14   **8.15**
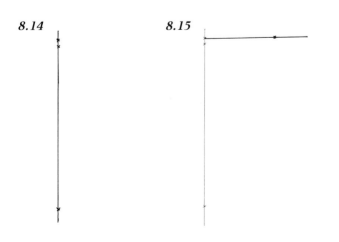

8.20

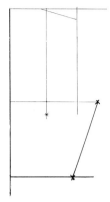

8.21

(c) Draw a vertical guideline down through the NP. Measure this line down from the top of the shoulder and mark a point on this line equal to the shoulder drop.

(d) Draw a line from this point to the point on the front neckline (*fig 8.23*).

11. Draw out your block and cut it out (*fig 8.24*). Check the curve at the neck and armhole and adjust the blocks if necessary (*fig 8.25*). The total of the front and back armhole circumferences should equal the measurement of the armscye neat plus 5cm for a fitted sleeve. If the measurement is too big you must raise the underarm line by 1.5cm.

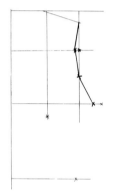

8.22

8.23

8.24

(c) Mark a point on this line equal to half X-front measurement. (This point should not be more than 1cm in from the vertical armhole guideline.)

(d) Mark a point 2cm in from the UP on the underarm line. (For bust sizes over 102cm, mark the point 3cm in from the UP.)

(e) Draw a line from this point through the lower third point on the armhole drop line, and then through the cross front line and on to the point at the top of the shoulder (*Fig 8.22*). This is your front armhole.

10. Front neck curve:

(a) On the CF line measure down from the CBNP and mark a point equal to half the back neck measurement plus 1cm. This is the FNP (front neck point = front neck drop).

(b) Draw a horizontal guideline at the FNP. Measure from the CF line and mark a point on this line equal to half the front neck drop.

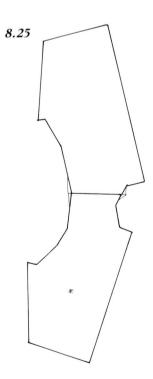

8.25

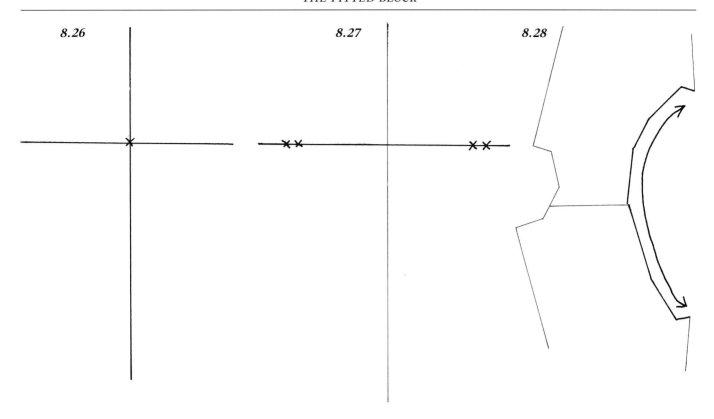

8.26   **8.27**   **8.28**

FITTED SLEEVE

1.   Draw a vertical guideline for the sleeve length. You do not mark the exact length at this point, so, to be on the safe side, make this line equal to SP to wrist (your sleeve length) plus half the armscye measurement.

2.   Measuring down from the top of this line, mark a point equal to $\frac{1}{2}$ the armscye measurement. Draw a horizontal guideline through this point (*fig 8.26*).

3.   Measuring from the centre to the right:

(*a*) Mark a point on this line equal to the UA (upper arm measurement) divided by 2. This is your upper arm width.

(*b*) Measure out from the UA point and mark another point equal to the UA measurement plus ease. The minimum for a fitted sleeve would be 2cm on either side of the centre line, but the ease can vary with style. This line is your sleeve width.

(*c*) Repeat from centre to left (*fig 8.27*).

4.   Measure *carefully* around the armhole on the pattern blocks (front and back), divide this number by 2 and subtract 1cm (*fig 8.28*).

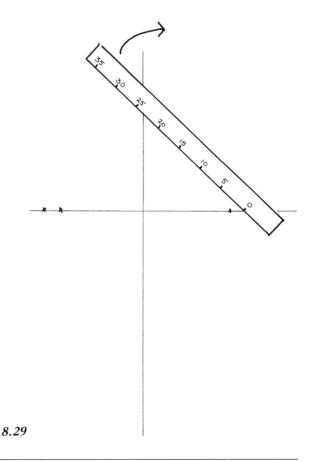

8.29

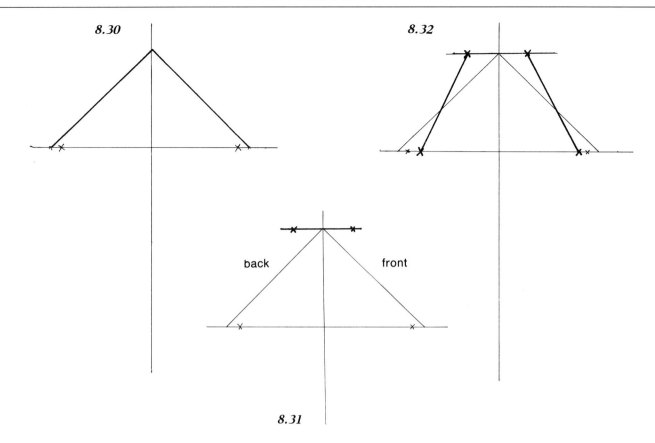

8.30

8.32

back   front

8.31

5. Draw a line from the UP (underarm point) at the end of the horizontal guideline to cross the centre sleeve line diagonally (*fig 8.29*). This line must equal half the pattern armhole measurement − 1cm, so place your ruler with 0 at the UP and pivot it until the correct number on the ruler is at the centre line. This is the height of your sleeve cap (*fig 8.30*). (The height of the sleeve cap is normally two thirds of the armhole height, or one third of the cross back measurement.)

6. Draw a horizontal guideline at the top of your sleeve cap (*fig 8.31*).

(*a*) To the right of the centre this line should be equal in length to your UA (without ease) divided by 8 (the front sleeve cap).

(*b*) To the left of the centre this line should be equal in length to your UA measurement (without ease) divided by 8 + 1cm (the back sleeve cap).

7. On the sleeve width line mark a point measured in from each end equal to UA measurement (without ease) divided by 8. Draw a guideline from these points on the underarm line to the end of the horizontal top of the sleeve cap line (front and back) (*fig 8.32*).

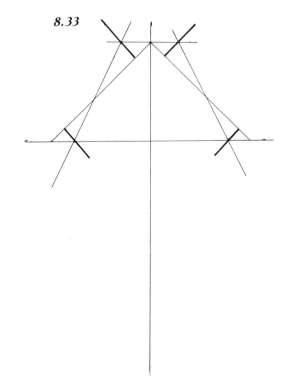

8.33

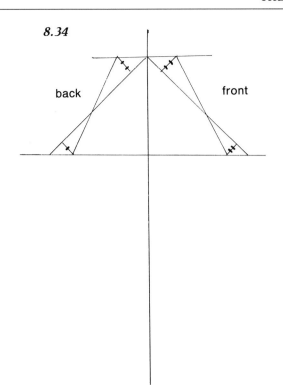

8.34

back   front

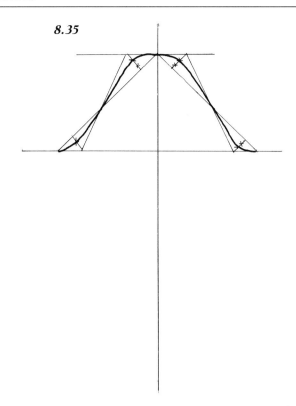

8.35

8. Using your set-square, draw guidelines at right-angles to your original sleeve cap triangle to cross the points where your two guidelines from 7 (above) meet the sleeve top and underarm horizontal lines (*fig 8.33*).

9. Divide and mark these right-angle lines as follows:

(*a*) underarm back in 2

(*b*) sleeve top back in 3

(*c*) sleeve top front in 3

(*d*) underarm front in 3 (*fig 8.34*)

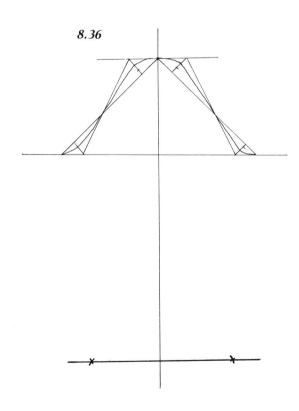

8.36

10. 'Join the dots'. Using the dots as a guide, draw in the sleeve cap curve. The dots to use as guides are the upper dots on the sleeve cap and the lower dot on the underarm front. The curve crosses the points F and B where the sleeve cap triangle is crossed by sleeve cap guidelines (*fig 8.35*).

11. Measure the vertical centre line from the top of the sleeve cap and mark the sleeve length equal to SP to wrist measurement. Draw a horizontal guideline at this point and mark the width of this line (equidistant from the centre) equal to the measurement of your closed fist (*fig 8.36*). (This measurement is variable.)

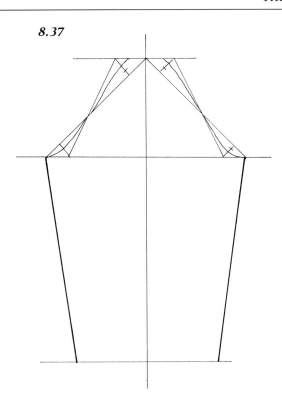

8.37

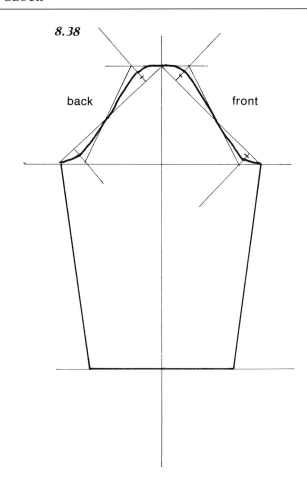

8.38

back   front

12.   Join the points at the ends of this line to the UA points (*fig 8.37*).

NB: This sleeve can be used with the basic fitted block where the back armhole has been made deeper than the front armhole (*fig 8.38*).

ALTERNATIVE FITTED SLEEVE

1.   Draw a vertical guideline equal to SP to wrist plus half AH. This line will be longer than you need. This is the centre sleeve line.

2.   Measure down from the top of the line (approximately half AH drop) and mark the line (*fig 8.39*).

3.   Draw a horizontal guideline from the centre at the mark. Make this line equal to UA divided by 2 plus ease (ease = 2cm). This is your sleeve underarm line and the length is equal to your sleeve width. Mark another point on this line to indicate the UA with ease divided by 12 (*fig 8.40*).

4.   Measure around the pattern armhole (front and back) *carefully*, divide by 2 and subtract 1cm (*fig 8.41*).

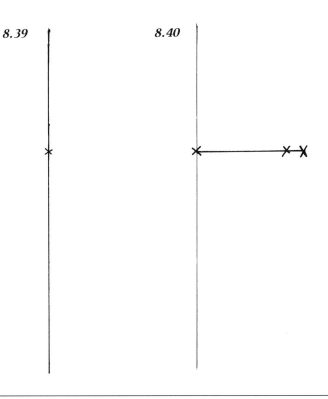

8.39   *8.40*

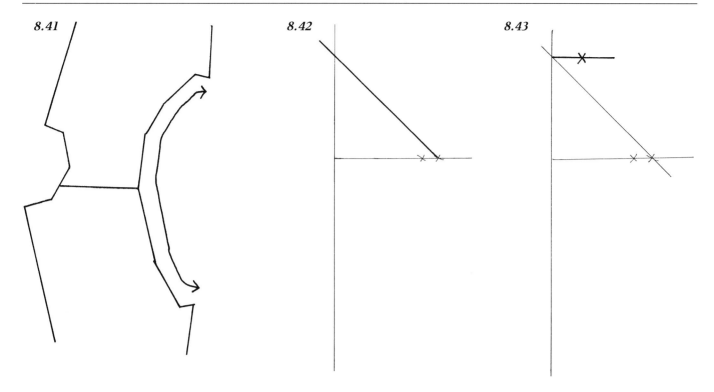

8.41   *8.42*   *8.43*

5. Draw a line from the end of the sleeve underarm line to cross the sleeve centre line. This line is equal to the measurement from stage 4 above. To do this place a ruler with the 0 on the point at the end of the horizontal underarm line and *pivot* the ruler until it crosses the vertical centre line at the correct measurement (*fig 8.42*).

6. Draw a horizontal line at the top of the sleeve cap equal to the measurement of the pattern armhole divided by 12 (*fig 8.43*).

7. Draw a line from the end of this line down to the point marked on the underarm line (*fig 8.44*). It is on this line that we will draw the sleeve cap curve.

8. The sleeve cap curve:

(*a*) The line that is drawn between the horizontal line at the top of the sleeve cap and the UA point on the underarm line is divided into two sections by the diagonal AH line. Divide each of these sections by 2.

(*b*) Draw the sleeve cap to curve out at the top section by 1cm. Curve the bottom section in slightly (*fig 8.45*).

9. Measure the vertical centre line from the top of the sleeve cap and mark the sleeve length equal to the SP

8.44

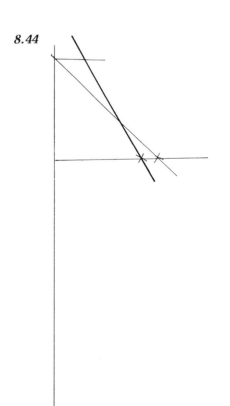

8.45

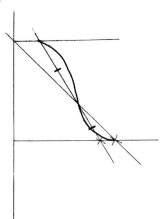

8.46

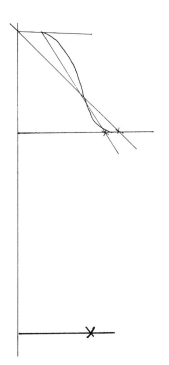

8.47

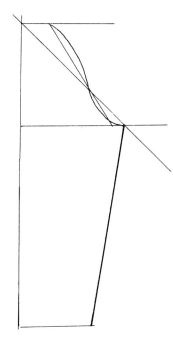

8.48

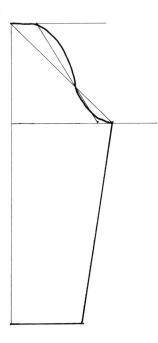

8.49

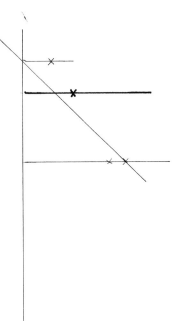

8.50

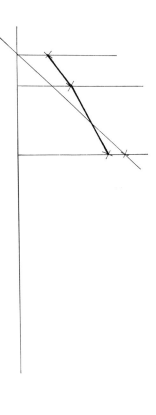

to W measurement. Draw a horizontal guideline (*fig 8.46*).

10.　Mark the width of this line equal to half the measurement of your closed fist (*fig 8.47*). (This measurement is variable.)

11.　Join the point at the end of this line to the point on your underarm line that indicates your sleeve width (*fig 8.48*).

YET ANOTHER SLEEVE CAP

After step 6:

7.　From the top of the sleeve, measure down the centreline and draw a horizontal guideline equal to one third of the measurement of the sleeve cap (between the top of the sleeve and the UA guideline) (*fig 8.49*).

8.　Mark a point on this line equal to the measurement of the pattern armhole divided by 5.

9.　Draw a line from the end of the top of the sleeve cap line to the point marked on the horizontal guideline marking one third of the height of the sleeve cap. Continue this line down to the point marked on the underarm line (*fig 8.50*).

　Continue to draft the rest of the sleeve (the wrist, etc.) as for the alternative sleeve above.

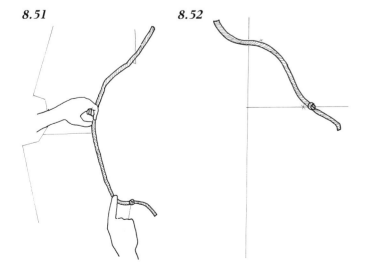

8.51　　　　*8.52*

ANOTHER EASY SLEEVE CAP

Use the same technique as above until step 5.

6.　Replace the measurement, pattern armhole divided by 12, with A = measurement divided by 6.

7.　As above.

8.　Replace pattern armhole divided by 5 with UA measurement divided by 3.

　This will give you a comfortable sleeve cap which includes quite a bit of ease.
　Continue to draft the rest of the sleeve (wrist, etc.) as for the alternative sleeve above.

AN EVEN EASIER ALTERNATIVE TO DRAFTING THE SLEEVE CAP

After step 3, measure around the pattern (front and back) armhole *carefully* with a piece of inelastic string (*fig 8.51*). Divide this in half and lay half of it carefully on your horizontal and vertical guidelines. Adjust the string to indicate your sleeve cap, with one point crossing the centre line and the other crossing the horizontal underarm line at the sleeve width point (*fig 8.52*). You can increase the length of this piece of string by 1cm to allow for ease in the sleeve cap. Then draw in your sleeve cap.
　Continue to draft the rest of the sleeve (wrist, etc.) as for the alternative sleeve above.

JAPANESE VERSION OF THE FITTED SLEEVE

1.　Draw a vertical guideline equal to SP to W plus half AH. This is the centre sleeve line, and will be longer than you need.

2.　Measure down from the top of the line (approx. half AH drop) and mark the line (*fig 8.53*).

3.　Draw a horizontal guideline from the centre at the mark. Make this line equal to UA plus ease (ease = 2cm). This is your sleeve underarm line, and the length is equal to your sleeve width. Mark another point in from the end of this line to indicate the UA (upperarm width) with ease divided by 12 (*fig 8.54*).

4.　Measure the armhole on the front block. Measure

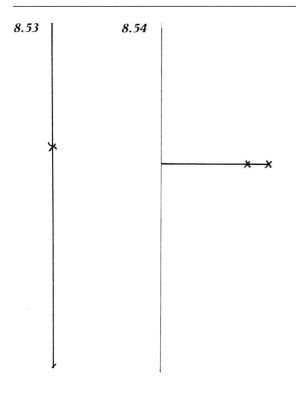

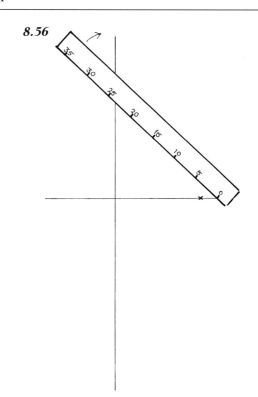

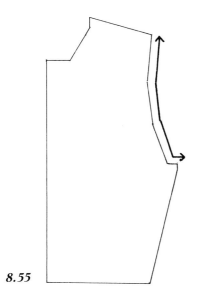

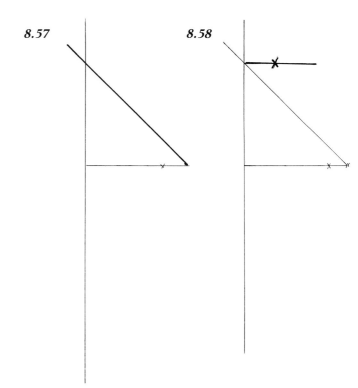

from the SP around the armhole line and down to the UP (*fig 8.55*).

5.   Draw a line from the end of the sleeve underarm line to cross the sleeve centre line (*fig 8.57*). This line is equal to the measurement from stage 4 above. To do this, place a ruler with the 0 on the point at the end of the horizontal underarm line and **pivot** it until it crosses the vertical centre line at the correct measurement (*fig 8.56*).

6.   Draw a horizontal line at the top of the sleeve cap equal to the measurement of (UA plus ease) divided by 6 (*fig 8.58*).

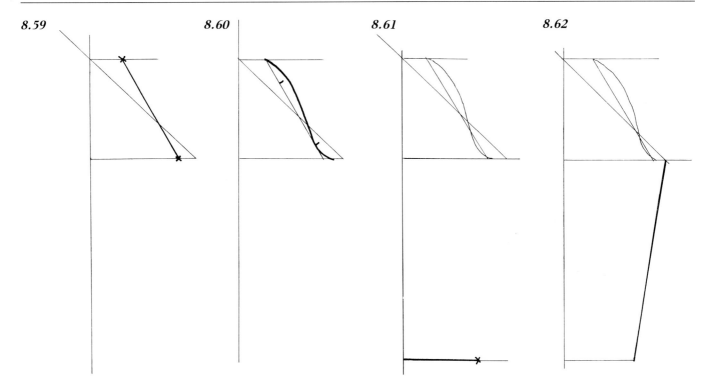

8.59   *8.60*   *8.61*   *8.62*

7. Draw a line from the end of this line down to the point marked on the underarm line (*fig 8.59*). It is on this line that you will draw the sleeve cap curve. (This line is divided in two where it crosses the diagonal guideline indicating the top of the sleeve head.)

8. The sleeve cap curve:

(*a*) The line drawn between the horizontal line at the top of the sleeve cap and the UA point on the underarm line is divided into two by the diagonal AH line. Divide each of these sections by two.

(*b*) Draw the sleeve cap to curve out at the top section by 1cm. Curve the bottom section in slightly (*fig 8.60*).

9. Measure the vertical centre line from the top of the sleeve cap and mark the sleeve length equal to the SP to W measurement. Draw a horizontal guideline (*fig 8.61*).

10. Mark the width of this line equal to half the measurement of your closed fist. (This measurement is variable.)

11. Join the point at the end of this line to the point on your underarm line that indicates your sleeve width (*fig 8.62*).

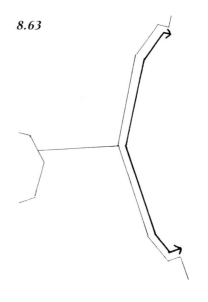

8.63

ALTERNATIVE JAPANESE FITTED SLEEVE

1. Measure around the armhole of the garment (*fig 8.63*).

2. Draw a vertical line. Mark the top of the line and measure down from the top. Mark a point equal to the

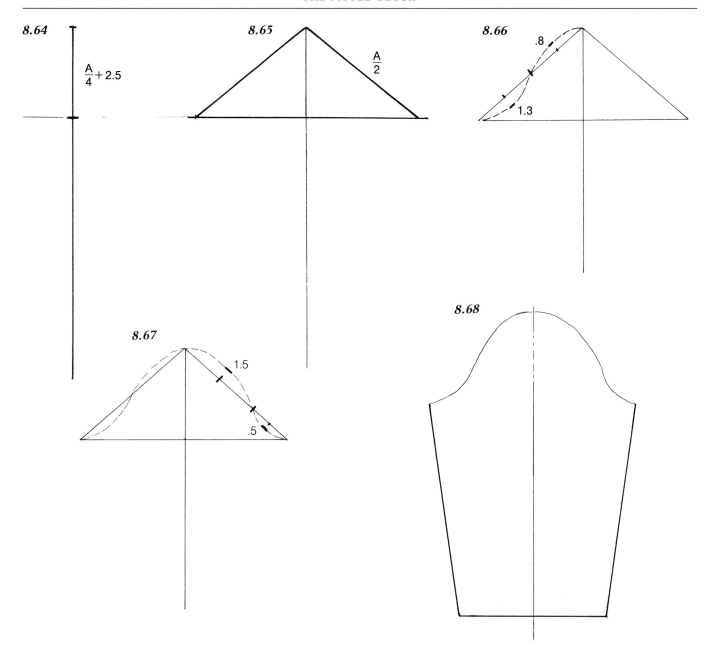

measurement around the armhole divided by 4 plus 2.5cm. This is your sleeve cap rise (*fig 8.64*).

3. Draw a horizontal line at the sleeve cap rise point. Measuring from the top of the vertical line, draw a diagonal line equal to the measurement around the armhole divided by 2 where it crosses the sleeve cap rise horizontal line (*fig 8.65*).

4. Divide the diagonal on the left into two equal sections. In the middle of the bottom section mark a point 1.3cm in from the diagonal. In the middle of the top section mark a point 0.8cm out from the diagonal. Draw the front sleeve curve (*fig 8.66*).

5. Divide the diagonal on the right into three equal sections. In the middle of the bottom section mark a point 0.5cm in from the diagonal. Between the top two sections mark a point 1.5cm out from the diagonal. Draft the back sleeve curve (*fig 8.67*).

6. Measure the vertical centre line from the top of the sleeve cap and mark the sleeve length equal to the SP to W measurement (*fig 8.68*).

7. Draw a horizontal line equal in length to the desired cuff measurement centred on the centre line.

8. Draw a line from the end of the cuff line to the UP.

9

Using the design doll to help draft garment patterns

1. Trace around the doll.

2. Draw and/or design the garment (*figs 9.1*, *9.2*) on top of your doll tracing. You can colour it in, cut it out with tabs to hang on your doll (*fig 9.3*), and so on (*fig 9.4*). You could also cut the garment shape out of the paper and leave a garment-shaped 'hole' through which you can view your swatches.

3. *Measure* the distance between the body of your doll and the edge of the drawn garment (*fig 9.5*).
    Divide the distance between the two by the body width. This will give you the *percentage* ease to add to your basic block when you come to draft your garment pattern.

4. Measure any other critical design features, such as sleeve length/yoke depth/design lines/distance between the waistline on the doll and the hem of the garment (*figs 9.6*, *9.7*). (Allow 2–4cm for vertical ease or 'blousing.') To convert the scale measurements from your doll to the drafted pattern, divide the cm measurement of the feature on the doll by 2 and move the decimal point one place to the right. This will give you the cm measurement for your pattern draft.
    When you are drafting the garment sections from your basic block, you must remember to take into consideration the type of fabric you are making. If it is very thick or not very stretchy, e.g. tuck stitch, double-bed fabric or woven fabric, you must allow at least 2–3 per cent extra ease.

5. Complete the drafting of your pattern and make all your tension swatches.

9.1

9.2

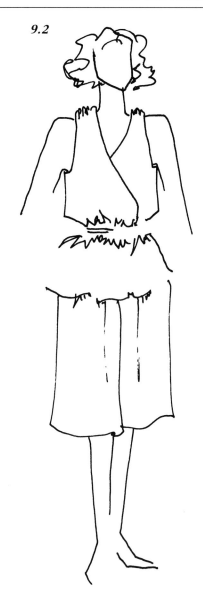

9.3

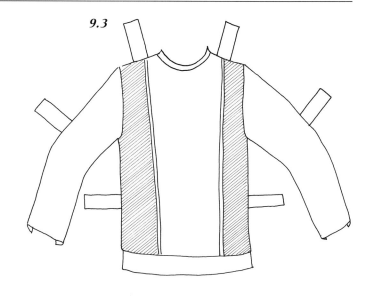

(*a*) Make the swatches for the fabric of the garment.

(*b*) Make the swatches for the edges and samples for any decorative details.

(*c*) Make samples of the 'construction' techniques you intend to use if they are to be a feature.

NB: When drafting a brown paper-bag jumper, the width of the body of the garment will be carried straight up to the shoulders, so you must draw the seam line accurately, e.g. if you have a garment which is 100cm at the bust the shoulders will be 50cm wide. If your shoulders are 40cm wide, you will have an overhang of 5cm at each shoulder.

9.4

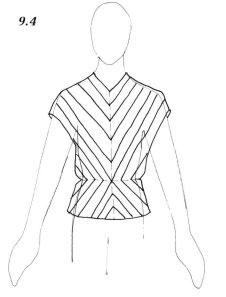
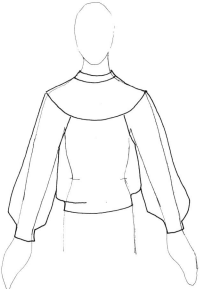

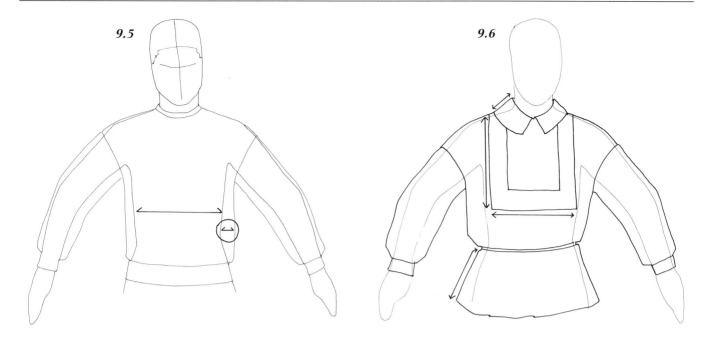

9.5

9.6

9.7

yoke

29cm

13cm

+23% ease

waist
ease for blousing

peplum 17.5cm

From pattern to garment – using the calculator

1. Draw the pattern out to the correct size and shape, preferably on squared paper. (The squares merely help you to draw your shape accurately: they are not intended to represent stitches.)

2. Measure all the horizontal measurements carefully and using the information from your tension swatch, calculate all the stitches required. If you use the Green or Blue Rulers and make your standard swatches to enable you to measure 40 sts × 60 rws (Green) or 20 sts × 30 rws (Blue), you will know how many stitches and rows are in 10cm and so merely have to move the decimal point one place to the left to get the number of stitches and rows in 1cm. If you measure your stitches and rows with any other measure, merely divide the number of stitches (and/or rows) by their cm measurement. The resulting number is the amount of stitches and rows in 1cm.

Then multiply the measurements of the pattern by the number of stitches or rows in 1cm to find how many you need to knit.

Measure the cast on and cast off lines and also the areas of gradual decreases (*fig 9.8*), e.g. bottom cast on; underarm cast off; armhole decrease; neckline cast off; neckline decrease; shoulder decrease and cast off.

9.8

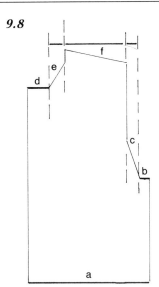

9.9

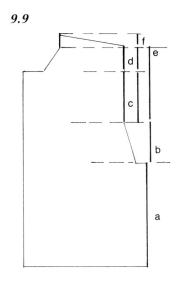

9.10

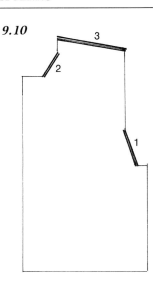

3. Measure all the verticals and calculate the number of rows required (*fig 9.9*), e.g. for hem to underarm; armhole decrease; neckline cast off (beginning of neckline); neckline decrease; beginning of shoulder; and shoulder decrease.

4. There are three places where the decreasings are gradual over several rows, and the rate of decreasing must be calculated (*fig 9.10*).

TO CALCULATE THE RATE OF DECREASING

1. Starting with the number of stitches you have, subtract the number of stitches you need to have at the end. This gives the number of stitches you need to lose (number of decreases).

2. You have a number of rows on which to carry out the decreases. Every row is an opportunity for a decrease, but you may not need that many opportunities – you may have more rows than the decreases you require. *So . . .*

3. How many of these opportunities (rows) will you have to miss between each decrease to distribute the decreases evenly? e.g. three decreases in 11 rows (3 balls into 11 boxes) (*fig 9.11*).

If you divide 11 by 3
you get 3 remainder 2 (*fig 9.12*)
so you can decrease once every 3 rows (*fig 9.13*)
3 times (*fig 9.14*)
but you will have 2 rows left over (*fig 9.15*).

We can distribute these extra rows between the decreasings (*fig 9.16*) (twice every 4 rows) (*fig 9.17*) *but* if we decrease twice every 4 rows (*fig 9.18*), we will only be able to decrease once every 3 rows (*fig 9.19*).

Where we add these rows the distance between the decreases will be greater, therefore the angle of the shaping will be shallower (*fig 9.20*).

To recap, this is what you did:

4. You had 3 stitches to lose and 11 opportunities to lose them. You divided 11 by 3 and found that 3 went into 11 3 times with 2 remaining. So you could decrease one stitch every 3 rows 3 times, but you would have 2 rows left over.

If you distributed these two rows between the decreasing, you will have no rows left over, but on two of the occasions you decrease you will have one extra row between the decreases. So you will have 3 rows between the decreases only once. The sum can be written like this:

(*a*) 3 goes into 11 3 times (rows between rows) rem. 2 (rows left over).

9.11 ① ② ③ □1 □2 □3 □4 □5 □6 □7 □8 □9 □10 □11

9.12

9.13

9.14

9.15

9.16

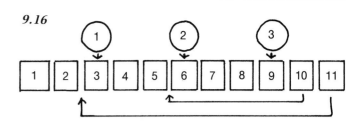

9.17

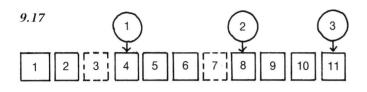

9.18

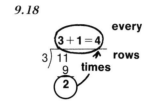

9.19

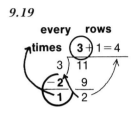

9.20

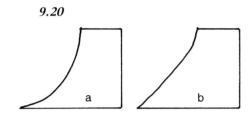

(*b*) Take the remainder from the number of decreases and add 1 to the number of rows between.

(*c*) So we can now see that the formula looks like this (*fig 9.21*):

decrease every 3rd row once

decrease every 4th row twice

9.21

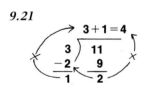

10

Calculating for circular sideways knitting

You must first determine the dimensions of the shape you wish to knit. This will be longer on one side than on the other, and could be a skirt, a yoke, a collar, a frill, a peplum, or a shawl, etc. It is really any shape that can be knitted sideways with internal shaping to make one edge longer than the other. You can draft the shape from a basic block: e.g. yokes on a bodice block, or skirts, or you can measure directly from the body.

When determining the shape you wish to make, one edge may be more critical than the other: e.g. the fitting of the top or yoke of a skirt is more important than the width at the hem; the bottom of a yoke on a bodice must fit the main garment section and the neckline can be adjusted slightly.

1.   You must make a tension swatch before you begin. Because your knitting will be 'hanging' vertically, there will be a greater tendency for it to drop. If you think about the way the fabric is formed, the yarn travels from side to side (*fig 10.1*). If the fabric is hanging on the body in the same direction it is made, the loops hang on to the yarn from the previous row. If, however, you turn the fabric through 90 degrees, the yarn travels up and down the fabric and there is nothing to stop it from straightening out and thus making the fabric longer and narrower (*fig 10.2*). If you are concerned about dropping in a skirt you may make a tension swatch *twice as wide as usual*. Hang the swatch up for several days (sideways) as it will hang on the final garment, with some small weight attached to the bottom, and then measure it (*fig 10.3*). This will give a more accurate measurement. Determine the number of stitches and rows per cm.

2.   **Width = stitches** (*figs 10.4, 10.5*)
Determine the width of your knitting (the length of the skirt or depth of a yoke) and convert this into stitches.

3.   **Length (long) = rows   Length (short) = rows**
Determine the length of the longest and shortest sides and convert these two measurements into rows.

4.   **Number of sections for shaping**
Find a number which will divide into both row numbers from stage 3 evenly. You may have to adjust the number of rows in either the longest or shortest side in order to get a satisfactory result.

5.   **Number of rows for shaping**
Subtract the smaller number from the larger one. This will give you the number of rows you can have in each shaping.
   If your shaping is going to be symmetrical, this number must be divisible by 4. If it is going to be asymmetrical, it must be divisible by 2.

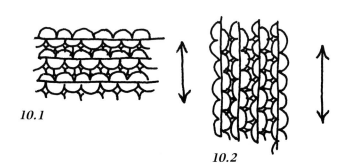

10.1

10.2

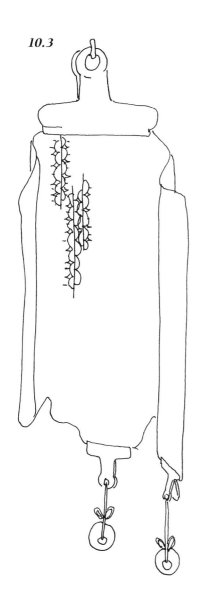

10.3

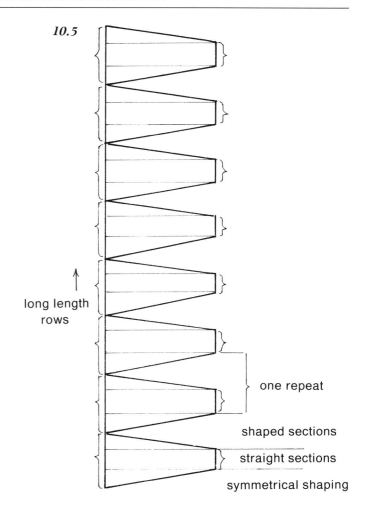

10.5

long length
rows

one repeat

shaped sections

straight sections

symmetrical shaping

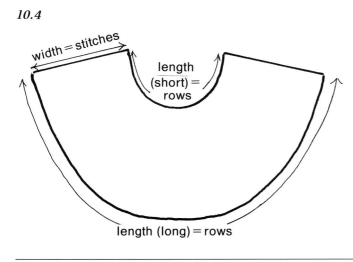

10.4

width = stitches

length
(short) =
rows

length (long) = rows

6. You can calculate regular shaping as explained on page 98–9. You know the number of stitches you have to shape because of the width of your section. You know the number of rows that are available for shaping. Remember that you will be able to shape only on alternate rows. Symmetrical shaping is really making two darts back to back.

For Shape I (fig 10.6)

(*a*) Gradually put the required needles into HP (on alternate rows on the side of the knitting opposite the carriage) until all needles required are in HP.

(*b*) Then return them to UWP (on alternate rows on the side of the knitting opposite the carriage), gradually copying exactly what was done in (a) above until all needles are back in WP.

(*c*) Knit straight section.

10.6   10.7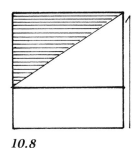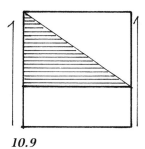

                                    10.8   10.9

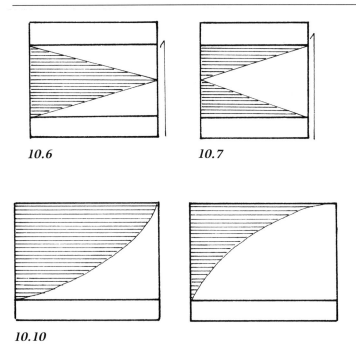

10.10

For Shape II (fig 10.7)

(*a*) Put all needles into HP and gradually put them back into UWP (on alternate rows on the side of the knitting opposite the carriage) until all needles are in WP.

(*b*) Then gradually put the required needles into HP (on alternate rows on the side of the knitting opposite the carriage) until all needles are in HP.

(*c*) When this shaping section is completed you can knit the straight section by putting *all* needles back to UWP at once. These two methods result in shapings that are symmetrical. The two following shapings are not symmetrical.

For Shape III (fig 10.8)

(*a*) Gradually put required needles to HP (on alternate rows on the side of the knitting opposite the carriage) until all needles are in HP.

(*b*) Put all needles back to UWP at once.

(*c*) Knit straight section.

For Shape IV (fig 10.9)

(*a*) Put all needles to HP and then gradually push required needles to UWP (on alternate rows on the side of the knitting opposite the carriage) until all needles are in WP.

(*b*) Knit straight section.

If you decide not to have regular shaping (*fig 10.10*), you *must shape on alternate rows* but you do not have to move the same number of needles every time! This can achieve very interesting shaping, e.g. fish-tail flares in skirts, and you can control where the fullness lies. You can use this technique to give flares or 'puffs.' The choice is yours.

11

Pattern drafting for bias knitting

If you want to knit a garment on the bias, you will first have to establish the angle of your shaping. This must be done regardless of whether you are calculating your garment or using a patterning attachment.

1. Knit a tension square and determine the stitches and rows in 10cm.

Either use the Green/Blue Ruler to find out the number of sts and rws in 10cm, then divide 10 by the number of stiches/rows and you will find out how many cm each stitch/row measures;

or measure 40 sts/60 rws (20 sts)/30 rws for chunky knitting) and then calculate for standard gauge (chunky) machines:

40 (20) sts = x cm

$$\frac{x}{40} \left(\frac{x}{20}\right) = \text{cm measure of each stitch}$$

60 (30) rws = y cm

$$\frac{y}{60} \left(\frac{y}{30}\right) = \text{cm measure of each row}$$

(Divide the measurement by stitches/rows to find out the measurement of each stitch/row.)

2. To determine the *bias line*:

(a) *For calculating on squared paper*
1. Draw a horizontal and vertical line meeting at a 90 degree angle. If you are going to decrease 1 st on every alternate row you can make a line on your graph that would give you the exact angle your knitting would make.
2. Mark a point on your vertical line that is the equivalent to the measurement e.g. 20 rws (measuring from 0). Draw a horizontal line from this point (*fig 11.1*).

3. Mark another point on your horizontal line that is the equivalent to the measurement of half the number of sts e.g. 10 sts (measuring from 0). Draw a vertical line from this point (*fig 11.2*).
4. Draw a line from 0 to the point where these two lines cross. This is the diagonal line for your bias knitting (*fig 11.3*).

(b) *If you are using a pattern attachment:*
1. Set the attachment up according to the information you have determined from your

11.1

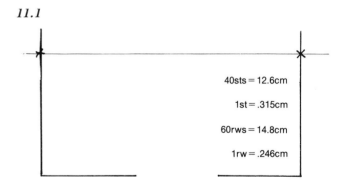

40sts = 12.6cm

1st = .315cm

60rws = 14.8cm

1rw = .246cm

11.2

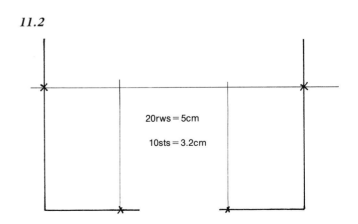

20rws = 5cm

10sts = 3.2cm

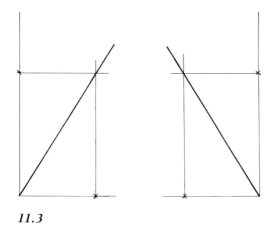

11.3

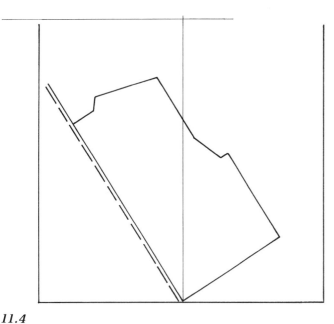

11.4

tension square regarding the stitch scale and row adjustment.

2. Feed a blank sheet into your attachment and roll it down. Adjust the row counter on the attachment (if it has one) to read 000.

3. Mark a point on your pattern sheet at the point where the stitch scale reads 0.

4. Roll your pattern sheet down carefully to equivalent of, e.g. 20 rws. Mark another point on your sheet where the stitch scale reads the equivalent of *half* the number of sts.

5. Remove the sheet from the attachment and draft a straight line through these two points. This will give you the bias line for your knitting.

Now you are ready to place your garment on this diagonal line (*fig 11.4*) and you can *either* calculate to determine how many sts and rws you will need to knit your shape, *or* draft your block on the sheet to be fed into your patterning attachment and then let *it* do all the work for you.

12

From pattern to garment using the charting device

1. Knit the tension swatch and allow it to rest.

(*a*) If knitting in acrylic, you must allow your swatch extra time to 'relax.'

(*b*) If knitting in oiled yarn, e.g. Shetland wool, lambs-wool, cashmere, etc., you must wash and block your swatch.

(*c*) If you are knitting in silk and plan to dry clean the finished garment, test it by pinning your swatch inside the pocket of a jacket and send the garment to the dry cleaner's.

It is very important that you knit swatches of all the stitch patterns you intend to use in the garment. Don't just knit a tension swatch in stocking stitch and assume that the measurements for Fair Isle knitting will be the same if you increase the tension dial number by one. The swatch may be the same width, but it will be quite different in length.

At this point it is also a very good idea to knit samples of all the hems and edges you plan to incorporate into your garment. Then you can decide whether you will be able to knit in the hem or edge or if it will be necessary to add it after the garment sections have been finished.

2. Once you have determined your stitch and row measurements, you can set up your patterning attachment. You must put the appropriate stitch scale (which resembles a ruler) at the front of your attachment. The point where the drawn pattern line crosses the stitch scale tells you which needles on your needle bed must be in working position.

You must set the row gauge on the attachment to correspond with the information of your tension swatch.

To check whether the patterning attachment on Brother and Toyota machines is accurate, mark the starting point on the pattern sheet. Then roll your pattern sheet down, counting the clicks (each represents one row). When you have rolled the sheet down for 60 rows (clicks), make another mark on it. The measurement of the distance between these two marks should be the same as the measurement of 60 (30 on a Brother chunky machine) rows of your tension swatch.

To check if your patterning attachment is accurate on a Knitmaster machine, mark your starting point on the pattern sheet. Make another mark on the sheet 5cm for half-scale patterns (10cm for full-scale patterns) above the first mark. Move the carriage backwards and forwards on the needle bed (without any needles in WP) or click the patterning attachment row tripper equivalent to the number reading you got on your Green (Blue) Ruler. When you have moved the patterning attachment row tripper the same number of times, you should have moved the sheet 5cm for half-scale and 10cm for full-scale.

(*a*) On the Jones-Brother KL116 you can draw your pattern out full-size and full-scale if you wish. However, it may be easier to draw out half the garment shape on the sheet where appropriate (*fig 12.1*) (e.g. a symmetrical front and/or back and sleeve). This will save you the bother of looking from side to side when shaping a symmetrical piece.

If you are drawing out a garment piece which is not symmetrical, e.g. a sideways knitted batwing, you would of course draw the full garment section.

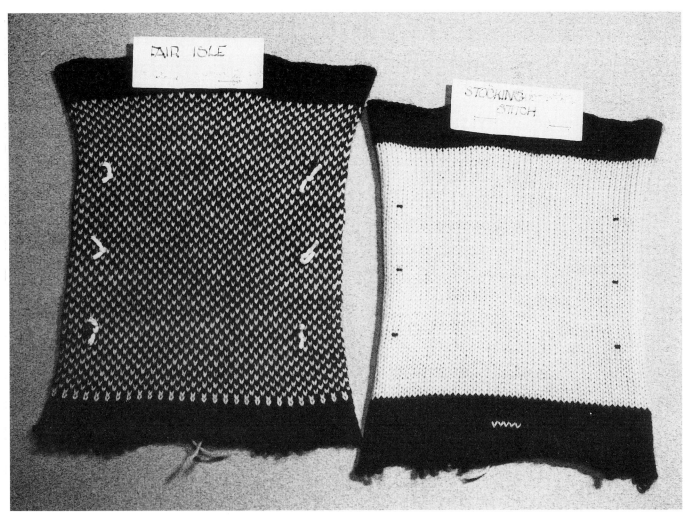

Comparison of stocking stitch and Fair Isle tension swatches

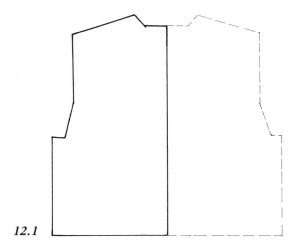

12.1

If the garment is symmetrical from top to bottom, you could draw your section out to the midway line. When you reach this point in your knitting, remove the sheet, turn it upside down, reverse it and reinsert it to knit the remaining half. The sheet is clear, so you should be able to see the pattern easily (*fig 12.2*).

(*b*) On Brother built-in Patterning Attachments, Toyota Knit Tracers and Knitmaster Knit Radars (later models with full-scale stitch scales) you will have to draw out the pattern to the equivalent of the 'fold line' on a dressmaking pattern. (*NB*: on the Brother built-in Knitleaders you cannot draw out your garment until you have ascertained which stitch scale you will need, as the 0 line on the sheet (the datum line) equivalent to 0 on the needle bed can be on either the left or right-hand side of the stitch scale, depending on which stitch scale you use.)

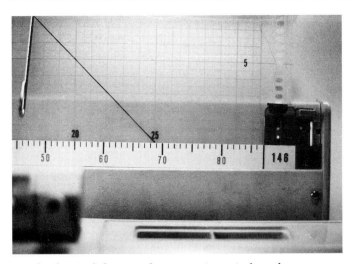

Knitleader with line on chart crossing stitch scale

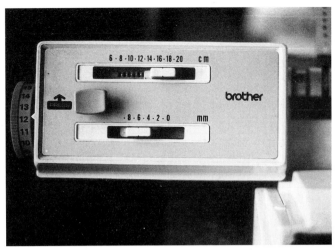

Row gauge on KL116

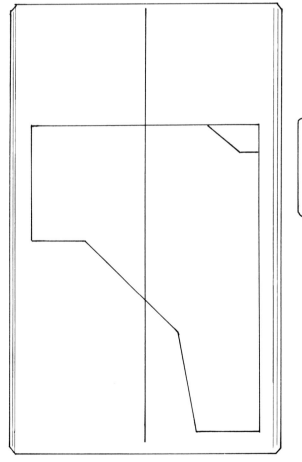

12.2

You can draw the pattern 'life-size' or full-scale, but you can only draw half of the shape, as the stitch scale corresponds with the needles that go from the centre to the edge of the needle bed, not edge to edge of the machine.

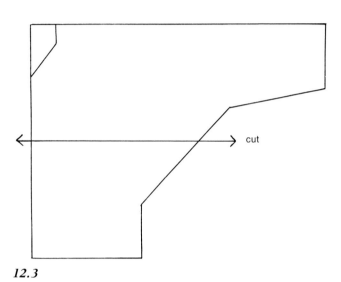

12.3

If you wish to draw out a pattern which is not symmetrical, e.g. a sideways knitted batwing garment, you may draw out the two sections you wish to knit in two colours as follows:

1. Draft your pattern as you wish it to look and cut it out.
2. Fold it exactly in half (*fig 12.3*) and cut it along the centre line (*fig 12.4*).
3. Mark a line on your patterning sheet equivalent to the centre 0 on the machine. This line lines up with the 0 on your stitch scale.
4. Place one half of the pattern on the sheet with the centre cut line on your marked centre line (*fig 12.5*). Draw around it with one colour.
5. Place the second half of the pattern on the sheet with the centre cut line on the marked centre

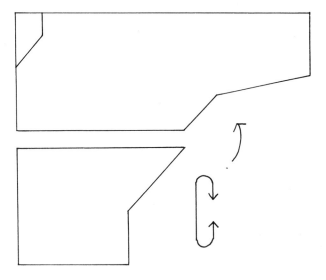

12.4

If two sides of a garment section are being shaped at the same time, the shaping can only be done on alternate rows at one edge, e.g. casting off stitches or putting needles into HP at the beginning of the row. You need only look at the patterning attachment once every two rows, and then repeat what you did at one side on the following row on the other side.

It is only possible to push a group of needles to HP on the side of the knitting opposite the carriage. If, however, you decide that you want to cast off or cast on, this can be done on both sides of the work simultaneously. Introduce an additional end of yarn at the edge of the work opposite the carriage so that while using the knitting yarn at one edge of your work, you can use the supplementary end at the other edge.

line and the edges of the second piece lining up with the edges of the first piece where they meet the centre line. Draw around the second piece in a second colour.

The first colour corresponds to the needles on one side of the needle bed and the second colour corresponds to the needles on the other side of the bed when you are knitting and shaping your garment section.

If you wish to knit a garment which is symmetrical from top to bottom and your pattern sheet is transparent, you can repeat the procedure mentioned for the KL116 as above. If your sheet is not transparent, you will have to draw out the whole shape.

(c) Knitmaster Knitradar
On older models of the Knitradar the patterning attachment is rather smaller and all garment shapes must be drawn half scale. To help with this, you can purchase a half-scale white triangle from Knitmaster dealers. This device is very easy to use. The two legs are half-scale measurements (one side is cm, the other is inches). The hypotenuse is full-scale. If you have drafted your block out full-scale, you will have to measure it and convert the measurements to enable you to draw out a half-scale pattern, or you can simply make your block up to half-scale and work directly from that, altering it to get your design lines. On older models you will still only be able to draw half your pattern on your patterning sheet. On later models you can draw out the *whole* shape half-scale or *half* the shape full-scale. It is up to you which you prefer.

Problems on patterning attachments

Some problems may arise when using the patterning attachment to knit up the garment shapes you have drafted on the knitting machine.

When measuring your tension swatch, you may find that the measurements are wider or longer than those you can use on your attachment.

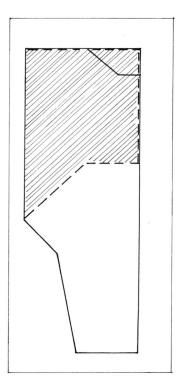

12.5

1. If your tension swatch is too long (i.e. the measurement of 60 rows is greater than the adjustment you can make on your attachment or the sample is longer than your Green/Blue Ruler), you must draft your pattern out half scale *in length only* (*fig 12.6*). For those knitters whose pattern is already in half scale, i.e. Knitmaster knitters, you must halve your scale again (i.e. use quarter scale). Then measure your rows again, divide by 2 and use this number on your attachment.

Knitmaster knitters must:

(*a*) Measure rows in cm.

(*b*) Divide this measurement by 2 and place that number against your ruler. Then you can see how many 'rows in 10cm.' This is not really the number of rows in 10cm, but it is the number you must put on your attachment to enable you to knit your (now quarter scale) garment accurately.

2. If the tension swatch measurement is wider than any of your stitch gauges, divide the measurement of 40 sts by 2 and use the gauge (ruler) that corresponds to that measurement, but halve the number indicated. For example, if the line on your pattern sheet crosses the gauge at 10, you must substitute the number 5.

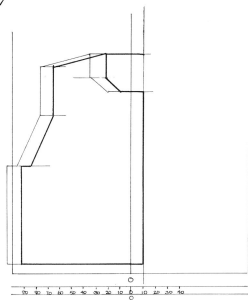

12.7

Knitmaster knitters must:

(*a*) Measure 40 sts.

(*b*) Divide the measurement by 2 and then place it against your Green/Blue Ruler to find out the 'number of sts in 10 cm'. Use this number to find the appropriate stitch gauge and proceed as above.

3. Use the following procedure if the garment is wider than your attachment sheet and stitch gauge but you would have enough needles to knit the required width. (It is easier to do this if your garment shape is symmetrical.)

Draw half the pattern shape on your patterning attachment sheet so that the centre line of the pattern is aligned with the right of the centre 0 on your stitch gauge (by 10 needles). (To do this, you must place your gauge at the bottom of the sheet before you draw out your pattern.) You may have to extend the stitch gauge by writing the additional numbers on the gauge to take you from the highest number indicated up to 100 (*fig 12.7*). When you come to knit your garment, take 10 on the R of 0 on the gauge to be 0 on the needle bed. Then 0 on the gauge would be 10 L on the needle bed, 10 would be 20 on the needle bed, and so on.

4. If the overall garment pattern outline is wider than the pattern sheet (*fig 12.8*) (and requires more needles than you have on your needle bed) but can be divided

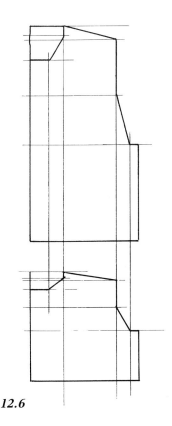

12.6

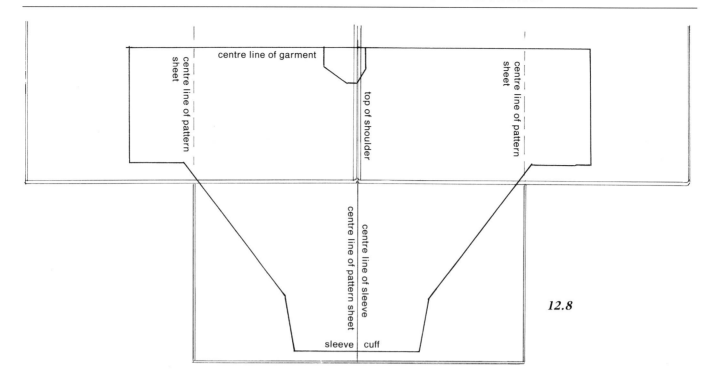

12.8

into sections, each not wider than the number of needles available, you can draw your pattern on the sheet in sections and remove and replace your work on the bed when you are knitting. You must make sure that all the stitch patterns are transferred accurately and that your Fair Isle repeats will match up. This can be done with both vertical and horizontal knitted dolman shapes and many others.

13

Alternative sources of pattern

Although I feel very strongly that the best approach to machine knitted fashionable garments to fit real people is to draft your own shapes based on the measurements of the person who is actually going to wear the garment, nevertheless there are other possibilities.

EXISTING GARMENTS

One way of arriving at a shape for a garment is to take a suitable, comfortable existing one and use it as a template. The disadvantage of this method is that if the garment is really comfortable, it has probably been worn and washed frequently, with the result that it is completely out of shape, which will give a totally distorted pattern if you try to draw around it accurately. You could use the measurements of the garment as a guide for the amount of ease required when drafting your own pattern from body measurements, but I wouldn't rely on the actual shape too much, as it will probably lead to confusion and disappointment.

SEWING PATTERNS

Another source of garment shape is the commercial sewing pattern, which can be used on the charting device. If you have an attachment that enables you to draw your shape full scale, you will find it easier than using a half-scale model. If, however, you have a half-scale charting device, you will have to reproduce the commercial pattern in half-scale, which will mean measuring it accurately and then re-drafting it to the correct size. If you have a device that enables you to reproduce only half the pattern and your pattern is not

going to be knitted symmetrically on the needle bed, you will have to follow the instructions for putting your garment shape on the charting device on page 107.

There are a few things to remember when using sewing patterns:

1. It is better to use patterns designed for stretchy fabrics. These usually require less easing of fabric and are usually designed with a minimum of darts.

2. On armhole shaping, the outward curve towards the shoulder point can be modified to a straight vertical line, which will make shaping easier and can result in less distortion of stitch pattern (*fig 13.1*). Remember, however, that the length of the line from the SNP to the SP must be the same on the front and the back of the garment. You will find that the armhole depth is different on the front and back of commercial patterns

13.1

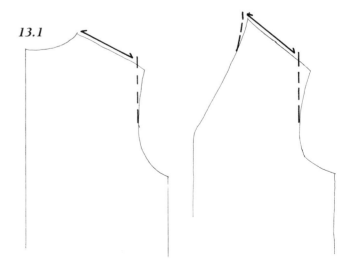

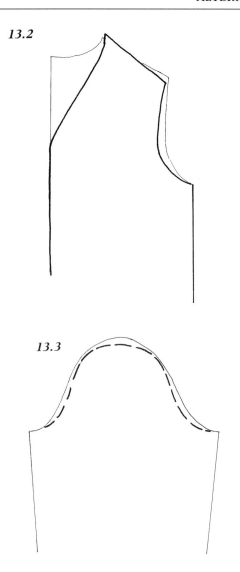

13.2

13.3

the cap area only. Be careful, however, that it does not end up smaller than your armhole. The circumference should measure the same as the whole armhole (plus 1–2cm).

4. When choosing patterns to adapt, avoid those that are too elaborate, with facings, darts, etc. You can modify patterns by knitting them in sections rather than shaping within the garment section. The best patterns are those which consist of very simple shapes, perhaps relying on gathering or smocking. Short row shaping can often be helpful.

5. Seam allowances should be deleted.

HANDKNITTING PATTERNS

Perhaps you have seen a pattern for a handknitted garment which you found intriguing but there was no diagram to go with it so that you wondered how it was achieved or exactly what the shaping looked like. You can use your charting device to help you to draft the pattern.

1. Note the tension specified in the pattern (the number of sts and rws in 10cm). For the Knitmaster charting device, the next step is to adjust your rows and choose your stitch scale to match the tension of the pattern. For other charting devices, you must find out how many cm 40 sts and 60 rws measure.

2. Set up your charting device with a blank sheet and do the pattern as a 'dry run' by rolling the sheet down manually according to the number of rows specified in the pattern. Mark the sheet according to the number of sts required by the pattern, using the stitch scale as a guide.

Mark the sheet to indicate the number of sts required in the cast on. Roll the sheet down according to the number of rows required. Mark the sheet indicating the sts to be increased or decreased according to the rows specified.

You can also mark any short row shaping in this way. Then when you want to reproduce the shape you will have the pattern drafted out and need merely to substitute your own tension swatch information and knit the garment.

(*fig 13.2*), which means that the shoulder seam comes towards the front of the garment. On most knitting patterns for garments, however, the armhole drop on the front and back is the same. Neither is 'right' or 'wrong'; these are merely two different approaches to design.

3. Usually, woven fabric tends to be less stretchy and more stable than knitted fabric, meaning that more ease has been added to the sleeve cap. You may therefore find that you have to decrease the circumference of the sleeve cap, otherwise it is too big and 'bulgy' for the armhole (*fig 13.3*). You can do this by reducing the height of the cap and by reducing the width slightly in

Green and white
poncho

White poncho

White Shetland dress

Green and black doughnut top

Ten-square jacket

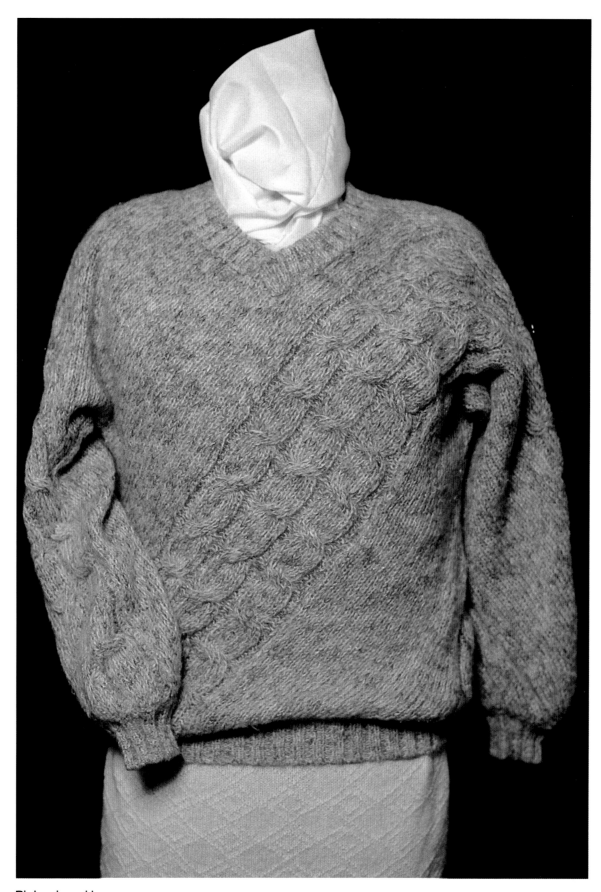

Pink origami jumper

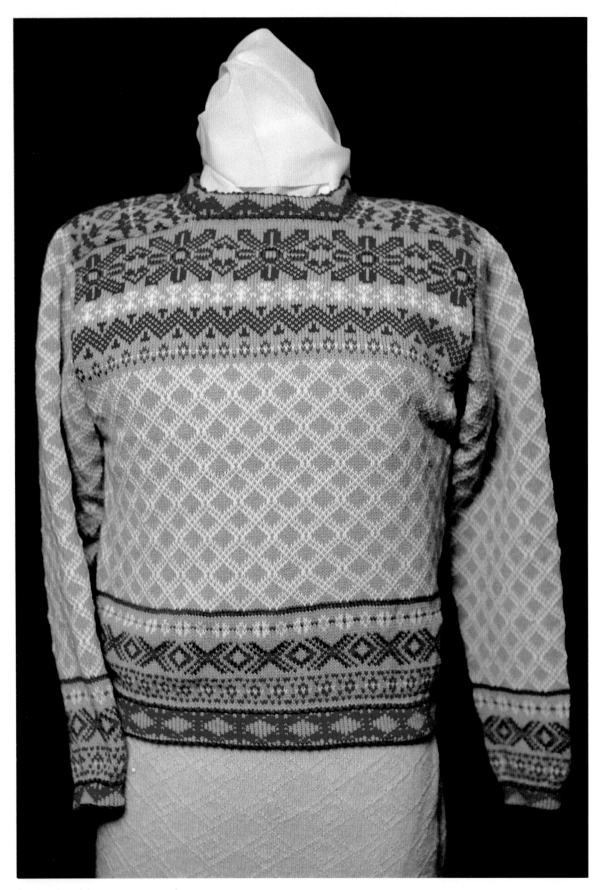

Strap shoulder percentage jumper

Black and white percentage jumper

Brown and white tuck stitch waistcoat

14

Bodice variations

Darts

For bust darts knitted horizontally:

1. Draft fitted body block. Note BP. Add required ease (*fig 14.1*).

2. Measure from SNP to waist front (over bust) and back. Subtract back measurement from front measurement (*fig 14.2*). The difference between the two is the depth of the dart.

3. Draw a horizontal line through the BP. Mark a point on the line 1cm away from the BP towards the side seam (*fig 14.3*).

4. Slash the pattern at the horizontal line and spread the two sections of the pattern equivalent to the depth of the dart.

5. Draw a line from the side seam of the lower section to the mark on the upper section 1cm away from the BP (*fig 14.4*).

6. Shaping is done by short rowing. The shaded section is not knitted.

14.1

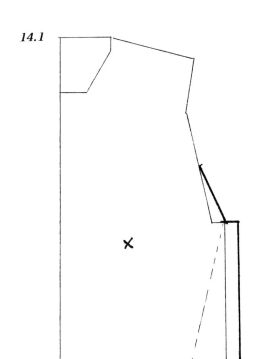

14.2

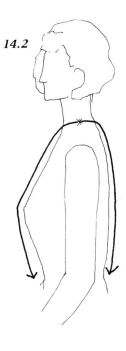

14.3

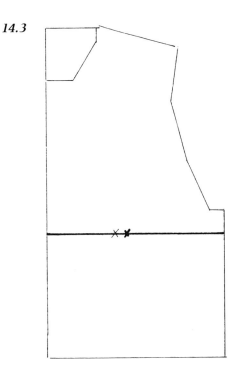

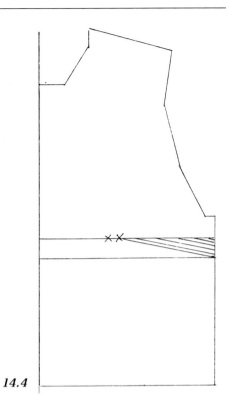

14.4

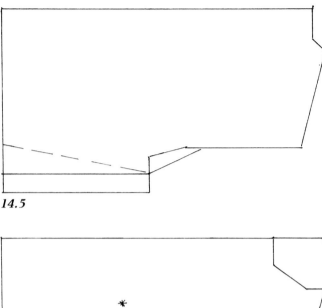

14.5

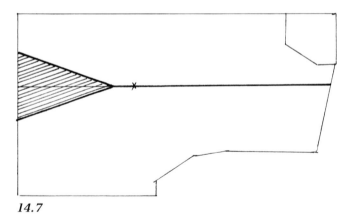

14.6

The following darts are knitted vertically.

SIMPLE BUST DART

1. Draft the fitted blocks (both front and back) with the centre line horizontal. Note the BP. Add required ease. Omit extra fitting in the front armhole (*figs 14.5, 14.6*).

2. On the front block, draw a horizontal line through the BP and mark a point on this line 1cm away from the BP towards the waistline (*fig 14.7*).

3. Mark two points equidistant from this line on the waistline. The measurement between these two points is 38 per cent of the difference between the bust measurement and the waist measurement.

4. Draw lines between these two points and the point 1cm below the BP. Shade in the area. This area is not knitted (*fig 14.8*).

5. On the back (half) block mark the centre point of the waistline. Draw a horizontal line through this point. Mark the point where this line crosses the line at the bottom of the armhole.

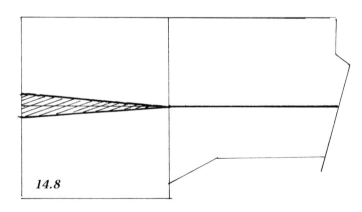

14.7

14.8

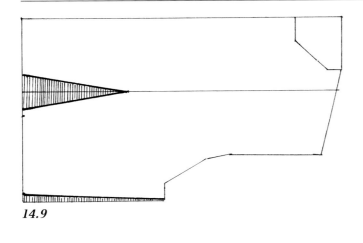

14.9

6. Mark two points on the waistline equidistant from the horizontal line. The distance between these two points is 12 per cent of the difference between the bust measurement and the waist measurement.

7. Draw lines between these two points and the point on the horizontal line where it crosses the armhole line. Shade in the area.

8. All shaping is done by short rowing and the shaded area is not knitted.

9. You can redistribute some of the shaping by making another dart by short-rowing at the underarm side seam (*figs 14.9, 14.10*). Your bust dart will then be smaller by the amount included in the new dart.

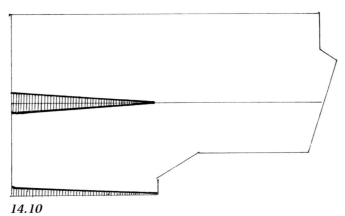

14.10

PEPLUM DARTS

1. Draft the basic fitted bodice (front and back) with the simple bust dart and the centre line horizontal (*figs 14.11, 14.12*). Add the required ease. Add the required length to the blocks below the waistline.

14.11

14.12

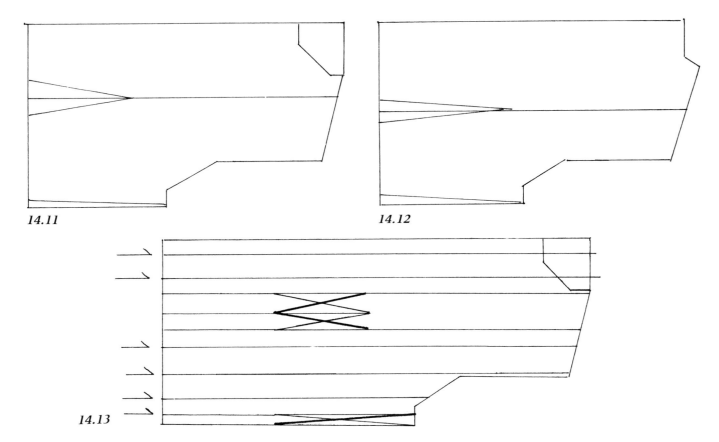

14.13

14.14

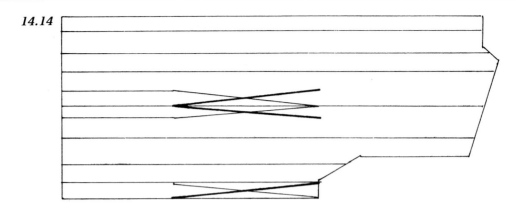

14.15

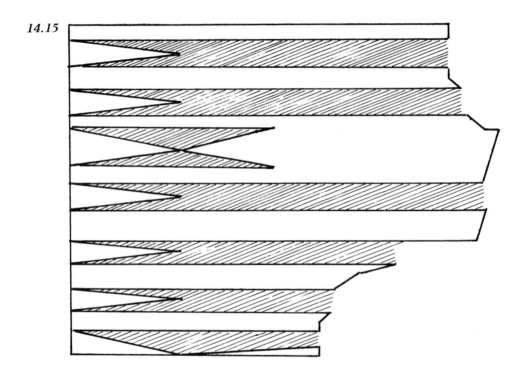

2. Extend the horizontal lines from the bottom edges of the darts. Redraft the bodice darts, reversing them (*figs 14.13, 14.14*).

3. Slash the blocks into horizontal sections. (The more the merrier!)

4. Spread each section apart equidistantly. Insert short-row knitted triangles into the spaces between the sections (*figs 14.15, 14.16*).

5. All shaping is done by short rowing.

Yoke variations

DRAFTING FOR HORIZONTAL KNITTING

1. Draft the basic fitted block front and back. Add required ease and length (*fig 14.17*).

2. Determine the depth of the yoke and slash the pattern horizontally front and back. The yoke may be straight or shaped. Re-draft the front neck if required (*fig 14.18*).

3. Divide the bottom of the pattern into vertical sections (*fig 14.19*). Slash the sections, spread them out equidistantly and re-draft the bottom part of the pattern (*fig 14.20*).

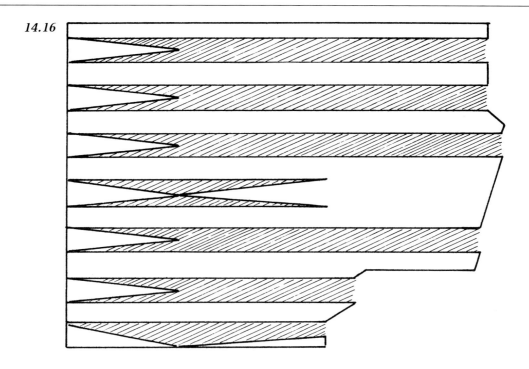

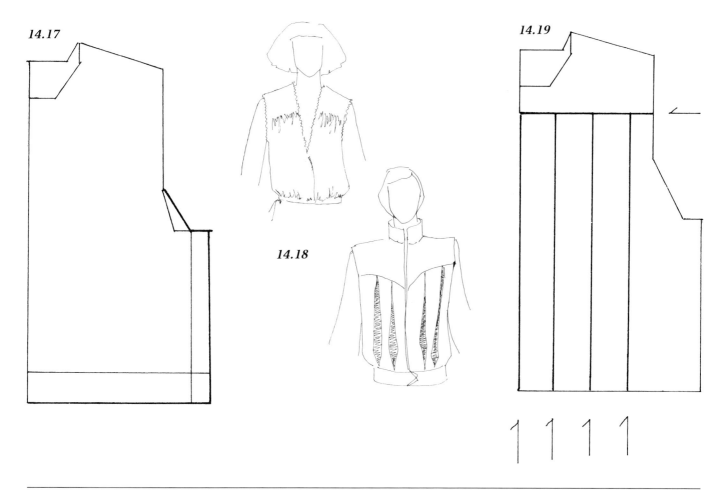

14.16

14.17

14.18

14.19

14.20

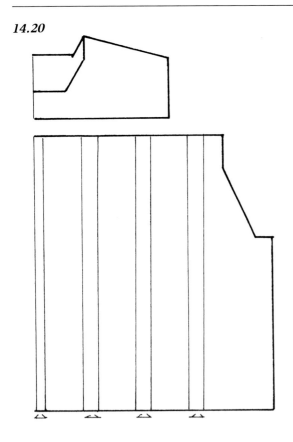

14.21

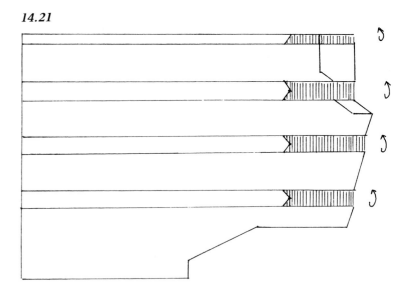

4. To knit the garment, cast on and knit the bottom and remove the work on to WY or a garter bar. Replace work on the number of needles required to knit the yoke, either gathering (decreasing evenly across the row) or pleating. The pleating must be done from WY. (*NB*: If the front and back are spread equally, there will be *no* decreasing in the centre section in the back if the neck is drafted down to the bottom of the yoke line at the front. You will only have gathered across the shoulders.)

DRAFTING FOR VERTICAL KNITTING

1. Draft the basic fitted blocks front and back with the centre line horizontal. Add required ease.

2. Determine the depth of the yoke. Draw a vertical guideline.

3. Divide the pattern into horizontal sections. Slash and spread the sections equidistantly. (It is usually a good idea to make more rather than fewer sections when drafting this sort of pattern.)

4. The yoke is created by:

(*a*) Short-rowing repeatedly over the *same* needles for several rows (*fig 14.21*). You must *carefully* wrap the end needle in HP each time. This results in quite a lot of yarn wrapped around this needle, so care must be taken when knitting it back into WP.

(*b*) Short-rowing, but only decreasing/increasing one needle every two rows. This results in a very deep 'dart' which becomes almost a gather, but avoids the problems encountered in (*a*) above.

(*c*) Picking up or making 'little hems' over the yoke section only.

Bodice modifications

When designing garments which will have a front closing, you may wish to add 1–2cm allowance for this. You need not add more than this if you are knitting an edge on each front section. If, however, you are knitting the crossover and facing in one piece with the front sections, you will have to make allowances for this.

A word of warning for garments with buttonholes (fig 14.22). Always plan your buttonholes starting with the first buttonhole *level with the bust point*. Work out from this point, planning the spacing of the remaining buttonholes. This is standard practice in dressmaking for a very good reason, as it prevents 'gappy fronts'.

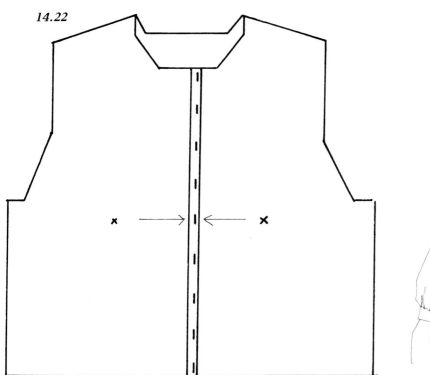

14.22

14.23

SLEEVELESS VESTS

1. Draft the basic fitted block front and back. Add required ease. For a fitted waistcoat, you may wish to include a fitted side seam (*fig 14.23*). For a pullover, you may wish to have the shape more casual. You may alter the neckline and the armhole to suit your design if required.

2. To make allowance for any garments worn underneath, i.e. a shirt or blouse, drop the UP 1.5–2cm or more if required (*fig 14.24*).

3. Adjust the hemline. For a fitted waistcoat you will have to allow for a centre closing. You can add 0.5–1cm to each half of the front section. You can also design a shaped hemline (*fig 14.25*).

CARDIGANS AND OUTERWEAR

The basic garment is drafted, but extra ease is added at specific points:

(*a*) Bust, 8–10cm plus.

(*b*) Across the front (to allow for closings), 2cm plus.

(*c*) At shoulder width 0.5–2cm plus (at each shoulder).

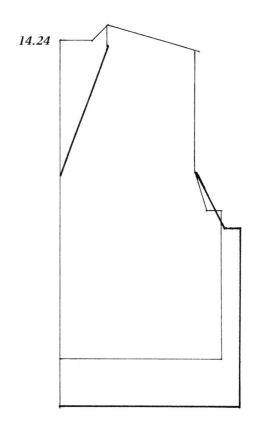

14.24

14.25

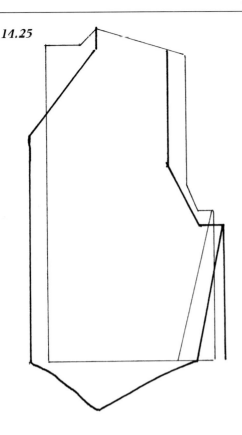

14.26

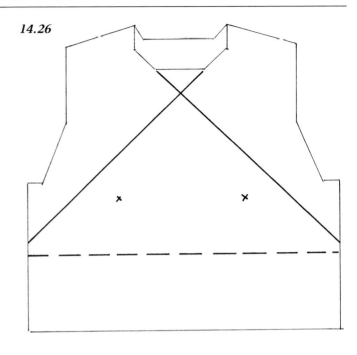

14.27

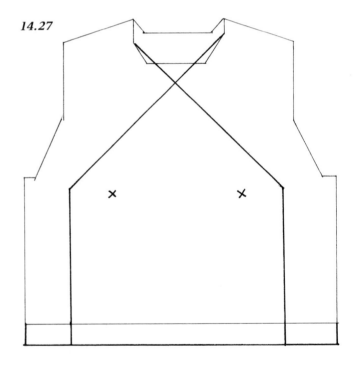

(*d*) The UP is dropped 1.5–4cm. The armhole drop is increased and the armhole itself made larger to accommodate garments worn underneath.

(*e*) Sleeves: the ease is increased by 2–4cm.

CROSSOVERS

1. Draft the basic front block in full and add the required ease.

2. Length is adjusted and the neckline and crossover drafted. You must then re-draft your pattern in two pieces (right front and left front). If the length is short, check the circumference of the body at the hemline point (*fig 14.26*). If the crossover is loose at this point, you may require a neat edge to keep the garment in place. Don't forget to allow for vertical ease or blousing if the garment is to be fitted at the hemline.

The minimum allowance is 1.5cm (*fig 14.27*). Remember not to make the neckline too deep or the crossover too minimal, as this can result in a 'gappy' neckline. To help in drafting your pattern, indicate the BP in your draft.

If the neckline does turn out to be a bit 'gappy' and loose, this can be adjusted by adding a firm edge to help it keep its shape.

Special techniques

By using short-rowing and knitting some areas with waste yarn, you can knit an entire raglan garment in one go. This variation can be adapted for other similarly shaped garments, such as peasant blouses.

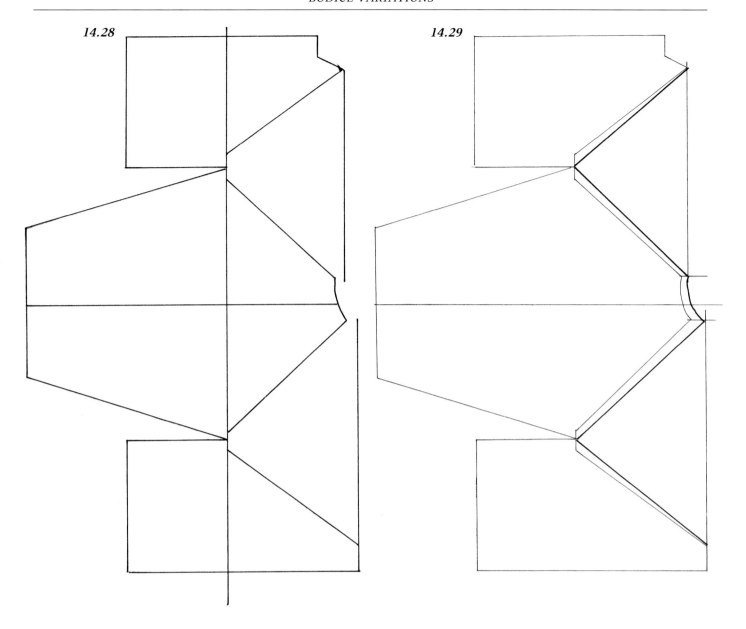

14.28

14.29

1. Draw horizontal and vertical guidelines (*fig 14.28*). Using your raglan pattern, line up each section in turn (i.e. front, sleeve, back) so that the centre lines of the pieces are all parallel to the horizontal guideline and all the UPs are on the vertical guideline.

2. Draw straight vertical guidelines from the SNP on the front and the SNP on the back (*fig 14.29*). Draft horizontal guidelines from the SNPs of the sleeve and adjust the top of the sleeve.

3. Re-draft the diagonal line between the SNPs and the UPs.

4. When knitting the pattern:

(*a*) Start and finish knitting at the CB or the CF (*fig 14.30*). The garment is drafted from the CB (CF) and knitted halfway. The pattern is then turned upside down and the other half of the garment knitted in mirror image (in reverse order).

(*b*) The underarm seam is separated from the sleeve by several rows of waste knitting.

(*c*) Extra needles required for the sleeve length are cast on (cast off) in waste knitting.

(*d*) The shaded areas indicate shaping by short rowing.

(*e*) Underarm side seams and sleeve seam and the CB (CF) seams are grafted after the garment is removed from the machine.

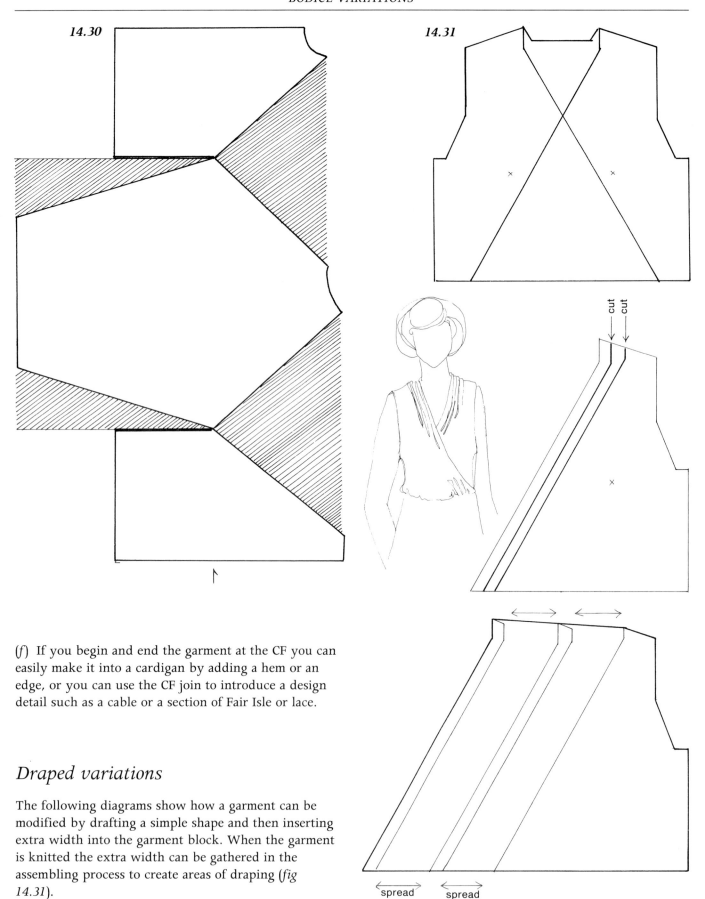

14.30

14.31

(f) If you begin and end the garment at the CF you can easily make it into a cardigan by adding a hem or an edge, or you can use the CF join to introduce a design detail such as a cable or a section of Fair Isle or lace.

Draped variations

The following diagrams show how a garment can be modified by drafting a simple shape and then inserting extra width into the garment block. When the garment is knitted the extra width can be gathered in the assembling process to create areas of draping (fig 14.31).

cut cut

spread spread

More draped variations

14.32

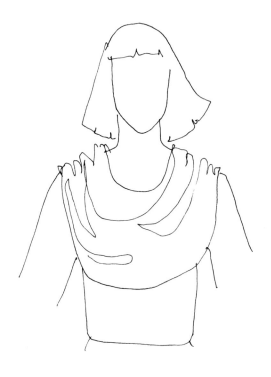

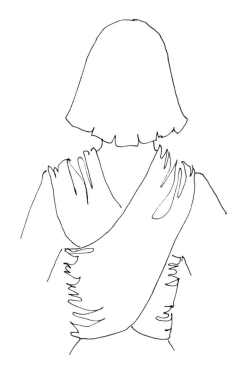

15

Sleeve variations

This section will consider the pattern drafting variations that are available to the knitter when designing the sleeve. Some variations can depend on whether the sleeve is knitted from top to bottom (cuff to sleeve head or vice versa), or sideways.

To add fullness to the sleeve width, a dressmaking technique called 'slash and spread' is used. Where you slash and how far you spread depends on where you decide you want the fullness to be. You must remember that a lot of knitted fabric is very unstable. The amount of fullness you choose to include can also depend on the type of fabric you are knitting: a thin stocking stitch fabric is much more 'compressible' than a thick double-bed tuck stitch fabric.

When you gather knitted fabric, it can ease in a great deal more than an equivalent amount of woven fabric. This means that when calculating the amount extra you must allow for gathering you should probably exaggerate this, otherwise your gathering may disappear. Although most of the examples here are drafted from the fitted sleeve, with a little ingenuity they can also be applied to other types of sleeve, such as the raglan.

Puffed sleeve

FULLNESS IN THE WHOLE SLEEVE

1. Draft a fitted sleeve. Draft both right and left hand sections (*fig 15.1*). Strictly speaking, you will not need both sections because your pattern will be symmetrical, but it will help you to decide proportions when designing.

2. Slash your pattern down the centre line (*fig 15.2*).

3. Spread each section equidistant from the centre line and re-draft your pattern. You will now have fullness at both the sleeve head and the cuff.

FULLNESS AT THE HEAD

1. Draft a whole fitted sleeve. Draft both right and left-hand sections. Strictly speaking, you will not need both sections because your pattern will be symmetrical,

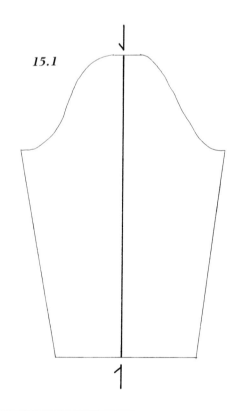

15.1

124

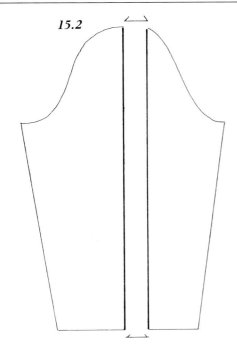

15.2

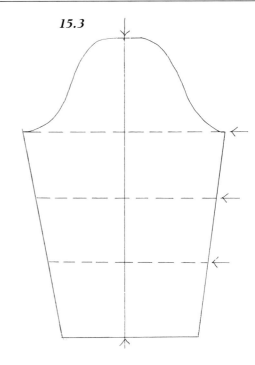

15.3

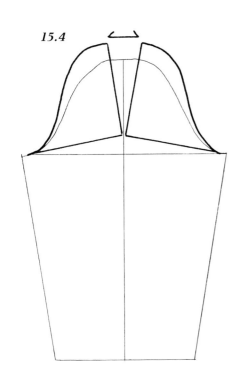

15.4

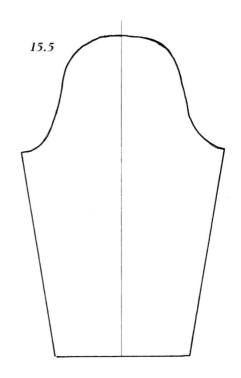

15.5

but it will help you in deciding proportions when designing.

2. Decide how far down the sleeve you want the fullness to be, e.g. underarm point (sleeve head only), elbow, wrist, etc., and cut your pattern horizontally at this point (*fig 15.3*).

3. Slash the pattern down the centre line to the horizontal slash line.

4. Spread the sleeve head apart equidistant from the centre line (*fig 15.4*), pivoting the two pieces from the outside bottom points, (a).

5. Re-draft the pattern (*fig 15.5*).

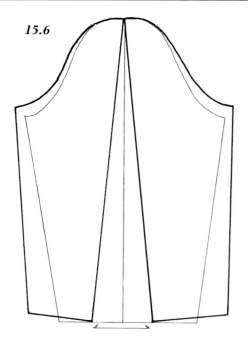

15.6

FULLNESS AT THE CUFF (BELL OR BISHOP'S SLEEVE)

1. Draft the whole fitted sleeve. Slash it down the centre line.

2. Pivoting the two sections at the top of the centre line, spread them apart at the bottom. Alternatively, slash the sleeve at the underarm and pivot the sections from the UP (*fig 15.6*).

3. Re-draft your pattern (*fig 15.7*).

FULLNESS WITHIN THE SLEEVE HEAD

This variation must be knitted sideways, using short rowing to shape the sleeve cap.

1. Draft the full sleeve with the centre line horizontal (*fig 15.8*). Divide the centre two thirds of the sleeve into five or six sections. Spread these sections apart equally (*fig 15.9*).

2. Draw a guideline from UP to UP and divide the cap into two sections, the top section being one third of the cap height.

3. Divide the space between each section in half and draw guidelines. Draw a line from the UP guideline and the sleeve cap line to the guidelines down the centre of each space. They will meet at the vertical line where the sleeve cap is divided (*fig 15.10*). These lines will be your guide for short-row shaping. (The shaded areas are not knitted.)

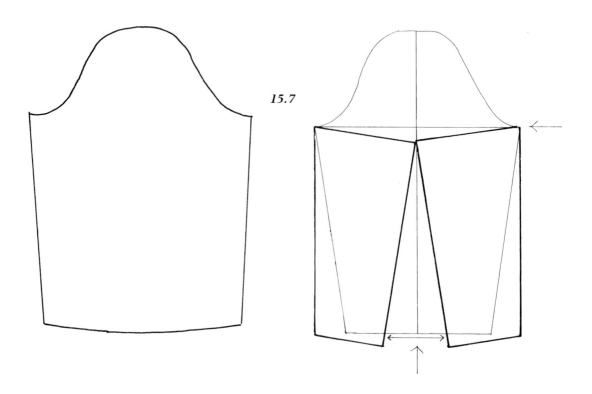

15.7

15.8

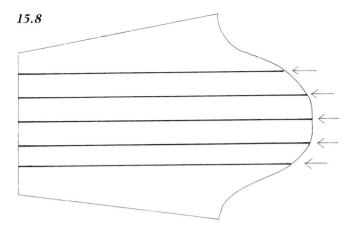

15.9

15.10

Sleeves with fullness combined with shaping

The transition between a full area of the sleeve and a shaped area can be done in two ways (*fig 15.11*). You can incorporate a pleat at the join, or you can gather the fullness by decreasing evenly across the row. In both cases you will have to remove the work from the machine and replace it on fewer needles. This can be done by taking the work off on WY, taking the work off on the garter bar, or by commencing the knitting with WY. Then, when you have finished knitting a section, remove the work and turn it upside down, replacing it from the WY to reduce the number of stitches.

1. Draft the whole sleeve. Decide what section will be full and what fitted.

2. Slash the pattern at this point (*figs 15.12, 15.13*). Divide into sections the portion to which you wish to add fullness (two or more, optional) (*figs 15.14, 15.15*).

15.11

15.12

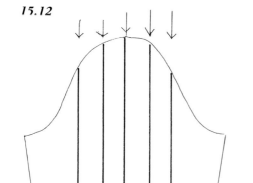

15.13

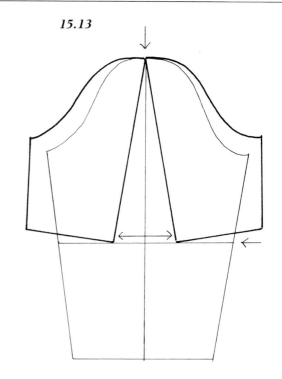

15.14

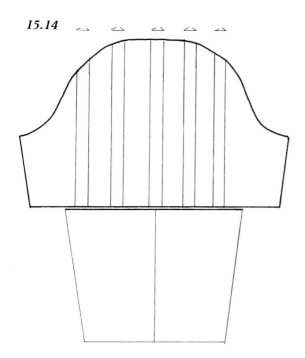

15.15

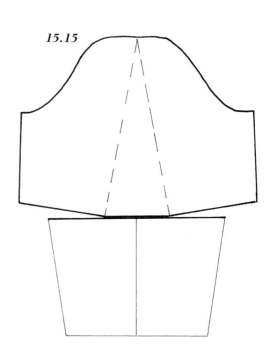

15.16

15.17

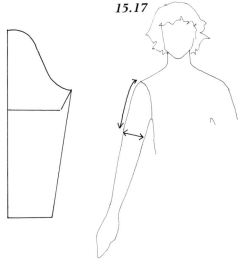

15.18

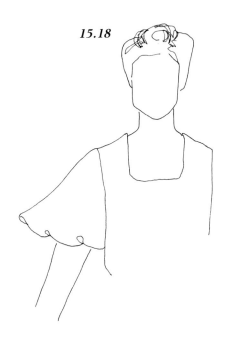

15.19

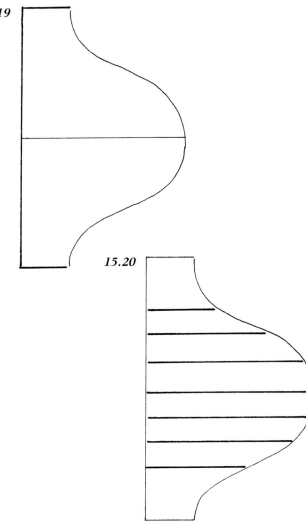

15.20

3. Alter the sleeve length and width at the cuff point (*fig 15.17*).

3. You can spread these sections apart or (if you have divided the pattern into two sections) pivot them from the top of the sleeve cap.

4. Re-draft your pattern.

Short sleeve

1. Draft half the fitted sleeve.

2. Measure from the SP down to the point where the sleeve is to finish. Measure the arm width at this point (*fig 15.16*).

Ruffled sleeve *(fig 15.18)*

This variation can be knitted sideways, using short-rowing to do the shaping.

1. Decide how long you want your sleeve to be.

2. Draft the whole fitted sleeve with the centre line horizontal. Draw a vertical line to indicate the chosen length. Extend the horizontal lines at the UP to the hemline (*fig 15.19*).

3. Divide the whole sleeve into sections and spread each section apart equally (*fig 15.20*).

15.21

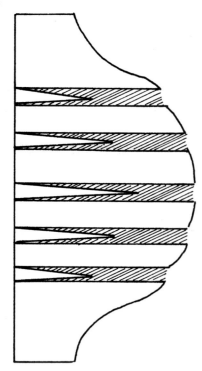

15.22

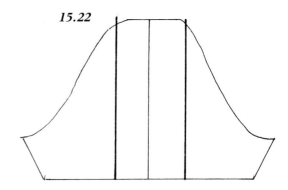

15.23

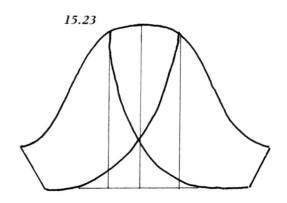

4. Draw a guideline down the centre of each space between the sections and decide where you want the fullness to finish. Draw a vertical guideline at this point.

5. Draft lines from the cuff edges of each section to the centre of each space at the point where they cross the vertical guideline. This will indicate where your short-rowing will occur. The shaded areas will not be knitted (*fig 15.21*).

Tulip sleeve (*fig 15.22*)

1. Draft the whole short fitted sleeve. Mark the cuff into thirds and draft vertical lines at each point to bisect the sleeve cap.

2. Draft two curved lines from each point on the sleeve cap to the opposite bottom edge of the cuff (*fig 15.23*). Make sure the curved lines cross three quarters of the way down the centre line.

3. Re-draft the pattern in two sections (*fig 15.24*).

15.24

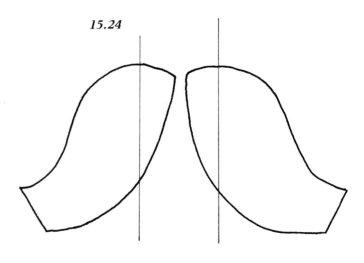

15.25 Draft for sleeve with pleat at shoulder

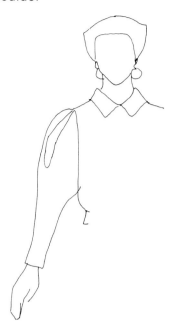

15.26 Draft for three-quarter fitted sleeve with ruffle at cuff

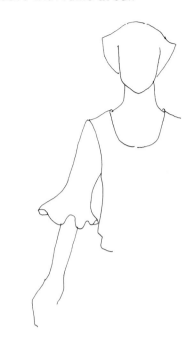

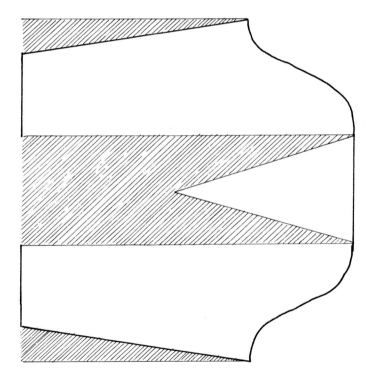

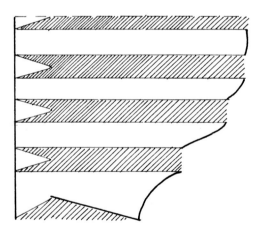

16

Shoulders

Saddle or shoulder strap garment

BODICE

1. Draft the back fitted body block twice (*fig 16.1*). On the second draft, place the front neck instead of the back neck.

2. Add required ease to the front and back and redraft the armhole slope (*fig 16.2*). Measure in 2–3cm from the new UP and mark this point. Draw a line from this new point to a point on the armhole drop line one third of the way up from the underarm line.

3. For a straight strap (*fig 16.3*), draw a line parallel to the shoulder slope line from the bottom of the side neck drop line on both (*a*) back and (*b*) front. For a shaped strap (*fig 16.4*), on the armhole drop line measure down from the SP 5–6cm. Mark this point on both (a) back and (b) front. Draw a line from this point to the bottom of the side neck drop line.

4. Cut off both straps and re-draft the body blocks (*fig 16.5*).

16.2

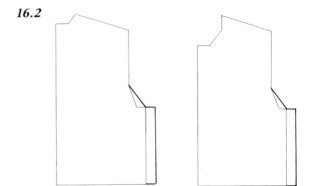

16.3

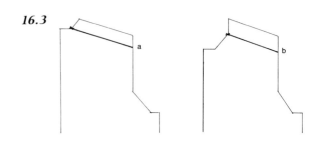

16.1

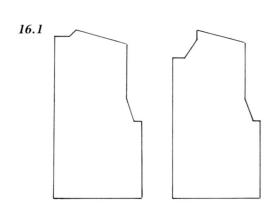

16.4

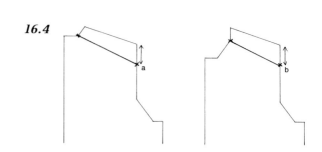

16.5

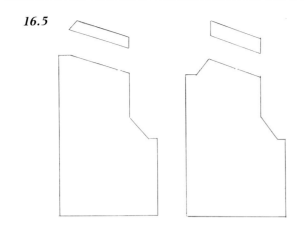

16.6 *16.7*

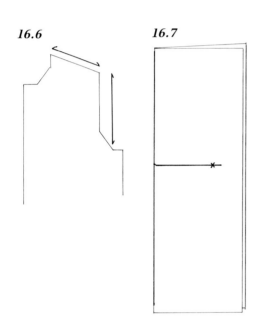

SLEEVE

1. Draft a new fitted sleeve from the new armhole. Draft a centre vertical line on the fold of your pattern paper (*fig 16.6*).

2. Measure down from the top of your paper the length of your shoulder slope line plus the armhole drop line.

3. Mark this point and draw a horizontal line equal in length to half UA plus ease (*fig 16.7*). (This is the underarm line on your sleeve.) Measure in from the UP plus 2–3cm and mark this point on your underarm line.

4. Measure around the armhole on your block. Include the strap (*fig 16.8*).

5. Use this measurement minus 1cm to draw a diagonal line from the end of the underarm width line to cross the vertical centre fold line. Mark this point (*fig 16.9*). This is the top of the sleeve cap.

6. Draw a horizontal line at the top of the sleeve cap equal to one-sixth the measurement of the UA plus ease (*fig 16.10*).

7. Measure down from the sleeve cap and mark a point equal to one third the measurement of the total sleeve cap height (from the top of the sleeve cap to the underarm line). At this point draw a horizontal line equal in length to the measurement of one-third UA plus ease (*fig 16.11*).

8. Draft the sleeve cap (*fig 16.12*) (join the dots).

9. Cut out the sleeve cap and open out the fold to give you the *whole* thing (*fig 16.13*).

16.9 *16.10* *16.11* *16.12*

16.8

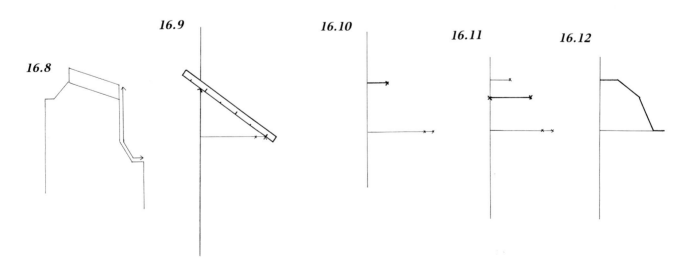

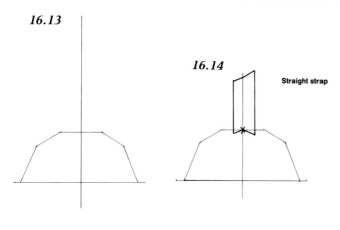

16.13

16.14

Straight strap

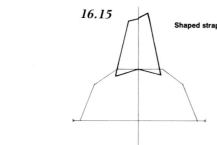

16.15

Shaped strap

16.16

16.17

Classic fully-fashioned shoulder

Use the simple block for this garment. Before you draft this pattern you must make a tension swatch because the back shoulder shaping will be done on the bias and you will have to calculate a bias line in order to make your shaping regular, i.e. decrease 1 st every row.

BODICE BLOCK

1. Knit a tension swatch and calculate the bias line (*fig 16.18*). Draw a vertical and horizontal line at right-angles to each other on your pattern paper. From the measurement of 40sts and 60rws calculate the measurement of 1st/rw. To do this, divide the measurement by the number of sts/rws. To get the measurement of 10sts/rws move the decimal point one place to the right. Mark a point on your horizontal line equal in length to the measurement of 10sts. Mark a point on your vertical line equal in length to the measurement of 10rws. Join the points.

2. Draw a simple back block over this bias line (*fig 16.19*). Make sure the line crosses the block at the SNP. Add the required ease at the bust.

3. To draft a new armhole (*fig 16.20*): measure in 2–3cm from the new UP; then measure down from the SP and mark a point equal to half the armhole drop. Join the points.

4. Cut the shoulder section above the bias line off your block and re-draft the back block (*fig 16.21*).

5. Draft the simple front block including the front neckline. Place the section you have removed from the shoulder of the back block on to the top of the front shoulder slope. Match the SNP and the SP. Re-draft the armhole to match the back block (*fig 16.22*).

10. Add to the top of the sleeve cap the two sections cut off the shoulder of the body block (*a*) straight strap and (*b*) shaped strap. Place the top shoulder line of the sections on the centre line of the sleeve. Allow the straps to overlap the sleeve cap (*figs 16.14, 16.15*).

11. Measure down the centre line from the new top of the sleeve (SNP) and mark a point equal in length to the measurement between the SNP and the wrist. At this point draw a horizontal line equal in length to the desired cuff width (optional) (*fig 16.16*).

12. Join the ends of this line to the UP (*fig 16.17*).

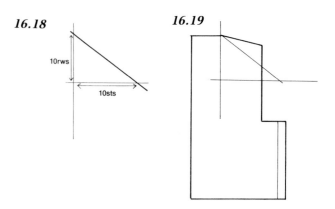

16.18

10rws

10sts

16.19

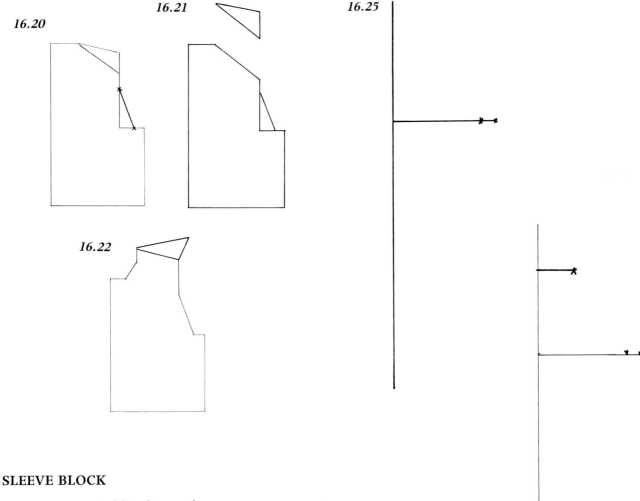

16.20 16.21 16.25

16.22

SLEEVE BLOCK

1.   Draw a vertical line longer than your measurement from SP to wrist. This line is the centre of your sleeve. Measure down from the top and mark a point equal to the measurement of the armhole drop on the basic body block (*fig 16.23*).

   Draw a horizontal line equal in length to half the measurement of your UA plus ease (underarm line).

2.   Measure in 2–3cm from the end of this line and mark this point.

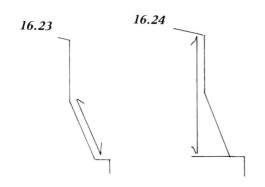

16.23 16.24

3.   On the vertical centre sleeve line, measure up from the underarm line and mark a point equal to two thirds the armhole drop (on the body block) (*fig 16.24*). Draw a horizontal line 5–6cm long at this point (*fig 16.25*).

4.   Using the bodice block, pivot from the bottom of the shoulder slope line (*fig 16.26*) to mark an arc from the point at the beginning of the sleeve cap shaping, equal in length to the armhole slope line (*fig 16.27*).

5.   Measure around the whole armhole on the body block (front and back). Subtract the measurements of

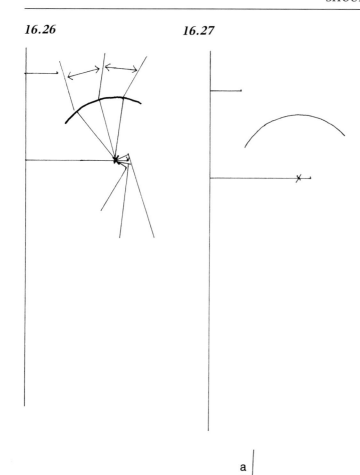

16.26   *16.27*

16.28

the front and back flat underarm section (*fig 16.28*).
Subtract the measurements of the front and back
armhole slope line. Using a ruler or a piece of string,
mark an arc equal in length to half the remainder
minus the length of the top of the sleeve cap. Use the
end of the sleeve top line as a pivot point for the ruler
or string.

6. Draft your sleeve cap through the point where this
arc crosses the arc drawn from the bottom of the sleeve
cap line (*fig 16.29*).

7. Measure down the centre vertical line from the top
of the sleeve cap and mark a point equal to your SP to
wrist measurement (*fig 16.30*). At this point draw a
horizontal line equal in length to half the required cuff
measurement. Draw a line from the end of the cuff line
to the UP.

Alternative classic fully fashioned garment

BODICE BLOCK

Proceed as for the above block through to step 5.

6. At the SP draw a horizontal line. Cut the pattern
off at this line (*fig 16.31*). This is your new shoulder
line.

7. Place the new shoulder line of the front block
against the slope of the back shoulder line and adjust
the armhole line (*fig 16.32*). These two sections are
your new blocks.

16.29   *16.30*

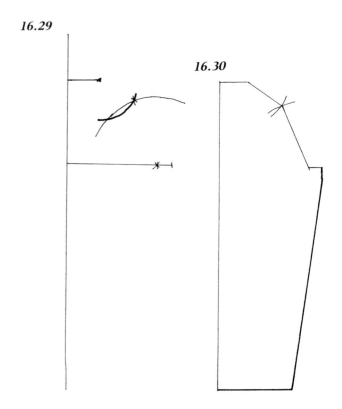

16.31

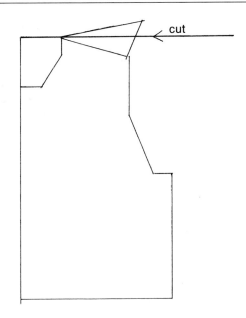

cut

16.33

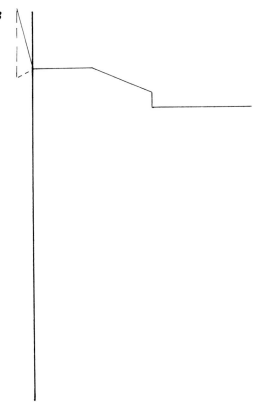

16.32

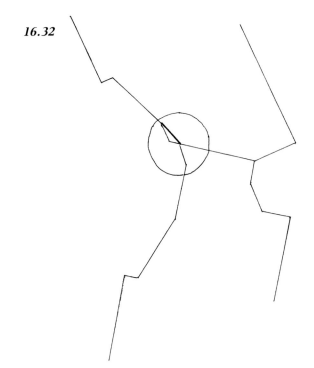

16.34

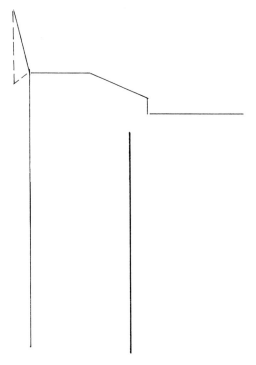

SLEEVE

1. Draw a vertical line. This is the centre sleeve line. Draft the front block horizontally (without the extension section at the shoulder) at the top of your vertical line with the SP of the block at the top of the vertical line (*fig 16.33*).

2. Draw a line parallel to the vertical centre sleeve line. The distance between the two lines equals the measurement of (half the UA plus ease) minus 2–3cm (*fig 16.34*).

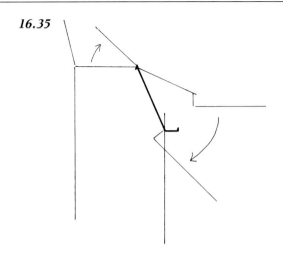

16.35

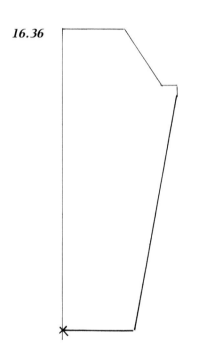

16.36

Raglans from the simple block

1. Draw in the neckline on your simple block.

(*a*) Back neck curve (*fig 16.37*): Mark a point 1.5cm down from the CBNP and draw a horizontal guideline at this point. Mark a point on this line equal to three quarters the width of half the back neck. Draw a line from this point to the SNP.

(*b*) Front neck curve (*fig 16.38*): Mark a point on the CF line equal to half the width of the Back Neck plus 1cm down from the CBNP and draw a horizontal guideline at this point. This is your front neckline drop.

Mark a point on this line equal to a quarter of the back neck width.

Draw a vertical guideline down from the SNP and mark a point on this line 4cm down from the SNP. Draw a line from the side neckline point to the front neckline point (*fig 16.39*).

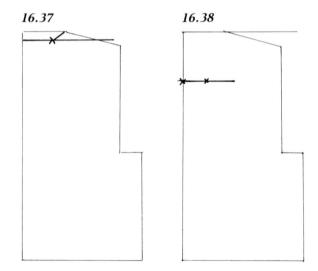

16.37   16.38

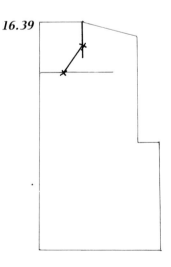

16.39

3. Pivot the body block at the top of the sleeve from the point at the top of the shoulder slope line (*fig 16.35*).

Mark the point where this line crosses the line parallel to the centre sleeve line. Join this point to the point on the horizontal line at the top of the sleeve.

Draw a horizontal line 2–3cm in length from the point on the parallel line.

4. Measure down the centre sleeve line from the SP and mark a point equal in length to the measurement of your SP to wrist (*fig 16.36*). Draft a vertical line equal to half the required cuff measurement.

5. Draw a line from the end of the cuff to the bottom right-hand corner of the square at the UP.

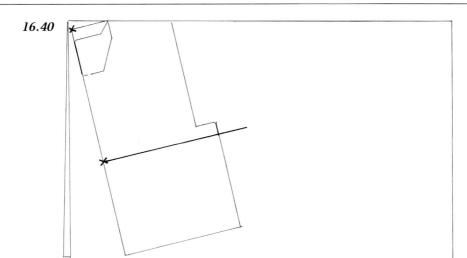

16.40

16.41

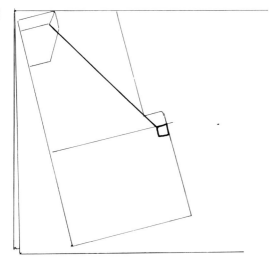

2. Fold your paper and place the front and back of the simple block on it with the shoulder line placed on the fold (*fig 16.40*).

3. Measure down from the top of the shoulder point on the centre line and mark a point equal to one quarter of your chest measurement. This will be your new underarm line (*fig 16.41*).

4. Mark the point where this line crosses the side seam line. Mark another point on this line equal to UA divided by 12in from the underarm seam line (*fig 16.42*).

16.42

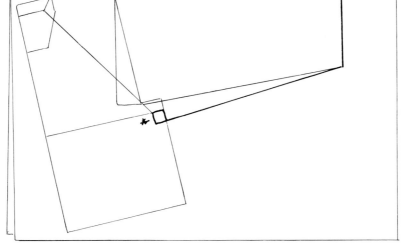

16.43

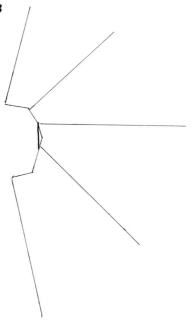

5.   Draw a square at the underarm point.

6.   Draw a line from the top left corner of the underarm square to the point where the back neck meets the side neck.

7.   Place the sleeve on the paper with the top of the sleeve at the top of the body and the centreline on the fold.

8.   Draw a line from the bottom right-hand corner of the underarm square at the sleeve wrist line.

9.   Trace and cut out half front, half back and the sleeve with the centre line on the fold of paper. The square at the UAP is included in both the front/back and the sleeve (*fig 16.43*).

16.44

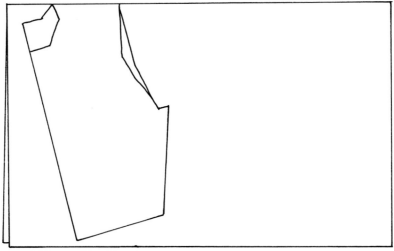

16.45

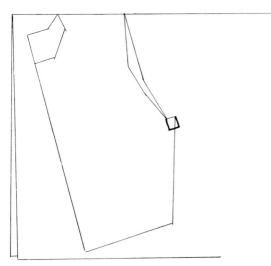

16.46

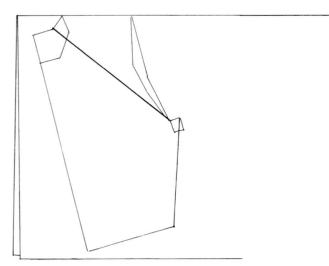

10. Open out the sleeve and place it between the front and back blocks. Correct the neckline.

Raglans from the fitted block

1. Fold your paper and place the front and back of the fitted block on the paper with the shoulder line on the fold line (*fig. 16.44*).

2. Draw a square at the underarm point with each side equal to UA measurement divided by 12 (*fig 16.45*).

3. Draw a line from the bottom of the armhole (the upper left corner of the square) to the point where the side neck joins the back neck (*fig 16.46*).

4. Measure the fold line of the paper from the SNP and mark a point equal to SNP to wrist measurement (*fig 16.47*).

5. Draw a vertical guideline at this point and mark a point on this line equal to half the closed fist measurement.

6. Draw a line from the bottom right-hand corner of the underarm square to the wrist point and to the waist (or hem) (*fig 16.48*).

7. Trace and cut out the front, back and sleeve (with the centreline of the sleeve placed on a fold of paper).

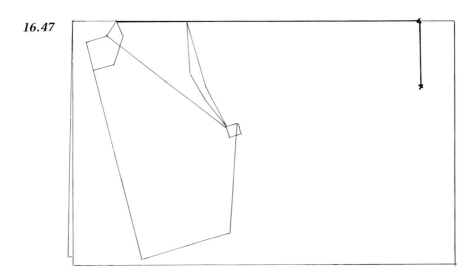

16.47

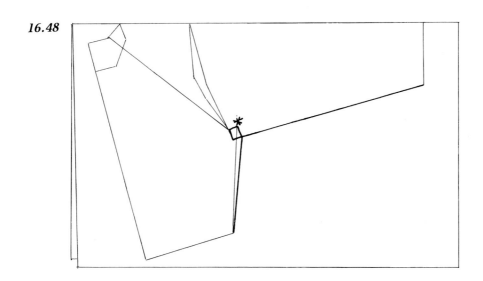

16.48

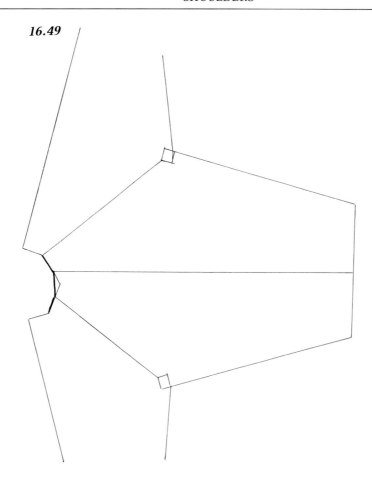

16.49

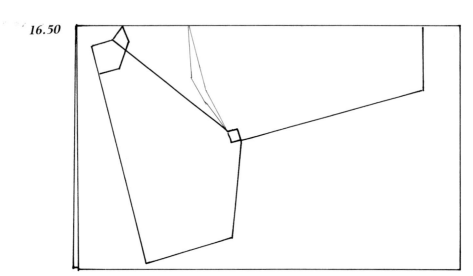

16.50

The square at the UP is included in both the front/back and the sleeve.

8. Open out the sleeve and place it between the front and back. Correct the neckline (*figs 16.49, 16.50*).

17

Dressmaking block for jersey fabric

BACK

1.   Draw a vertical guideline, which will be your CB line. Mark the CB length on this line (CB to waist point) (*fig 17.1*).

2.   Measure down from the CBNP and mark a point on the CB line equal to half the armscye (neat). Draw a horizontal guideline at this point. Mark a point on this line equal to one quarter of the bust measurement plus 2cm (*fig 17.2*).

3.   Measure down from the CBNP and mark a point on the CB line equal to one quarter of the armscye (neat). Draw a horizontal guideline at this point. Mark a point on this line equal to half X-back measurement plus 0.5cm (*fig 17.3*).

4.   Measure down from the CBNP and mark a point on the CB line equal to one-sixteenth of the armscye (neat). This is the shoulder slope from the CBNP. Draw a horizontal guideline. Mark a point on this line equal to half the X-back measurement plus 1cm (*fig 17.4*). This is your SP (shoulder point).

5.   Draw a horizontal guideline at the CBNP and mark a point on this line equal to neck divided by 5, plus 0.25cm (round it up to the nearest 0.5cm) (*fig 17.5*).

6.   Mark a point 1.5cm up from the side of your neck.

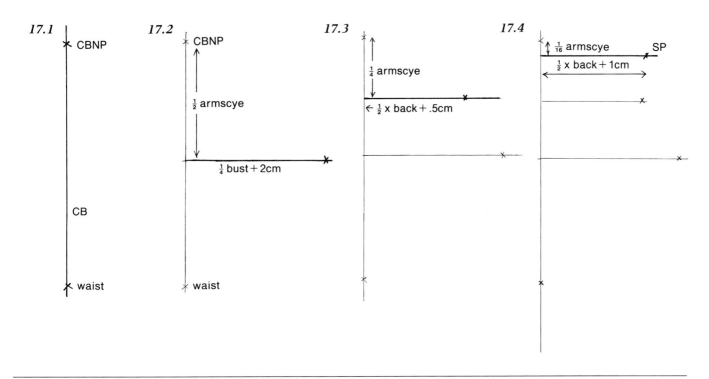

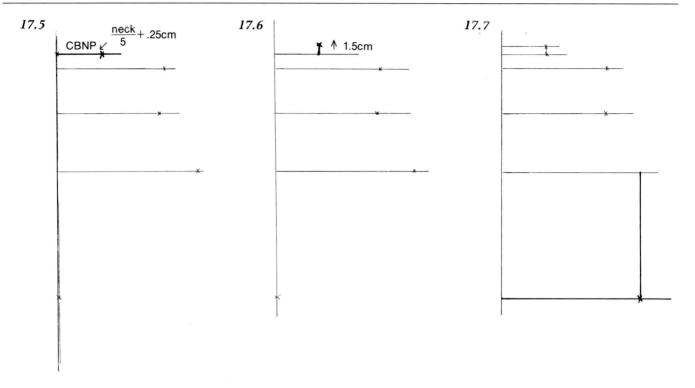

17.5 CBNP $\dfrac{\text{neck}}{5} + .25\text{cm}$ *17.6* ↑ 1.5cm   *17.7*

This new point is your SNP (side neck point). Draw a line from this point to your SP (*fig 17.6*).

7. Draw a horizontal line at the waist point and a vertical straight line up to the UP (*fig 17.7*).

8. Join all the dots (*fig 17.8*).

FRONT

The front is drafted in exactly the same way as the back, except for the front neck. The front neck drop (the distance between the CBNP and the front neckline) is equal to the neck divided by 5, minus 0.5cm. Mark this point on the centre line (*fig 17.9*) and then draw two guidelines, one at the front neck point, and join at the side neck point (*fig 17.10*). Curve a line between these two points.

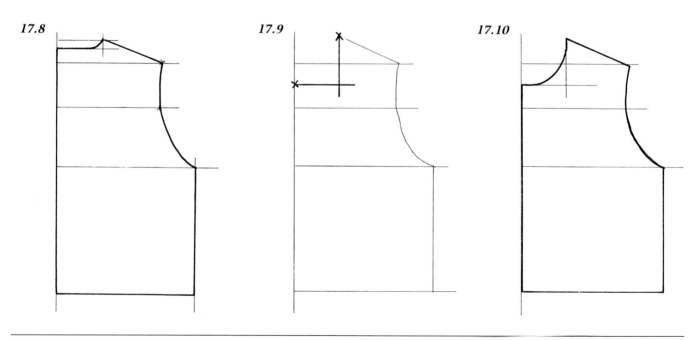

17.8   *17.9*   *17.10*

SLEEVE

1. Draw a vertical line. This line is the centre fold of your sleeve. Mark the length of your sleeve on this line. Draw a horizontal guideline at the wrist point (*fig 17.11*).

2. Mark a point on the line measuring down from the top equal to one quarter the armscye neat plus 1cm.

This is the depth of your sleeve cap. Draw a horizontal guideline at this point (*fig 17.12*).

3. Place your ruler with 0 at the top of the sleeve centre line (*fig 17.13*). Pivot the ruler until it crosses the underarm horizontal guideline equal to the measurement on the body block between the SP to the UP (shoulder point to the underarm point) plus 2cm (*fig 17.14*).

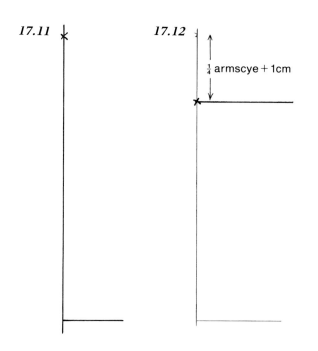

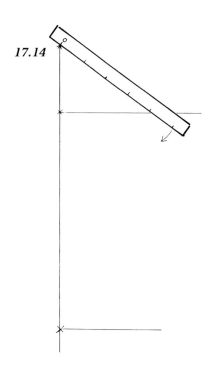

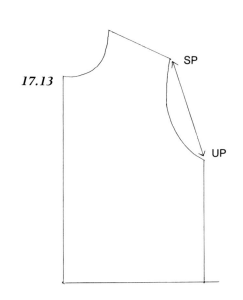

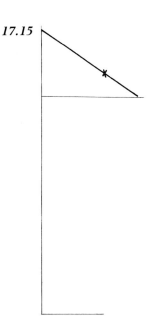

4. Mark a point on this line measuring back from the UP equal to one third the measurement of this line (*fig 17.15*).

5. Draw the sleeve head. The lower third is curved below the guideline by 0.6cm. The upper two thirds of the sleeve head is curved above the guideline by 1.75cm (*fig 17.16*).

6. Draw a vertical guideline (parallel to the centre sleeve line) from the UP down to the guideline at the wrist (*fig 17.17*).

7. Mark a point on the wrist line measuring from the centre equal to two thirds the measurement of this line.

8. Draw a line from this point to the UP (*fig 17.18*).

Raglan from the jersey block

1. Trace out the front and back body block from the centreline (*fig 17.19*).

17.16

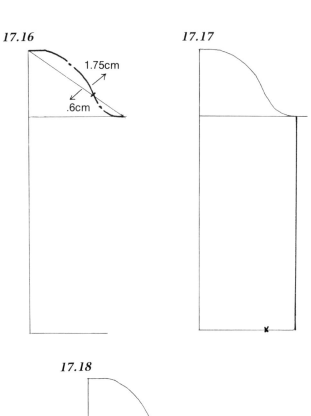

17.17

17.19

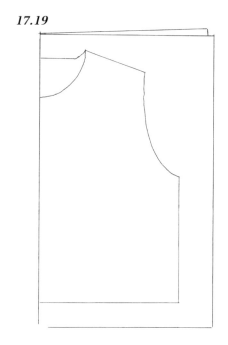

17.18

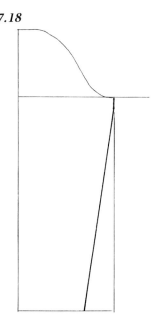

17.20

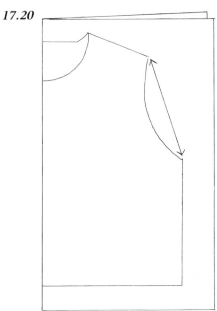

2. On the body block, measure between SP and UP plus 2cm. Divide this measurement by 3 (*fig 17.20*).

3. Place your ruler with the 0 on the UP and pivot the ruler until it crosses the vertical armhole guideline at this measurement (*fig 17.21*). Mark this point on both front and back blocks. Draw a new underarm curve below the guideline by 1.5cm (*fig 17.22*).

4. Mark a point on both the front and back neckline 3cm from the SNP (*fig 17.23*).

5. Draw a line from these points to the new points you have just marked in stage 3 on the vertical armhole line (*fig 17.24*).

6. Cut away the shoulder sections of the body blocks.

17.25

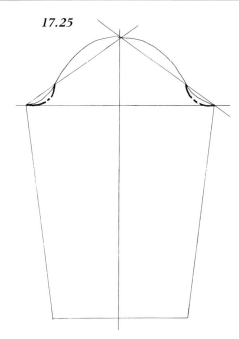

17.26

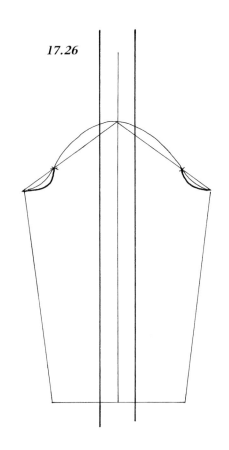

17.21

17.22

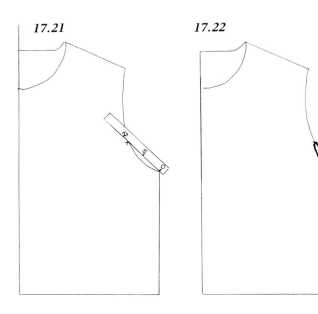

17.23

17.24

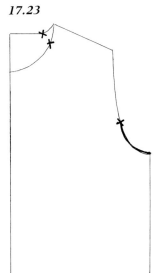
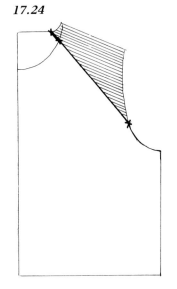

7. Trace out the whole sleeve block (both front and back sections) (*fig 17.25*).

8. Draw a new underarm curve below the guideline of the sleeve cap. Curve this line down by 1.5cm.

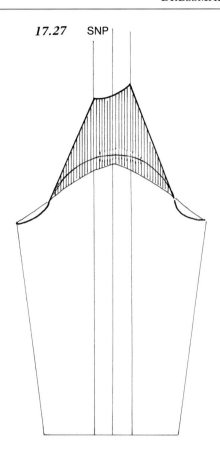

17.27 SNP

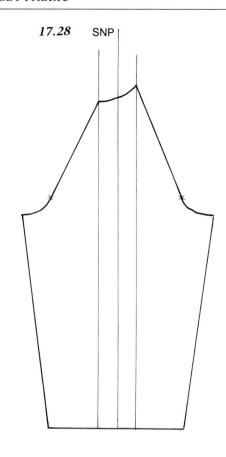

17.28 SNP

9. Draw parallel lines 3cm either side of the sleeve centre line (*fig 17.26*).

10. Place the cut out sections from the front and back body blocks on the top of your sleeve so that the marked points on the armholes match. Swivel the sections so that the SNPs cross the vertical guidelines each side of the centreline (*fig 17.27*).

11. Draw in the new side neckline at the top of the sleeve. Square across from the front SNP to the centre line and draw a line from there up to the neck SNP (*fig 17.28*).

12. Place the front, sleeve and back sections together to check the neckline. Adjust if necessary.

18

Yoke garments

When you are designing a yoke on a garment you can start with any of your blocks. If you choose to use a raglan (*fig 18.1*) or a dolman block (*figs 18.2a & b*) you will be able to make your yoke deeper than if you use the simple basic block or the fitted block. If you use a block with a sleeve (*fig 18.3*) you will limit the depth of the yoke to the length of the shoulder seam. If you use a dropped shoulder block you will be able to design a deeper yoke than if the sleeve seam is placed at the shoulder point as with a fitted sleeve.

Another point to remember when designing yoke garments is that if the yoke width (at the bottom) requires more needles than you have on the machine, the yoke must be knitted in two sections (front and back) and then joined.

You must also make sure that the number of stitches in the pattern you choose will fit *evenly* into the needles in WP without any extra sections of pattern at the edges because when you make up the garment you want the yoke to appear to be knitted in one piece. In order to do this you may have to adjust the number of needles in WP in any given section in order to get rid of extra bits of pattern at the edges. Any stitch pattern you use must match at the seams.

18.1

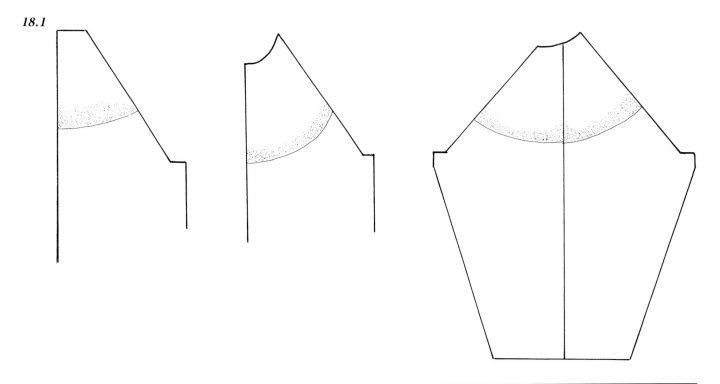

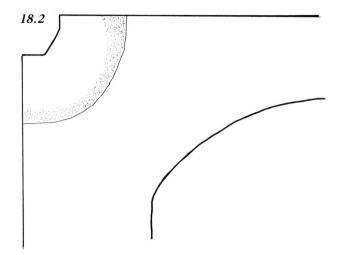

18.2

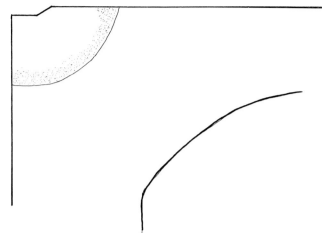

18.3

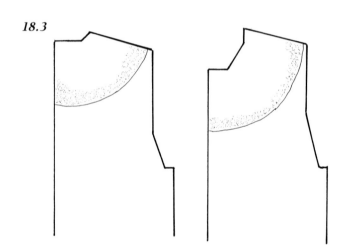

1. Trace out the front and back of the block for a garment with sleeves or a dolman garment. For a raglan garment trace out the front, back and whole sleeve of the garment.

2. Determine the depth of the yoke. This is optional. It can be the width of the shoulders or deeper, depending on the block you use and your design criteria.

Using a ruler, mark points on the block as follows (*fig 18.4*):

Front
1. Centre front
2. Front side neck
3. Front armhole seam

18.4

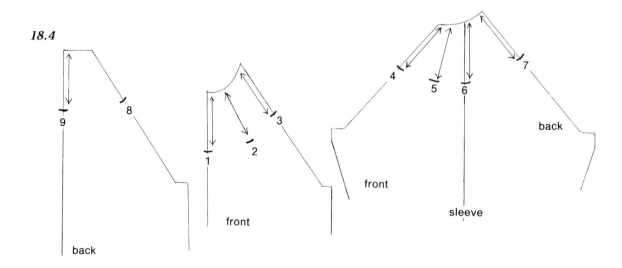

18.5

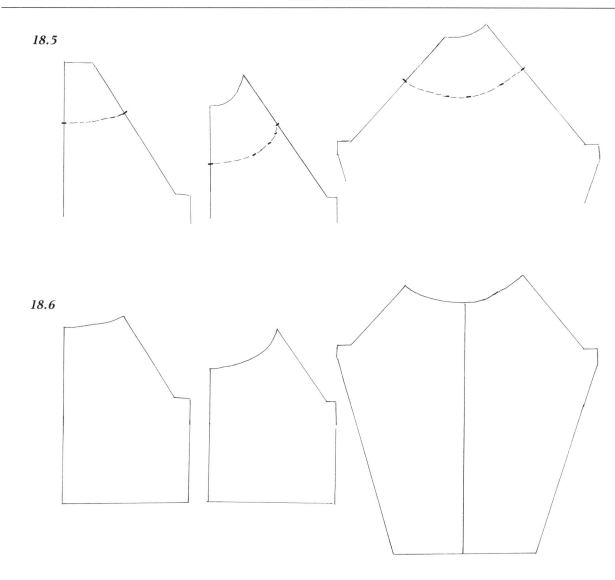

18.6

18.7

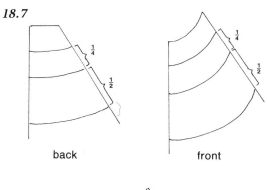

back   front

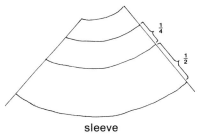

sleeve

Sleeve

4.   Front armhole seam
5.   Side neck point
6.   Centre line
7.   Back armhole seam

Back

8.   Back armhole seam
9.   Centre back

3.   Join the dots. This will give you the shaping for the main garment pieces as well as the yoke piece (*fig 18.5*). All shaping (where possible) must be done using short-rowing (putting needles into HP). Re-draft the main garment sections without the yoke (*fig 18.6*).

4.   Divide the yoke into sections. On your block the yoke is usually divided into three. The first decreasing comes at the half-way mark (*fig 18.7*). The next decreasing comes at the three-quarters mark. You will need to fit your pattern row repeats into the rows needed to knit each section. So the longest pattern would come at the bottom of the yoke. Each section is separated from the next by at least *one plain row of stocking stitch*.

5. Carefully measure the width of the bottom of each section (*fig 18.8*). (When measuring around the base you must measure *either* in two bites, e.g. half sleeve, front, half sleeve in one bite and half sleeve, back, half sleeve in the second bite; *or* measure around the whole base of the section, i.e. front, sleeve, back, sleeve and

divide by 2. Either use a tape measure on its side *or* 'walk' a ruler around the bottom of each yoke section.)

When you are calculating the number of stitches required for each section to make the pattern match at the edge, it is usually safer to opt for fewer rather than more stitches.

6. Draw a horizontal line equal to the measurement of the bottom of the first section. Mark the centre point and draw a vertical line at this point.

7. Mark the depth of each section on the vertical line and draw horizontal lines through each of these points (*fig 18.9*).

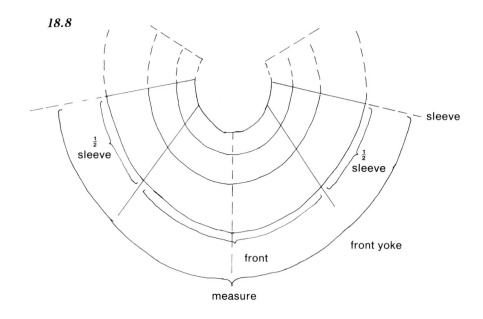

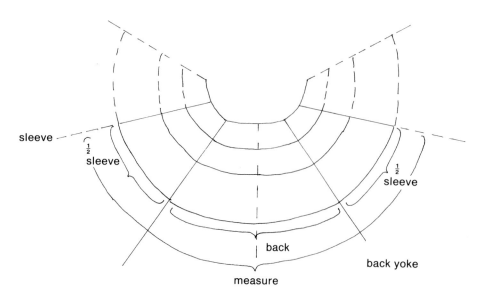

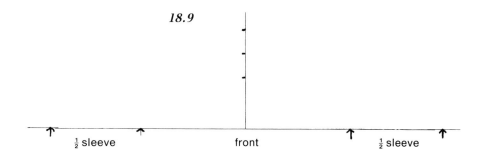

18.9

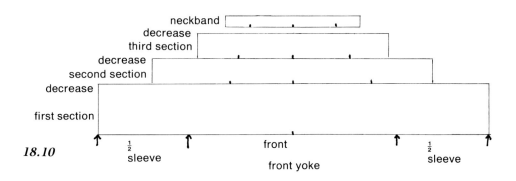

neckband
decrease
third section
decrease
second section
decrease
first section

18.10   ½ sleeve   front
front yoke   ½ sleeve

8. Mark each section equal in width to the section on the block (*fig 18.10*).

9. When knitting: knit each section straight. Add one extra stitch at each end for the seam. When you come to the end of the section you must decrease evenly across the row. If you are knitting in a Fair Isle pattern you must make sure that the pattern matches at the edges and you have finished one section of the pattern before you need to decrease. It is easier to decrease by transferring the stitches you need to lose with the transfer tool and pushing empty needles back to NWP *before* you remove the work from the machine. You can take the work off onto WY or use the garter bar. Remember to reset the number of needles required into WP before replacing your work on the machine.

Sideways knitted yoke garments

For sideways knitted yoke garments the initial pattern drafting stage is the same. The difference occurs when you draft the actual yoke.

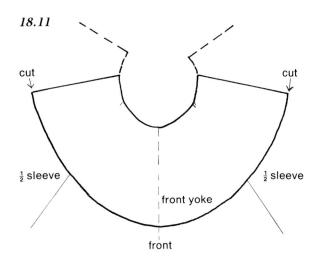

18.11

cut   cut

½ sleeve   ½ sleeve

front yoke

front

1. You will not need to measure anything in this case, but you will have to draft out the yoke sections (*fig 18.11*). Draft out the front and back sections. What follows is a favourite pattern drafting technique for dressmaking, called slash and spread.

Cut out the yoke and divide it evenly into vertical sections. The number of sections is optional, but

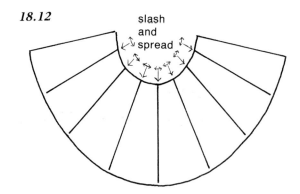

18.12

slash
and
spread

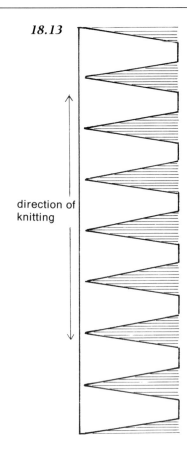

18.13

direction of
knitting

remember that the more sections you have, the more
short-row shaping you will do, while the fewer
sections you have, the less rounded in shape your
outside yoke edge will be.

2.   Slash each section from the neckline almost to the
base of the yoke (fig 18.12).

3.   Draw a vertical line and line up the bottom edge of
the yoke with this straight line. The sections will
spread apart.

4.   You can now trace this cut-out yoke on pattern
paper and shade in the areas between each section (fig
18.13). This area will be shaped by short-rowing. The
pattern can be used on a pattern attachment, or you
can calculate the shaping for each section.

19

Special variations

This section could equally well be called 'knitting in circles' or 'origami knitting.' We will see how the basic block can be twisted and turned, and cut and folded until you get the most unlikely looking pattern pieces which will, when knitted up and put together, make quite attractive and intriguing garments.

The first garment we will look at is the 'surprise jacket,' created by the American handknitter Elizabeth Zimmerman and later adapted for the knitting machine by Susanna Lewis. To draft a pattern for this garment from the basic block:

1. Draft the basic simple front block (*fig 19.1*). Add the required ease at the bust line. Don't worry about the hemline; this will be dealt with later.

2. Draw a horizontal line at the top of the CB (*fig 19.2*). Measure from the CB point and mark a point on this line equal to the measurement between the CB and wrist (measured with the arm held straight out horizontally). This is the top of the pattern line.

3. Draw a vertical line at the end of this horizontal line (*fig 19.3*). The length of this is equal to the measurement of half the bust plus ease (the whole garment front). Mark the mid-point on this line. Draw two horizontal lines, one at the end and one at the mid-point mark. These two horizontal sections are your sleeve width and measure the same as the width of the whole front of the garment (*fig 19.4*).

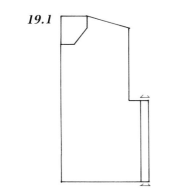

19.1

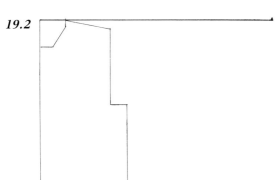

19.2

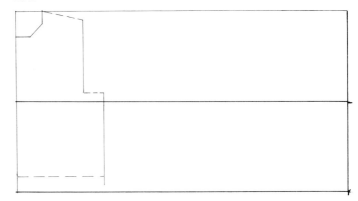

19.3

19.4

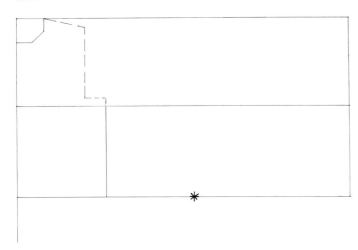

4. Measure out from the side seam and mark a point on the horizontal line at the bottom of your sleeve draft equal to the measurement of half the front.

5. Extend the vertical lines at the bottom of the front of the pattern and from the marked point from stage 4 above (*fig 19.5*). The length of the extension is equal to the measurement of half the bust plus ease (the whole front of the garment). Mark the mid-point on these lines.

6. Draft two more horizontal lines at the bottom of the extension and at the mid-point (*fig 19.6*). The bottom line is the centre back of the pattern and the pattern is mirror imaged from this line.

7. Determine the measurement you require for the length of the garment (*fig 19.7*). On the pattern, measure from the CB to the bottom of the front (the second horizontal line down from the top). Any additional length required will be added as a strip placed vertically to the left side of the pattern below this point.

8. Draw diagonal lines:

(*a*) from the UP to the bottom of the front (*fig 19.8*).

(*b*) from the UP to the bottom of the sleeve point.

(*c*) from a and b to c.

These lines give you a 'square' balanced on one corner.

9. Shade in the central area. This area is not knitted but shaped by short-rowing. This is an interesting garment to knit, but if you have a large bust size can result in an overly wide sleeve, because the

19.5

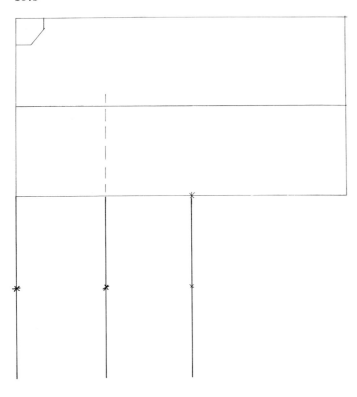

19.6

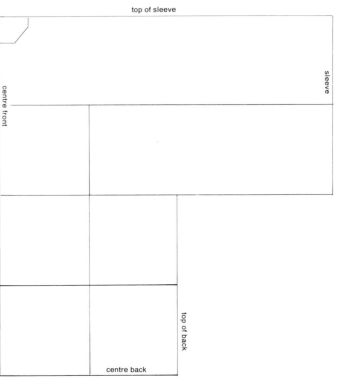

19.7

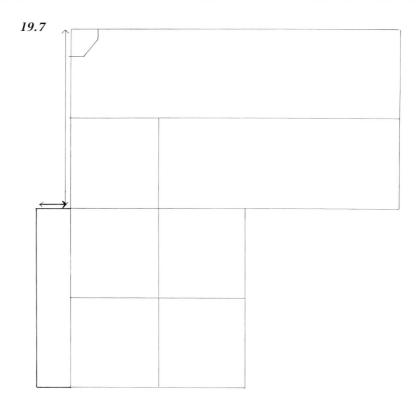

19.8

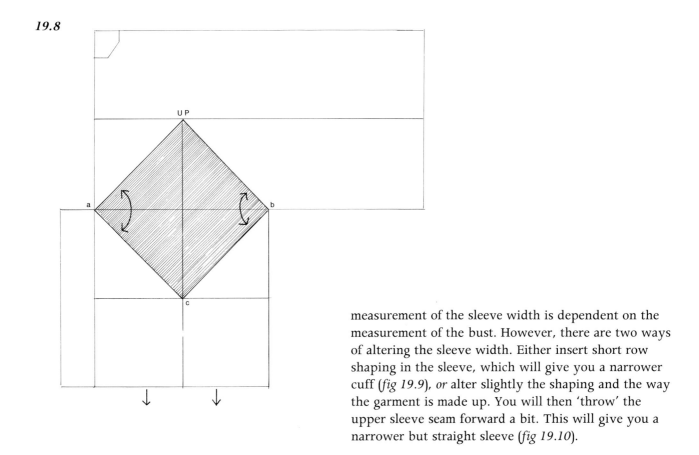

measurement of the sleeve width is dependent on the measurement of the bust. However, there are two ways of altering the sleeve width. Either insert short row shaping in the sleeve, which will give you a narrower cuff (*fig 19.9*), *or* alter slightly the shaping and the way the garment is made up. You will then 'throw' the upper sleeve seam forward a bit. This will give you a narrower but straight sleeve (*fig 19.10*).

19.9

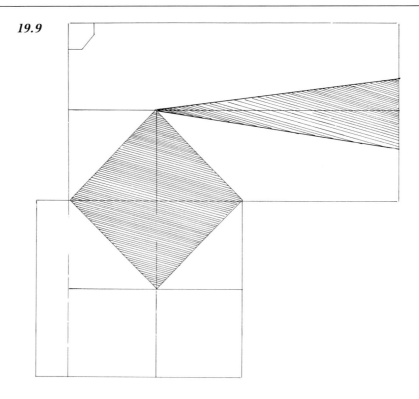

19.10

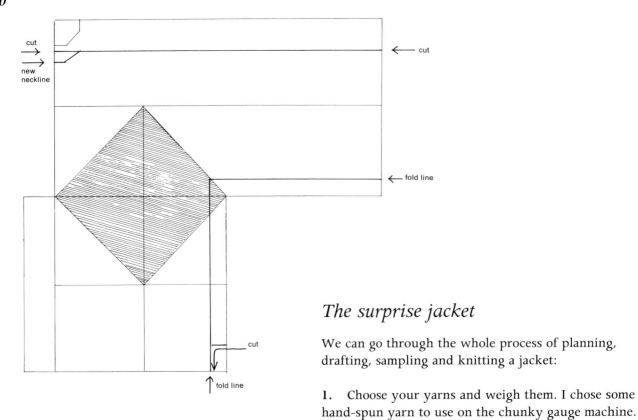

The surprise jacket

We can go through the whole process of planning, drafting, sampling and knitting a jacket:

1.   Choose your yarns and weigh them. I chose some hand-spun yarn to use on the chunky gauge machine. See Table 4.

Jacket, half assembled

TABLE 4

	Weight at beginning	Weight at end	Amount used
Dark purple	150g	0g	150g
White	360g	275g	80g
Purple	380g	260g	120g
Light blue	425g	80g	345g

Tension square

#10   20 sts = 14cm   1.4 sts in 1cm
             30 rws = 18.5cm   1.6 rws in 1cm

Back neck to wrist = 66cm
Chest (incl. ease)   = 104cm
Back neck to hem = 52cm

This is all the information you need to 'write' the pattern.

2.   Draft the pattern. The critical measurements I have used are:

If you draft a pattern according to these instructions you will find that the sleeve is 52cm wide. I did not want such a wide sleeve, so I decreased the number of rows knitted before I began the short row shaping to make the sleeve narrower (*fig 19.11*).

19.11

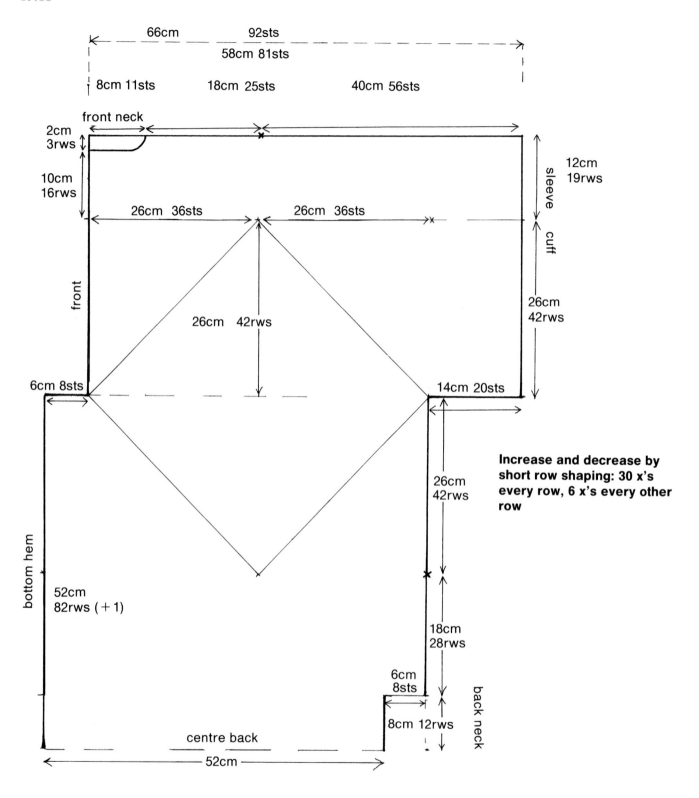

66cm   92sts

58cm 81sts

8cm 11sts   18cm 25sts   40cm 56sts

front neck

2cm 3rws

10cm 16rws

26cm 36sts   26cm 36sts

12cm 19rws

sleeve

cuff

26cm 42rws

front

26cm 42rws

6cm 8sts   14cm 20sts

Increase and decrease by short row shaping: 30 x's every row, 6 x's every other row

26cm 42rws

bottom hem

52cm 82rws (+1)

18cm 28rws

6cm 8sts

back neck

centre back

8cm 12rws

52cm

Tension Square: Tension 10

20sts = 14cm   1.4sts in 1cm
30rws = 18.5cm   1.6rws in 1cm

To knit shaped section

19.12

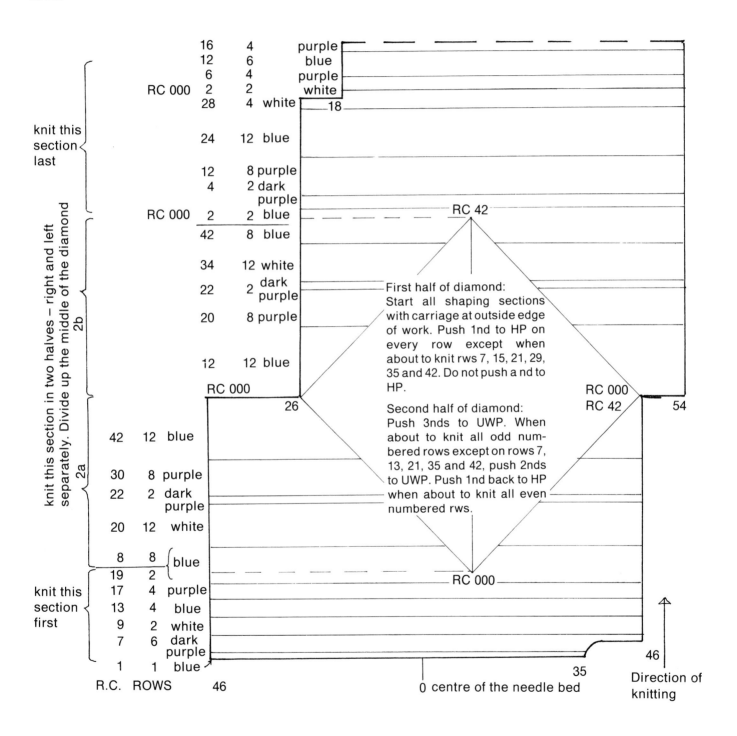

It is easier to knit this jumper in two halves. Reverse the
shaping for the second piece and graft the centre back.

3. The next step is to 'write' the pattern. This means using the information from the tension swatch to calculate the number of stitches and rows needed to get the shape of the drafted pattern. Most of the calculations are straightforward, but you do have to calculate the short row shaping carefully. I had to first decrease and then increase 36 sts at each side; I had 42 rows for the decreasing and another 42 for the increasing, so if I pushed needles to HP 30 times on every row and 6 times on every other row I would have made the correct number of decreases and knitted the correct number of rows. But I wanted the decreasing as even as possible, so I had to distribute the number of decreases on alternate rows evenly within the shaping. (42 divided by 6 equals 7, so every seventh time, the decreasing was done on an alternate row.) The first draft shows all the relevant measurements plus all the stitches and rows calculated from them.

4. In order to determine the colour striping, I made a model from tracing paper and coloured it in to indicate the colours. I then cut it out and folded it to get a clearer picture of what the garment would look like when it was knitted.

I then transferred this information to the second draft, which was the one I would use when knitting the garment. The stitches on the needle bed are indicated on the draft, and the row counter readings are indicated at the column on the left. For the sake of clarity I turned the row counter back to zero every time I began a shaped section (*fig 19.12*).

The garment was knitted in two halves, starting at the centre front both times and then grafting the centre back. The casting on (top of the sleeve) was done on WY and that seam then sewn by hand.

5. *The finishing*: I knitted a small swatch to sample for the edge, using Card 1 as a Fair Isle pattern. The sample was 20 sts and measured 15cm. The neck was 45cm and used 60 sts for the edge. I used the whole machine for the bottom edge, and 74 sts for the front edge, which measured 55cm.

(*a*) Cast on with WY. Knit several rows.

(*b*) Push all needles to HP and using dark purple *upside-down 'e' wrap all needles.*

(*c*) Pick up the edge of the garment with the right side of the garment facing the machine.

(*d*) Knit the outside of the hem first. If the first row is difficult to knit with the machine because of the upside-down 'e' wrap, you may have to knit this row by hand. I put the Fair Isle pattern on the outside of the hem only. The inside of the hem was plain.

(*e*) When you have finished the hem, pick up the edge of the garment again and cast off loosely.

(*f*) Because I had already sewn up the sleeves, I had to knit the cuffs, taking them off on WY and sewing them on afterwards. You could do the cuffs the same way you did the rest of the edges, if you remember to do it before you sew the garment up!

The origami jumper

If you take the basic shape, cut it up, fold it and twist it, you could end up with a very strange pattern indeed. This next sample appeared in a Japanese magazine some years ago. It looks strange as a pattern, but the garment made from it is very effective indeed.

1. Take a piece of paper folded over in half (*fig 19.13*). The paper must be equal in width and length to the measurement taken from wrist to wrist with the arms held straight out horizontally at each side. Place the fold of the paper at the top. Mark the fold line equal to the measurement of wrist to wrist. Mark the mid-point and draw a vertical line equal in length to half the wrist to wrist measurement. This is your centre front/back line.

2. Draw diagonal lines from the bottom of the CF line to each end of the horizontal line at the fold.

3. Draw a horizontal line at the bottom of the CF line. This line is equal in length to the measurement of half the bust + ease and the ends are equidistant from the centre line.

4. Draw vertical lines at the ends of the horizontal lines at the top and bottom of the pattern.

5. Draw a horizontal line parallel with the top line for the bottom of the sleeve. The distance between these two lines equals the required width of the sleeve (the depth of the armhole drop).

6. At the centre of the top of the pattern draft a V neck for the front. The neck drop can be 8cm. The back neck width can be 16cm (*fig 19.14*). (These measurements are optional.)

19.13

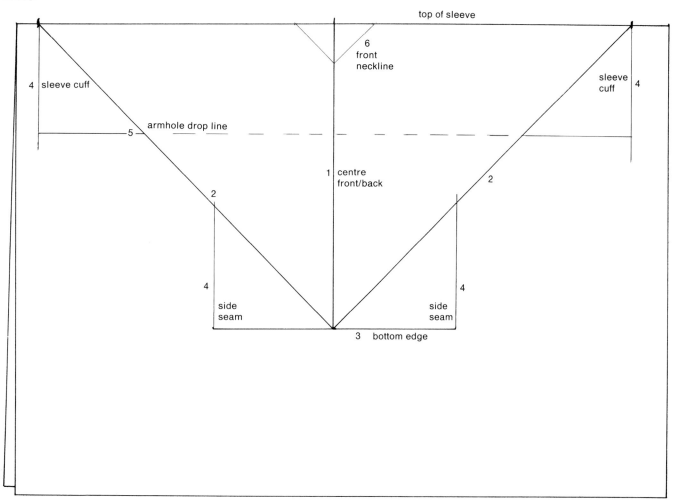

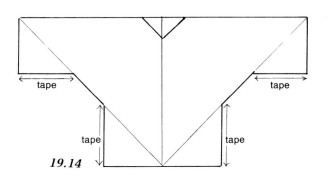

19.14

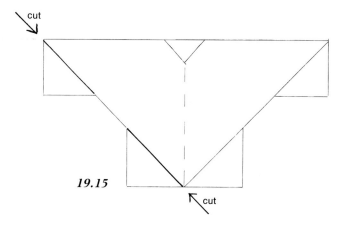

19.15

7. Cut out the pattern and secure the vertical and horizontal (not diagonal) seams with tape (*fig 19.14*).

8. Cut diagonal lines as indicated (*fig 19.15*). First cut the body and the adjacent sleeve on the diagonal line on one side. Then turn the pattern over and repeat exactly the same thing on the reverse.

19.16

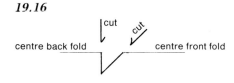

19.17

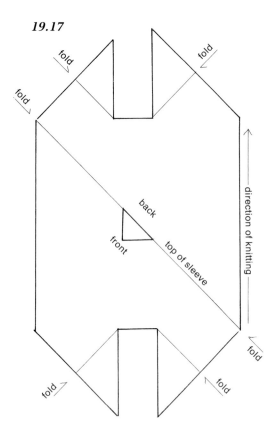

19.18

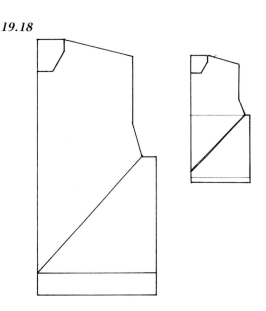

9. Open out the pattern. To cut out the neck, fold the pattern down the CF/CB line and cut out the neck on the front of the pattern (*fig 19.16*).

This is your pattern (*fig 19.17*). If you knit from bottom to top your stitch pattern will appear diagonally on the garment and will wrap over the shoulder and around your arm. If the pattern piece is too wide for your needle bed you can knit the pattern in vertical sections and piece them together, but you will have to be very careful in making up to disguise your seams.

NB: The central area *must be square*, so the length of the garment is directly dependent on the wrist to wrist measurement (cuff to cuff on the garment). If you alter one, you must alter the other. The width of the body and of the sleeves is entirely optional.

As you can see, you can have quite a bit of fun playing about with your basic block. A bit of tape, a pair of scissors, courage and a touch of imagination can work magic. For example, you can make your basic square block into a paper garment. Tape the seams together and then attack it with a pair of scissors. Try cutting through some of the seams and body sections. Cut through right angles, such as the underarm. Cut from UP to neck, UP to CF, UP to sleeve. When you have cut, open out your paper pattern. Look at it carefully and decide how short-row shaping might give you an interesting garment.

You can also take one pattern section, such as the body and cut that into pieces. These pieces can be shaped and put together again by short-rowing. If you bisect the UP at right angles and have a seam CF or CB (graft the two ends of your knitting together), you can knit doughnut shapes with holes in the middle for the arms (*figs 19.18 and 19.19*). You can also cut through the body block horizontally at the underarm point. This may lead to interesting directions in terms of directional knitting (*fig 19.20*).

The jigsaw effect

In addition to adding interest by directional knitting, you can approach your basic block as if you were about to create a jigsaw. This will liberate you from the dictates of having to knit the garment in horizontal sections. You will still have to make your fabric by moving the carriage across the needle bed from side to side, but each section can be considered separately and

19.19   **Two donut jumpers**   **19.20**

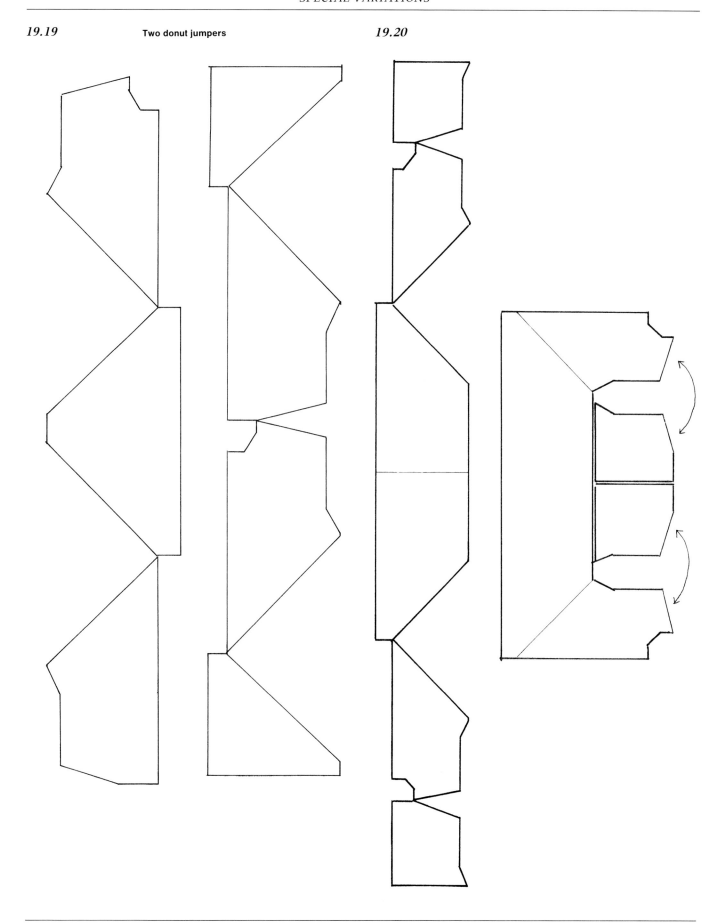

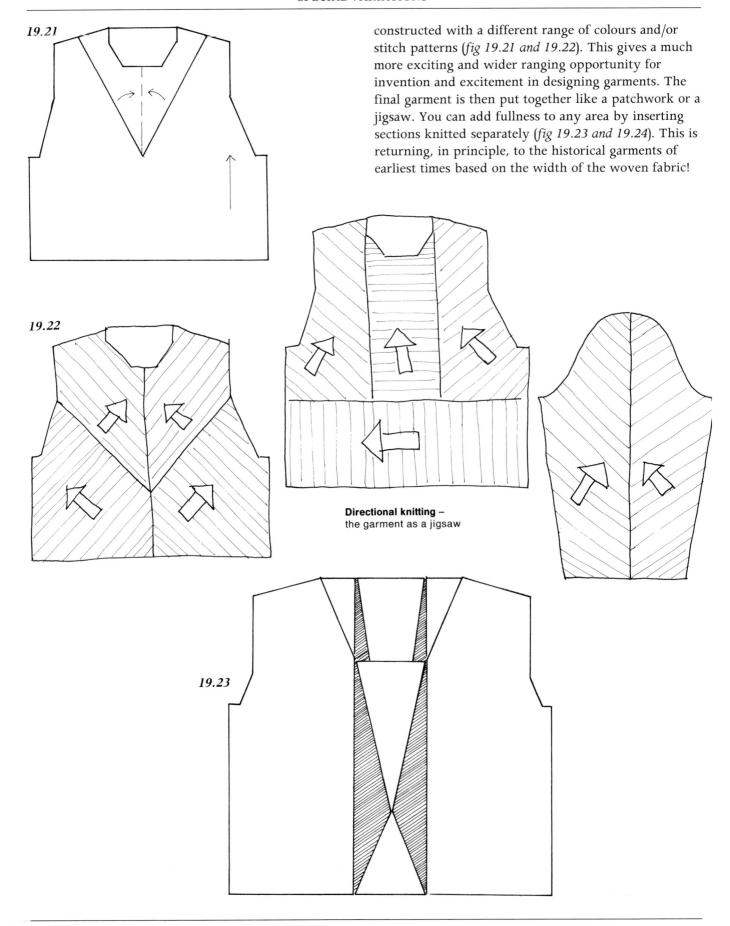

19.21

19.22

constructed with a different range of colours and/or stitch patterns (*fig 19.21 and 19.22*). This gives a much more exciting and wider ranging opportunity for invention and excitement in designing garments. The final garment is then put together like a patchwork or a jigsaw. You can add fullness to any area by inserting sections knitted separately (*fig 19.23 and 19.24*). This is returning, in principle, to the historical garments of earliest times based on the width of the woven fabric!

Directional knitting –
the garment as a jigsaw

19.23

Dart manipulation

19.24

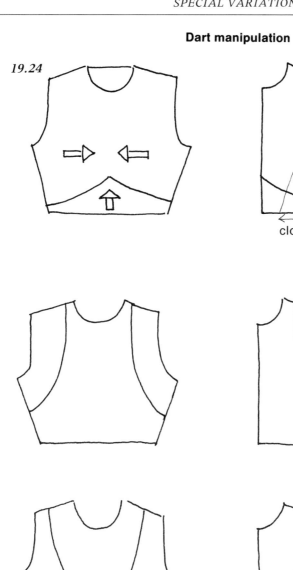

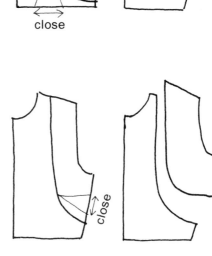

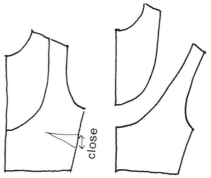

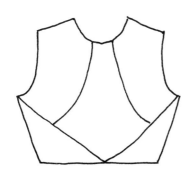

The jigsaw garment

This garment can make quite a splash. Because it is knitted in so many totally independent sections it can use any combination of colour, technique or stitch pattern. You can also use various techniques for joining the sections, making a feature of the joins. If you put it together very carefully, it becomes a reversible jacket.

The critical measurement for this garment is the chest measurement, with the measurement from wrist to CB as the second most important (*fig 19.25*).

The basic dimensions for each body section are determined by the chest measurement. When taking this measurement, remember that you are making a garment using a *double-thickness fabric*, so you must allow lots of extra ease. The weight of this garment will probably make it outdoor winter wear, so you will also have to allow for the fact that it will be worn over other clothing. I would suggest you allow at least a *minimum* of 35 per cent ease over your basic chest measurement!

The body of the garment is a patchwork of ten squares. Each can be as different as you like. To calculate the dimensions of the square:

1. Draw a right angle with long legs.

2. Draw an arc with a compass, using the corner of the right angle as the centre.

3. Draw two arcs with the compass, using the two points where the first arc crosses the two legs of the right angle (*fig 19.26*).

4. Draw a line from the corner of the right angle through the point where the two arcs cross. This line bisects your right angle and represents the diagonal of your square.

5. Mark a point on this diagonal line equal to half the chest measurement plus ease (*fig 19.27*).

6. Draw a vertical and horizontal line from this point to cross the legs of the right angle. This is the dimension of the squares you will knit to make your garment.

You must now make your tension square(s). Knit ten of these squares and fold them in half diagonally. You can then assemble the body of your garment (*figs 19.28, 19.29*), and will see how long your sleeves will be. You will have to knit from two to six additional

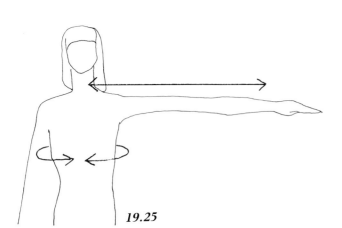

19.25

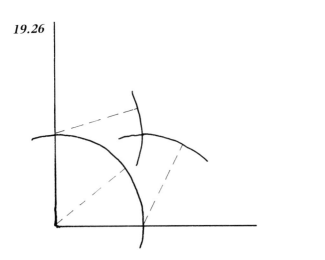

19.26

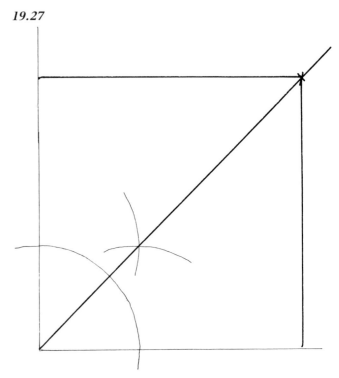

19.27

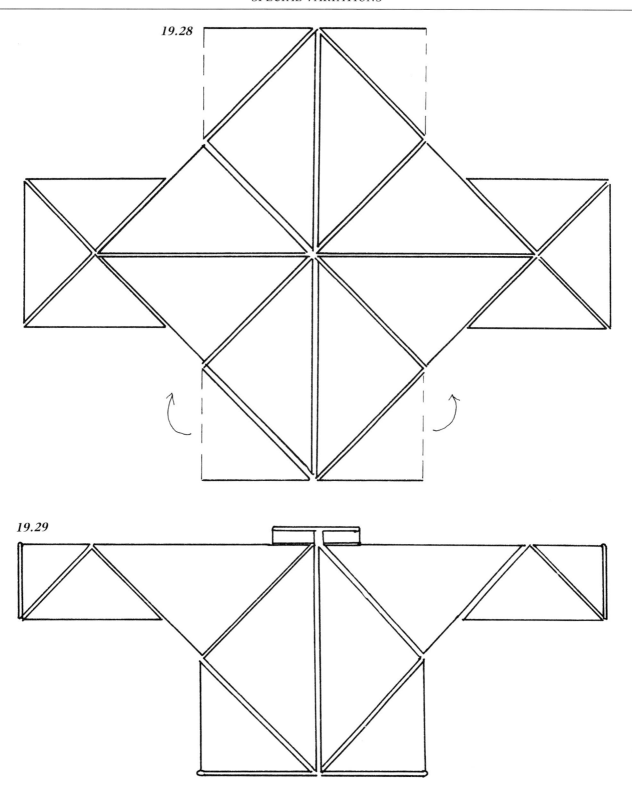

19.28

19.29

smaller squares to complete the sleeves. If your arms are long or you want long sleeves, you may need six squares.

To calculate the size of your sleeve squares, decide how wide you want the sleeve to be at the cuff. This will be the diagonal of your sleeve squares, calculated in the same way as you worked out the body squares.

The collar is optional. You can knit a simple rectangle, or you can be more adventurous. It's entirely up to you!

20

Construction of collars

Dressmakers often draft their necklines front and back and then design the collar by drawing it out on top of this draft (*fig 20.1*). The shoulder lines of the blocks are arranged so that the NPs touch and the SPs overlap by 2cm. As they draft, the collar becomes a flat pattern. If the pattern is altered so that the circumference of the outer edge decreases and the curve of the inner line of the collar (the neckline) becomes straighter, the collar has a more pronounced 'stand,' as can be seen on a mandarin collar, as the length of both the outer and the inner lines are the same and the collar stands straight up around the neck.

Doodling with collars in this way can be a help in giving you new ideas or seeing what effect a particular design will have, but there is one big problem. Knitters have great difficulty in knitting the shapes that dressmakers design. This approach is therefore interesting, but not necessarily relevant. For machine knitters, there are basically three approaches to knitting collars.

METHOD I

The collar is knitted horizontally on the single bed from or towards the neckline edge and folded in half where the fold line is the outside edge of the collar (*fig 20.2*).

This collar is quite thick as it is doubled over. The shape is a mirror image pivoting on the fold line. The collar can be knitted in a stitch pattern where the underside is plain. You can also include a decorative effect on the folded edge by transferring stitches or using HP or tuck stitch.

1.   The collar is begun either on WY or by picking up the neck edge of the garment.

2.   The collar is usually begun and finished on a small tension. The tension (stitch size) is increased as the knitting nears the folded edge, with a very big row for the folded edge. It then diminishes as it re-approaches the neckline.

The effect of this change in stitch size is to increase the width of the collar, making the measurement of the outside (folded) edge greater than the neckline edge.

20.1

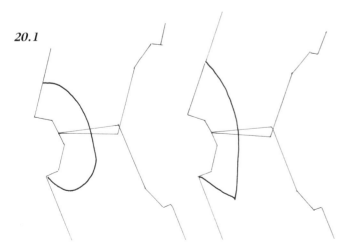

20.2

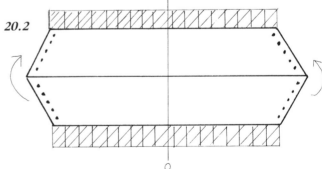

3. The other methods of increasing the width of the collar at the outside edge are to increase stitches at each edge of the knitting, to increase stitches evenly across the row, or to use stitch patterns to make the knitting wider. The disadvantage of increasing (decreasing) evenly across the rows is that it means more work; you will have to remove your knitting from the machine and then replace it on fewer (more) needles. While this is fiddly, it can be worthwhile if it achieves the desired effect.

4. Another way of getting more shaping into your collar is by short-row shaping within it (*fig 20.3*). You can use the sock-heel effect (needles in HP) at the fold line to help get a natural curve into your collar shape.

METHOD II

The collar is knitted horizontally on the double bed from or towards the neckline edge where the collar is a single thickness of fabric (*fig 20.4*).

1. The collar can be cast on or begun by picking up the neck edge of the garment. The cast on end is usually preferred for the outer edge. Sometimes you can include decorative features such as tucked effects on the cast-on edge.

2. Stitch size plays a part in the construction of this collar in much the same way as for Method I above.

20.3

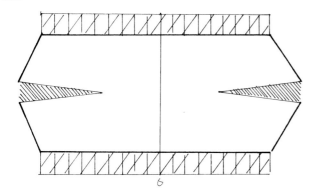

20.4

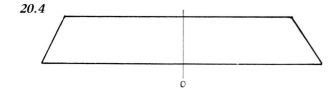

20.5

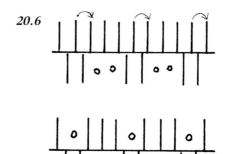

20.6

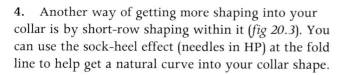

The cast on edge must be loose so that the edge of the collar lies flat. Then the size of the stitch can be decreased as you knit towards the neckline edge.

3. To have a ribbed collar that is not too pulled in, it is usually a good idea to arrange your needles to achieve a relatively flat rib. Either use a FNR (full needle rib), or use a 'flat rib.' This is achieved by having your machine at half pitch (needles are not opposite each other on the two beds) (*fig 20.5*). Then you will have *all* the needles on one bed in WP and an arrangement of needles on the other bed. This will give the effect of a ribbed fabric without the elasticity or pull.

4. In addition to altering your tension (stitch size) to decrease the width of your collar as you knit from the outside edge towards the neckline, you have three choices. You can decrease stitches at the edges of your knitting; you can decrease the number of needles in WP evenly across the bed by merely transferring the stitches to adjacent needles (*fig 20.6*) (in other words, altering the needle arrangement); or you can alter the stitch pattern, e.g. tuck stitch to stocking stitch.

5. You can make the collar a more curved shape by introducing short-row shaping if you wish.

METHOD III

Collars knitted vertically, parallel to the neckline edge.

This type of collar is knitted separately and sewn on the garment after it is finished. It can be knitted on a single or double bed. You can draft a pattern from dressmaking basic techniques for this type of collar, as you can knit curves.

1. The easiest way to tackle a collar like this is to draft it as a flat pattern and then to cut it out (*fig 20.7*).

2. Divide it into sections (*fig 20.8*) and slash it to the outside edge. Flatten it and make the outside edge a straight vertical (*fig 20.9*). You will have triangular gaps where your slashes are. These sections are shaped by short-rowing and are not knitted (*fig 20.10*), but before you knit the collar you must re-draft the pattern so that increases and decreases (at the edge of the collar for differences in the width of the collar) occur at the edge where there is no short-row shaping.

3. If you are knitting the collar on a single bed machine you will be folding it over in the middle. Leave a needle in NWP to indicate the fold line.

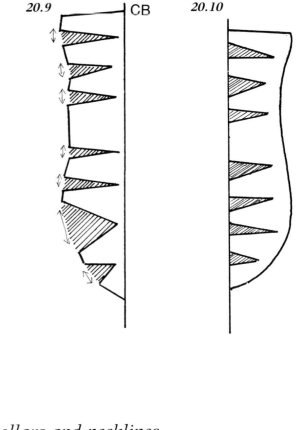

20.9   CB   20.10

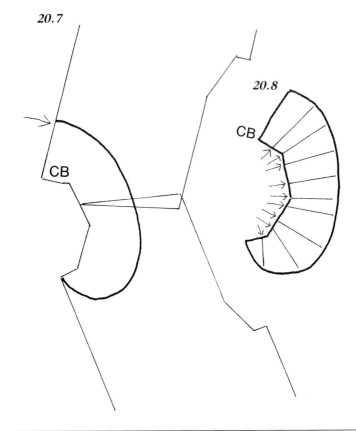

20.7

20.8

CB

CB

Collars and necklines

SIMPLE COLLARS

Collars can be knitted either folded over on the single bed, or single thickness on the double bed. If you are knitting a collar on a garment with a front placket or one that is opened down the front, you may be able to pick up the edge of the garment to knit on your collar. If, however, your neckline is smaller, you will have to knit the collar separately and then attach it to the garment either by sewing it on or by picking up the edge of the garment in sections and casting off the collar and garment together.

Collars can be joined to all sorts of necklines: crew necks, scoop necks, necklines with plackets, necklines with ribs already on them; the choice is infinite. They can be knitted in plain stocking stitch, mock rib or Fair Isle (doubled over), single thickness tuck stitch, lace, knitweave or a variety of ribs.

1. Draft the required neckline on the garment (*fig 20.11*). Measure around the neckline (*fig 20.12*).

2. Draw a horizontal line equal in length to half the neckline measurement. Determine the collar depth at the narrowest point and draw a guideline (*figs 20.13, 20.14, 20.15*).

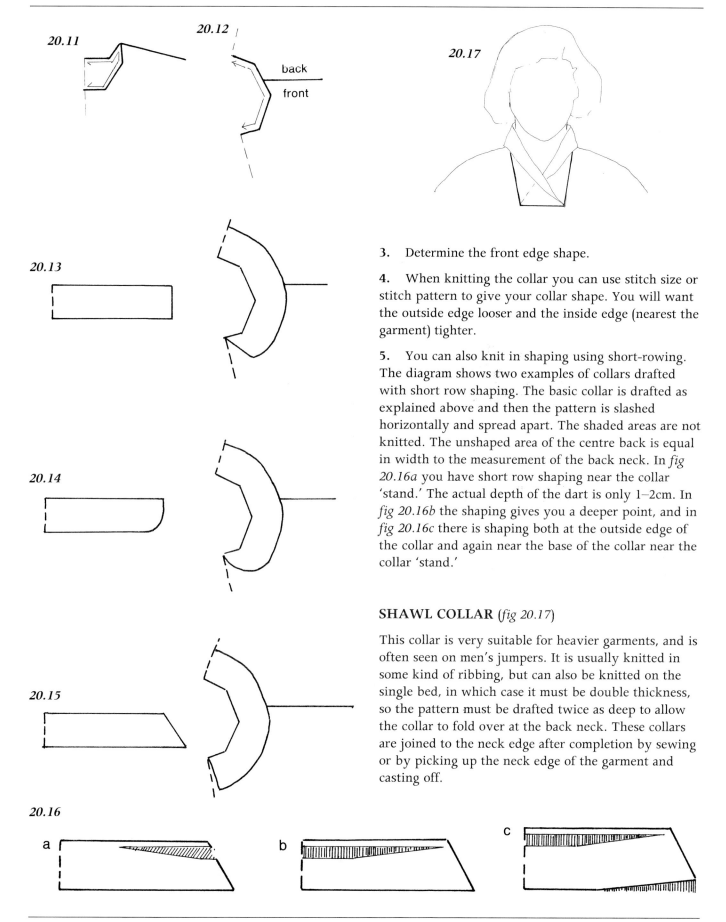

20.11

20.12

back

front

20.17

20.13

20.14

20.15

20.16

a

b

c

3. Determine the front edge shape.

4. When knitting the collar you can use stitch size or stitch pattern to give your collar shape. You will want the outside edge looser and the inside edge (nearest the garment) tighter.

5. You can also knit in shaping using short-rowing. The diagram shows two examples of collars drafted with short row shaping. The basic collar is drafted as explained above and then the pattern is slashed horizontally and spread apart. The shaded areas are not knitted. The unshaped area of the centre back is equal in width to the measurement of the back neck. In *fig 20.16a* you have short row shaping near the collar 'stand.' The actual depth of the dart is only 1–2cm. In *fig 20.16b* the shaping gives you a deeper point, and in *fig 20.16c* there is shaping both at the outside edge of the collar and again near the base of the collar near the collar 'stand.'

SHAWL COLLAR (*fig 20.17*)

This collar is very suitable for heavier garments, and is often seen on men's jumpers. It is usually knitted in some kind of ribbing, but can also be knitted on the single bed, in which case it must be double thickness, so the pattern must be drafted twice as deep to allow the collar to fold over at the back neck. These collars are joined to the neck edge after completion by sewing or by picking up the neck edge of the garment and casting off.

Square front (*fig 20.18*)

1.   Draft the neckline on the body block front and back. Widen the neckline by 1–3cm front and back. To determine the dimensions of the front neckline: draft a horizontal line to indicate the required depth, and for the width at the bottom, make the horizontal line the correct width. Draw a line from the edge of the bottom of the neckline up to the SNP.

2.   Draft the collar. Remember that the outside edge of the collar is to fold over and must therefore not be tight! (*a*) Measure side front neckline. (*b*) Measure half the back neckline (*fig 20.19*). Draw a horizontal line equal in measurement to (*a*)+(*b*) (half the collar). To determine the depth of the collar, measure the *whole* horizontal line at the bottom of the front neckline (*fig 20.20*).This is the depth of your collar at each end, but if you wish to have the collar deeper at the back you

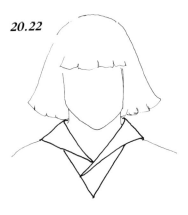

20.22

may do this by short-row shaping (*fig 20.21*). If you are knitting the collar on a single bed you must remember to double-up the depth of the pattern.

V-neck shawl collar (*fig 20.22*)

1.   Draft the V-neckline on the body block. Widen the neckline front and back by 1–3cm (*fig 20.23*).

2.   Measure half the neckline (front and back) (*fig 20.24*).

20.18

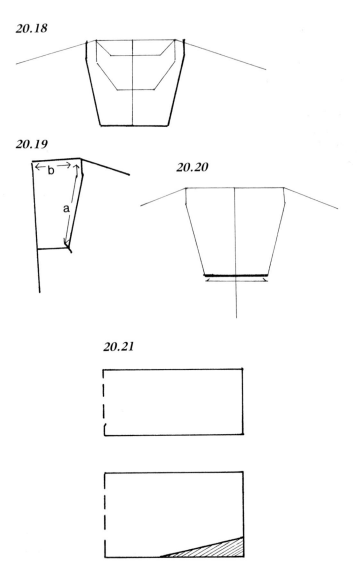

20.19

20.20

20.21

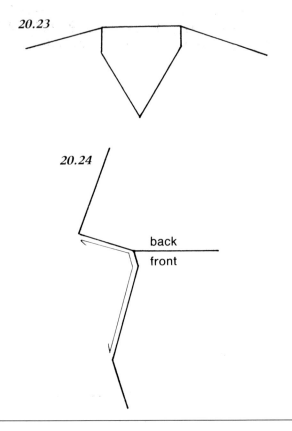

20.23

20.24

back

front

20.25

3. Draft the collar. Draw a horizontal line equal to the measurement of half the front and back neckline (*fig 20.25*). Draw a second horizontal line. This is a guideline parallel to the first line. The distance between the two lines is equal to the desired width of the collar which is, in this case, entirely optional. However, the collar need not be the same width throughout. If you decide to make the back of the collar deeper, you may do this by short-row shaping.

SHAWL COLLAR KNITTED IN ONE WITH FRONT FACINGS

This collar is designed to be knitted on garments with a front closing.

1. Draft the front block and add required ease (*fig 20.26*). Adjust the length of the garment.

2. Draw a vertical line up from the SNP equal in length to the measurement of half the back neck (*fig 20.27*).

3. Draw a horizontal line from the top of the vertical line and extend the horizontal line at the bottom of the garment (*fig 20.28*).

4. Draw a line parallel to the CF of the garment. The distance between this line and the CF of the garment

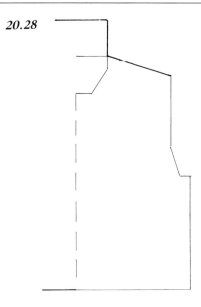

20.28

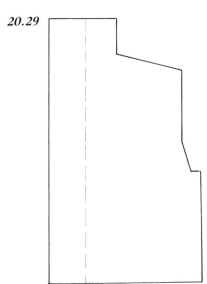

20.29

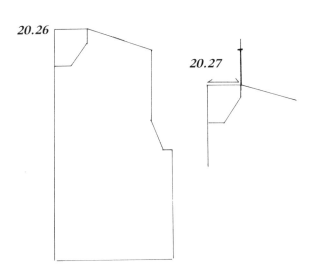

20.26

20.27

must be equal at least to the measurement of half the back neck.

5. This is your pattern. You can add 1–2cm at the CF to allow for closing (*fig 20.29*), but you should have added extra ease for this at the beginning. If you leave a needle in NWP at the centre line, this will mark your fold line.

SHAWL COLLAR KNITTED VERTICALLY FOR GARMENT WITH FRONT CLOSING

This collar is often knitted in one piece with the front band for a cardigan or jacket. It can be knitted on the single bed, in which case you must mirror image the knitting so that it can be folded in half lengthwise, but it is more successful when knitted on the double bed. This collar is drafted so that the straight edge is attached to the neckline. If you wish to knit it on the single bed and fold it over, the curved edge will need to be equal in length to the neck measurement, and the curved edge (where the shaping occurs) will be attached to the garment neckline.

Double bed neckband

1.   Draft the front block and add required ease. Adjust the length of the garment. Draft the front V-neckline (*fig 20.30*).

2.   Measure from the front hem to the beginning of the neckline a (*fig 20.31*). Measure from the beginning of the neckline around to the CB b (*fig 20.32*).

3.   Draw a vertical line equal in length to the measurement of the front band plus half the neckline. Draw a horizontal line at the top. Mark the point where the band meets the neckline.

4.   Draw a line parallel to the first vertical line from the hem up to the point where the neckline begins. The distance between the two lines will be equal to the required depth of your front band.

5.   Determine how deep you require the collar (*fig 20.33*). Remember that the collar will fold over at the back and you must draft your collar twice as deep. Starting at the CB line, draft the collar straight down for 4–6cm then curve it gently to meet the front band.

6.   When knitting a single-bed thickness of fabric on a double bed machine, if you wish to have the collar shaped so that it won't stand up so much, you can: divide it into sections; slash the sections and spread them apart equidistantly; or insert short-row shaping between the sections, thus making the outer edge wider than the inner neck edge (*fig 20.34*).

Single bed neckband

1.   Draw a vertical line for the front band with a parallel line on either side (*fig 20.35*). The distance between the centre line and the parallel line is equal to the desired width of the front band, and their length is equal to the length required.

2.   Draw two more vertical guidelines parallel with the centreline (*fig 20.36*). The distance between the guideline and the centreline is equal to the greatest desired depth of the collar.

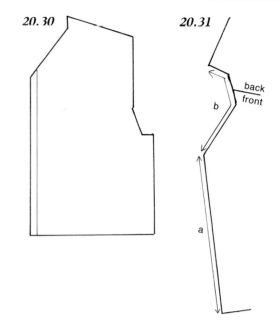

20.30   *20.31*

back
front

b

a

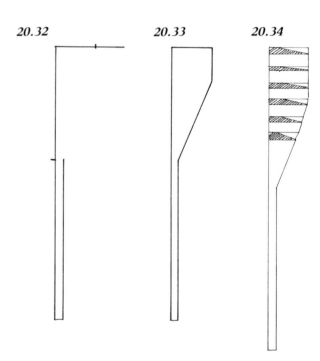

20.32   *20.33*   *20.34*

3. Measure half the front neckline and half the back neckline. Pivot a ruler from the top of the front band and mark the point where it crosses the vertical guideline for the collar depth (*fig 20.37*). The length of this line is equal to the measurement of half the front neckline (*fig 20.38*). Draw a line between this point and the top of the front band. Measure up from the point on the collar depth line and mark a point equal to the

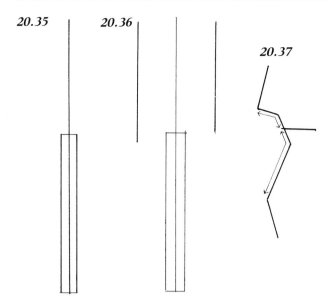

20.35 *20.36*

20.37

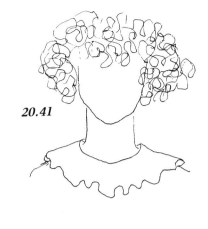

20.41

20.42

CB

CF

20.43

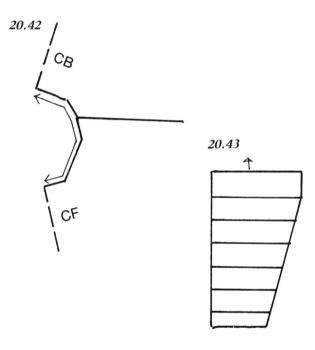

measurement of half the back neckline. Draw a horizontal line at this point (*fig 20.39*).

This is half your collar band. You must knit the other half as an upside-down mirror image. You may leave a needle in the centre of the collar in NWP to indicate the fold line.

You can also insert short-row shaping to give the collar a graceful curve (*fig 20.40*).

20.38

20.39

20.40

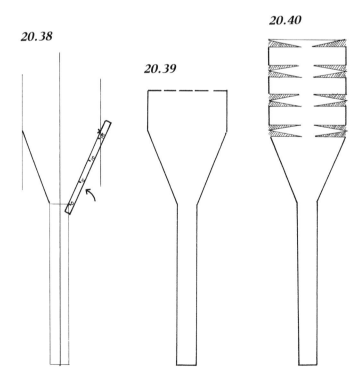

RUFFLED COLLAR (*fig 20.41*)

This edging can be attached to any kind of neckline. It is knitted as a single fabric to allow it to ruffle. It can be done in lace, tuck or open tuck stitch as well as plain stocking stitch. The lighter the fabric in weight, the more effective it is.

1. Draft the required neckband on the garment and measure it from CF to CB (*fig 20.42*). Draw a straight line equal to this measurement.

2. Determine how deep the ruffle will be (the depth need not be constant). Draft the outer edge of the ruffle.

3. Divide the pattern into sections (*fig 20.43*). Slash

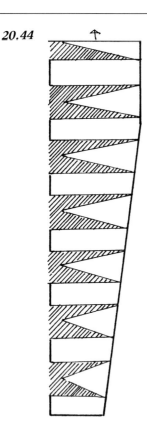

20.44

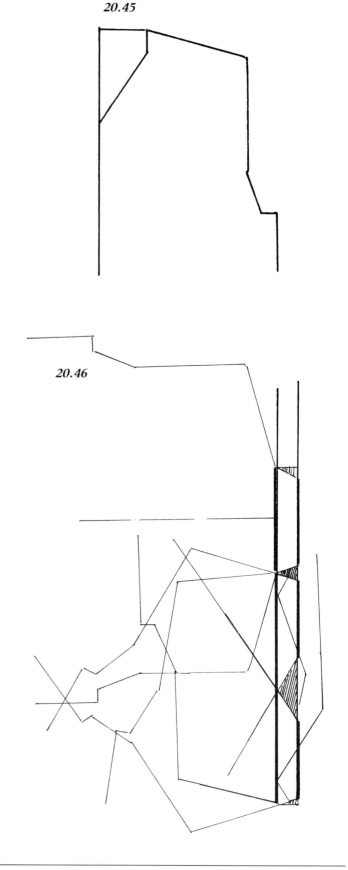

20.45

20.46

each section and spread it apart (*fig 20.44*). The more you spread it, the more ruffled your band will be. Shaping is done with short-rowing.

SOME VARIATIONS FOR V NECKS

Using short-rowing techniques

1. Draft the V neck on your block (*fig 20.45*).

2. Draw a vertical line to represent your neckband. Draw another line parallel to the first line. The distance between the two lines is equal to the depth you require for your band.

3. Place your block with the edge of the neckline at the edge of your band (*fig 20.46*). Mark the SNP and the CF points on the band. Using the block as a guide, mark the angles where the short rows will give your band the required shape at the shoulder and at the centre front. Repeat this for the rest of the band, marking the other side of the front both at the centre and the shoulder, and then for the back band.

4. This can be knitted in rib or on the single bed, but in the latter case the pattern will have to be knitted as a mirror image. Remember to get the short-rowing the right way round.

Using fisherman's rib

If knitting in a racked fisherman's rib pattern where you are racking *every* row, the result is that your fabric will have a strong bias. When you have knitted a strip long enough to go from one shoulder to the centre front of your V neckline, knit one row without racking, then resume racking on every row. Knit the second strip long enough to go up the second side of the front neckline and then around the back neckline. You need not draft the pattern for this band, but two warnings to consider are: don't make the neckline too deep! and don't make the band too wide!

SAILOR COLLAR

1. Draft the front block and add the required ease. Draft a V neckline (*fig 20.47*).

2. Draw a vertical line for the centre of the collar. At the bottom of this line, draft a horizontal line equal to half the required width of the back of the sailor collar (*fig 20.48*).

3. Draw a vertical line at the edge of the collar.

4. Measure up from the bottom of the collar and mark a point on the centre vertical line equal in length to the required depth of the collar at the back. Draw a horizontal line at this point equal to the measurement of half the back neck (*fig 20.49*).

20.49   *20.50*

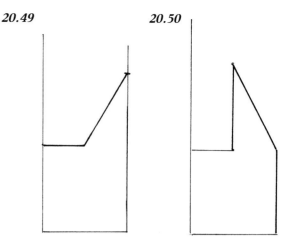

5. Draw a diagonal line from the edge of the back neck to cross the vertical line extended from the edge of the collar. The length of this line equals the measurement of one side of the front neckline.

A variation on the shaping of this collar would be:

Steps 1 and 2 as above.

3. Measure up from the bottom of the collar and mark a point on the vertical line equal in length to the required depth of the collar at the back. Draw a horizontal line at this point equal to the measurement of half the back neck (*fig 20.50*).

4. Draw a vertical line up from the edge of the back neckline. This line is equal in length to the measurement of one side of the front neckline.

5. Draw a diagonal line from the end of the back of the collar to the end of this line.

INSERT DRAPED NECKLINE

1. Draft the body block with the required ease added. Draft a V neckline. Widen the neckline by 1–3cm and draft it quite deep (*fig 20.51*).

2. Draft the V shape from the body block and slash it at the centre line (*fig 20.52*). Pivot the two sections outward from the point and re-draft the new shape. Draft a new top line from point to point (*fig 20.53*).

3. If you wish to knit the collar vertically using short row shaping, draw a vertical line equal to the measurement of the width at the top of the triangle.

20.47   *20.48*

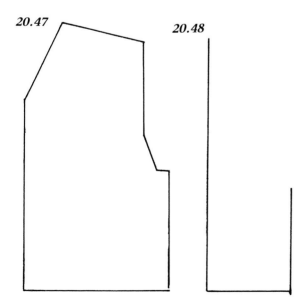

20.51

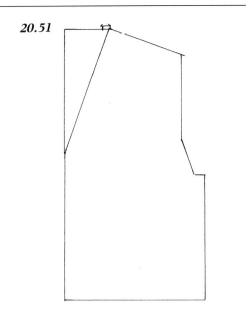

20.54

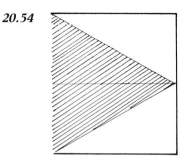

20.52 **20.53**

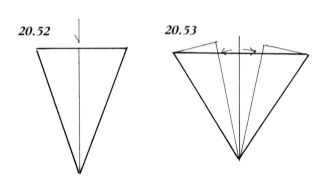

Mark the mid-point. Draw two horizontal lines equal to the measurement of the depth of the triangle at the outside edge, one at the top of the vertical line and one at the bottom. Draw two diagonal lines from the end of the two horizontal lines to the mid-point on the vertical line. Shaping is done by short rowing. The shaded areas are not knitted (*fig 20.54*).

Examples of other neckline variations which could be drafted on your body blocks are: front plackets, cowl necklines, square necklines, and scoop necklines. These can be done in conjunction with your design doll. Turtle necklines and high mandarin collars are really just extended plain crew necklines and do not require special drafting.

21

Measurements for skirts and trousers

Now we come to the easiest and the most difficult aspects of pattern drafting. The skirt is one of the easiest patterns to draft successfully and trousers are the most difficult. If you are going to make a garment that is attractive, fashionable and becoming, there is certainly at least one golden rule you should observe: allow sufficient ease. Do not make the garment too clingy or too tight. Even if you are pencil slim, any knitted garment that leaves no room for manoeuvre is bound to search out any figure fault, no matter how minute, and reveal it: you certainly don't want to look like 'two little boys having a fight in a paper (or knitted) bag!' Knitted garments can, however, be comfortable and easy to wear, even for the generous figure, if enough tolerance is allowed. They can be just as complimentary to your figure as a garment made of woven fabric; the elasticity of knitted fabric can even hide a multitude of sins.

Measuring for pattern drafting must be done very carefully, but the give in knitted fabric does make allowances for minor discrepancies. One of the aids in measuring the circumference is a stiff piece of card measuring about 20cm × 30cm. This should be held over the stomach when measuring the upper and lower hip, which will forestall any possibility of the skirt clinging to lumps or bumps that you don't want to be noticed.

Horizontal measurements (figs 21.1, 21.2):

1. Waist circumference.

2. 'Upper' hip circumference (taken at about the hip bone, over the abdomen).

3. 'Lower' hip circumference (taken over the bottom or at the top of the thigh, whichever is the greater).

4. Upper thigh circumference (taken around the top of the leg).

Vertical measurements:

1. Waist to 'upper' hip.

2. Waist to 'lower' hip.

3. Body rise (this is taken at the side seam from the waist to the seat of a hard chair when the subject is sitting down. This indicates the position of the crotch seam) (*fig 21.3*).

4. Waist to knee (a reference point).

5. Waist to ankle (another reference point).

6. Through the crotch. (This is a very useful check measurement to use once you have finished your basic draft. It is taken from the waistline at CF through the legs, with a comfortable amount of tolerance, to the waistline at CB.)

Basic skirt pattern

Having taken your basic measurements, the drafting of a skirt is simplicity in itself. It is just common sense.

1. Draw a vertical line. This is your CF/CB line. The length of the line equals the desired length of your skirt. Draw a horizontal guideline at the top and bottom.

2. Measure down from the waistline and mark points equal to the distance between waist and upper hip, and between waist and lower hip. Draw horizontal guidelines at these points (*fig 21.4*).

3. Mark the width of the lower and upper hip guidelines equal to one quarter of the measurement

taken at this point *plus ease*. This will be anything from 2cm. The amount of ease depends on the thickness of the fabric; you will have to allow more ease for a thicker and less elastic fabric such as Fair Isle or knitweave.

4. Mark a point on the waistline about half-way

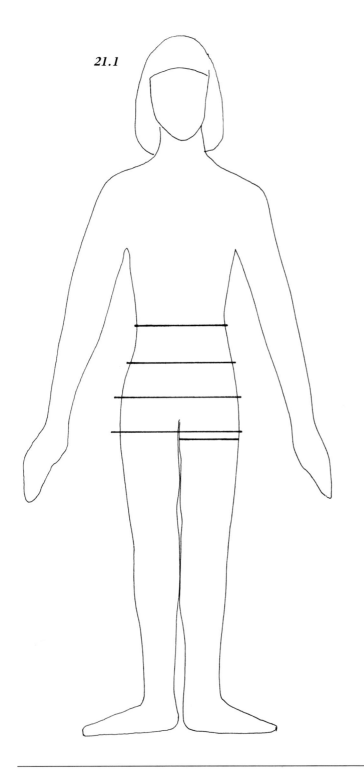

21.1

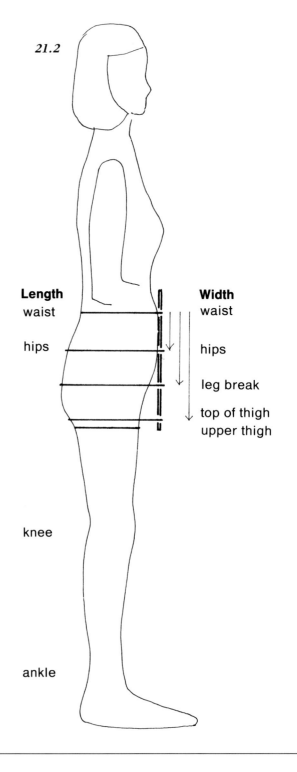

21.2

between the measurement of one quarter waist plus ease and the upper hip measurement. Mark a point on the hemline equal to one quarter the desired width of the skirt at this point (*fig 21.5*).

It is important to remember that the skirt will probably have to be fairly elastic at the waist, as knitted skirts generally do not have a closing, and rely on being pulled over the head or hips in order to put them on. To achieve a waist shaping you can decrease above the widest point (the upper or lower hip) but you must not decrease too much, otherwise you will

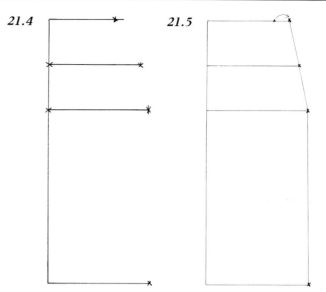

21.4   *21.5*

21.3

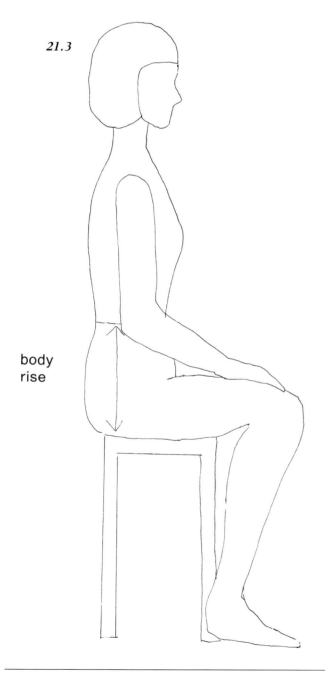

body rise

not be able to get the garment on. There are several possibilities for decreasing:

(*a*) Decrease at both edges of the knitting.

(*b*) Decrease the stitch size or tension number.

(*c*) Decrease the number of needles in WP.
Either remove the work, decrease evenly across the row and replace the work on the machine on fewer needles.
Or transfer some stitches to adjacent needles. Move those empty needles to NWP and knit the remaining section on fewer needles. (**NB**: although this will result in a narrower fabric, it may also make the fabric longer.)

(*d*) Change the stitch pattern, e.g. from tuck stitch to stocking stitch, for the 'yoke' area.

For the same reason, it is very important to remember to cast off or finish the knitting *very loosely*. Even if you make a hem or an edge into which you will insert elastic, it won't do any good if the casting off edge won't stretch enough to go over your head in order to get the garment on.

Skirt variations

Skirt variations are very simple. The most important point about any pattern you draft is that it must be easy over the hip area. Once you have realized this, you can add fullness wherever you like; you can use

21.6   *21.7*

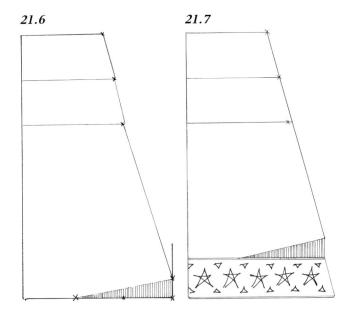

width of the panel of the skirt – narrower panels require a smaller dart and less shaping. Draw a line from this point to the skirt side at the lower or upper hipline (depending on which is wider).

3. Divide the hemline into thirds and draw a line from the point at the bottom of your diagonal side seam line to the first third (from the vertical centre line) mark on the hemline. This will indicate the area to be shaped by short rowing. This will prevent drooping at the seams. If, however, you decide to have a bottom border on your skirt, it is advisable to draft a straight area at the bottom edge of the skirt and to do the short row shaping after the patterning has been completed (*fig 21.7*).

This is the basic technique for drafting a flared or A-line skirt. You can also use this technique to draft a four or six gored skirt if you divide all horizontal measurements by the appropriate number.

your plain skirt pattern and slash and spread it to knit pleats or gathers; you can even, if you wish, knit a wrap-around skirt.

A-LINE OR GORED SKIRTS

1. Draft your basic front. Adjust the length. Decide how wide you want your skirt to be at the hemline. Draft a horizontal line at the base of your skirt equal to one quarter the width of the skirt at the hemline (*fig 21.6*).

2. Draw a vertical line at this point. Mark on this line a point 2–3cm up from the hemline, depending on the

CULOTTES

1. Front: draft half the A-line skirt front.

2. Measuring down from the waistline, mark a point equal to the measurement of the body rise on the centre front line and draw a horizontal guideline at this point (the crotch line). Mark a second point halfway between the waist and the body rise on the centre front line (*fig 21.8*).

3. Measuring from the centre line, mark a point on the horizontal guideline equal to one-eighth of the hip measurement minus 2cm.

21.8   *21.9*

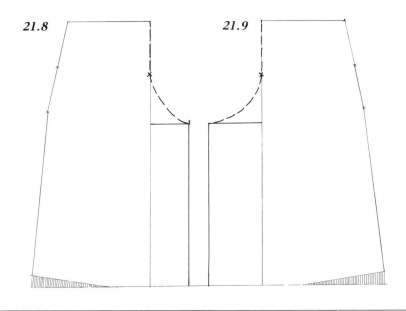

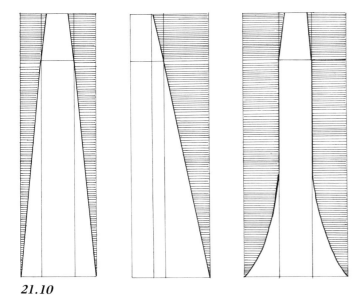

21.10

4.   Draft a curve from the point marked on the centre line to the end of the horizontal guideline. Draw a vertical line straight down to the hemline.

5.   Back: draw half the A-line skirt back (same as front) (*fig 21.9*).

6.   Measure and mark the draft as for the front, *except* that the horizontal guideline at the crotch is equal in length to one-eighth of the total hip measurement *plus* 2cm.

SIDEWAYS KNITTED SKIRTS

Although you can draft these skirts, it is more usual to calculate them. If you do draft them, base them on your critical measurements.

   Determine the desired width at the hemline (*fig 21.10*). Divide your skirt into sections by finding a number that will divide evenly into the width you want at the hem and the width you *need* at the hipline. (This is a critical measurement and cannot be adjusted to a smaller number; it will indicate the *minimum* width you will need in your panel at this point.) You need then draft only one of the sections. You can draw it as a rectangle with the height of the section equivalent to the maximum width required. You can then draw the design line for your short row shaping, which can be at any angle you require. You can even draft a shape that will give you a fish-tail effect.

   You must only ensure that you knit enough rows at the hip level to give your skirt plenty of ease at this point!

SPECIAL EFFECTS *(figs 21.11, 21.12)*

Just as with the bodice, you can approach the skirt as if it were a jigsaw; in other words, you can cut up the pattern and knit each section in a different way with a different stitch pattern, in a different colour, or even in a different direction.

RIBBED SKIRTS

Ribbed skirts are very seldom drafted, as the shaping for a rib skirt depends on two major factors.

Tension size

In order to design a ribbed skirt the most important thing is to knit an accurate tension swatch. For a skirt that depends largely on the stitch size to give the garment shape, you may knit a swatch 60 rows long. Divide it into three sections of 20 rows each and use a different stitch size for each section (gradually decreasing the stitch size).

1.   Length. Measure the whole swatch. Calculate how many rows you will need to knit to make a skirt the required width (length of skirt in cm divided by length of swatch in cm times number of rows). Divide the number of rows you need to knit into thirds. Knit the first third at the largest stitch size, the second third at the middle stitch size and the final third at the smallest stitch size.

21.11

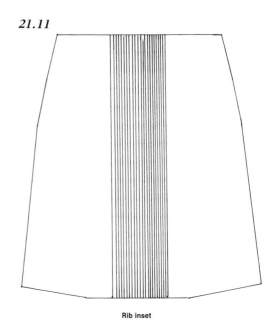

Rib inset

21.12

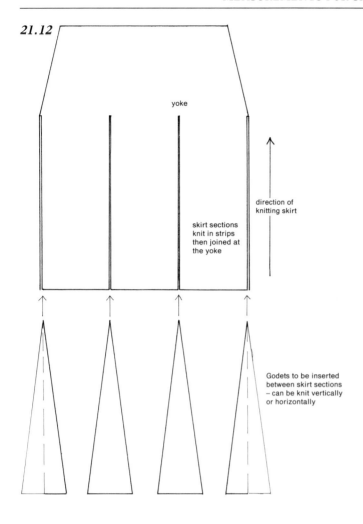

yoke

direction of
knitting skirt

skirt sections
knit in strips
then joined at
the yoke

Godets to be inserted
between skirt sections
– can be knit vertically
or horizontally

2. Width. When calculating how many stitches will be needed for the skirt, allow the swatch to relax and then measure a given number of ribs rather than of stitches. You know how wide your widest part is and will want the skirt fabric at this area to be easy and not cling, so don't pull the fabric flat while measuring.

Determine the width of a given number of ribs, then divide your width measurement by this number. Multiply by the number of ribs you have measured and you will find out how many ribs you require. This will have to be divided evenly into sections because you will probably not be able to knit the skirt in one go.

Needle arrangement

You may alter the needles in WP to alter the width of the fabric (*fig 21.13*). You may decide to knit the garment in different needle set-ups. In order to calculate, or to use the patterning attachment, you will have to knit a separate swatch for each needle set-up. You can then measure each swatch and, starting with the number of ribs or needles needed to make a skirt to fit you at the hips, you can work from there. You will be concerned mainly with the length of each section, which must be decided from each swatch. The number of needles that you begin with at the bottom of your garment will be determined by the number of needles you will need in WP when you reach the hip area.

21.13

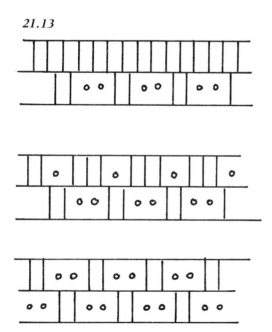

Trouser block

To draft a trouser block is an exacting but not impossible task. Be warned, however, that making a block that will fit perfectly is not easy. Not everyone can wear trousers, and of those who can, not all can wear knitted trousers. Having said this, however, even the most generously proportioned of women can often get away with loose trousers or 'palazzo pants' when fashion permits. It really depends on the wearer. Knitted trousers are certainly very comfortable to wear.

Because the wearer sits, stands, kneels, etc., in trousers, they get more push-me-pull-you wear than any other garment, so it is very important to make them of a very firm fabric, to avoid bagginess and stretching at the knees (unless they are very full and flowing indeed, more like a divided skirt than a pair of trousers). This means that you will need to use the smallest stitch size you can get away with. You may also decide that you wish to use a firmer stitch pattern, such as Fair Isle (the same yarn in Feeder A and Feeder B and a 1 × 1 stitch pattern) or slip stitch (1 × 1 stitch pattern). Trousers are also often made in wool rather than any other fibre because it holds its shape better.

When you have measured the figure you will notice that you have two hip depths and two hip widths. Which do you use for your trouser pattern? To be safe, draw the horizontal hip line at the average distance below the waistline, i.e. approximately 18cm, but use the greater hip width measurement.

FRONT

1. Draw a vertical line equal in length to the required length of the trousers. Draw horizontal guidelines at the top and bottom. Measure down from the top and mark a point on the vertical line equal to the drop of the hip line and the body rise plus 1.5cm (the crotch line). Draw horizontal guidelines outwards from both sides of the vertical line at these points (*fig 21.14*).

2. On the crotch line, measure from the centre to the left and mark a point equal to one twelfth of the hip measurement plus 1.8cm. Draw a vertical guideline up to the waist. This is the CF guideline.

3. On the hip line, measure to the right from the vertical centre front guideline and mark a point equal to one quarter of the hip measurement plus 1cm (*fig 21.15*).

4. On the crotch line, measure to the left of the CF guideline and mark a point equal to one sixteenth of the hip measurement plus 1cm.

5. On the waistline, measure 1cm to the right of the CF guideline and mark a point (the centre front waistline point). Draft the front curve: draft a line down through the hip line where the CF line has crossed it, then curve it down to join the crotch line at the left-hand point marked (*fig 21.16*).

6. From the centre front waistline point measure along the waistline and mark a point equal to one quarter of the waist measurement plus 2.5 to 5cm. This is your pattern waistline.

7. At the bottom line of the trousers, measuring from the centreline, mark two points, one on either side equal to one quarter the total trouser width at the hemline (optional) minus 0.5cm (*fig 21.17*).

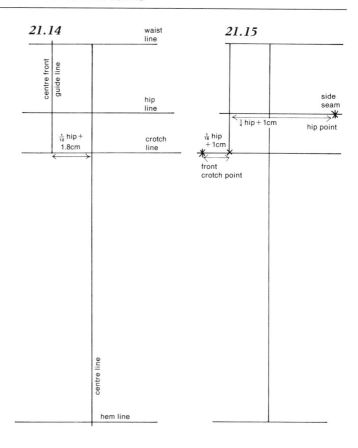

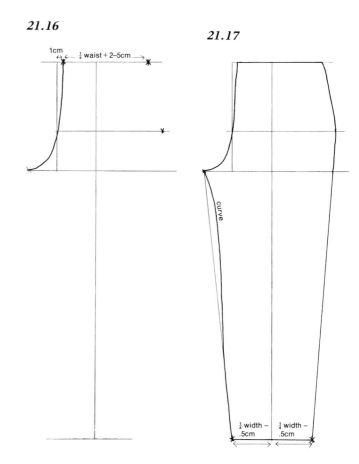

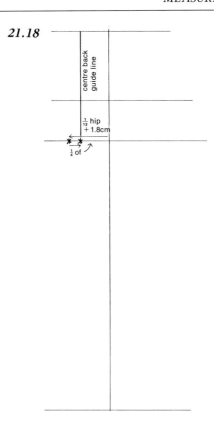

21.18

centre back guide line

$\frac{1}{12}$ hip + 1.8cm

$\frac{1}{4}$ of

21.19

centre back

side seam

waist

waist point

$\frac{1}{4}$ waist + 4.5–6cm point

8. Draft the sides of the legs, curving the inner leg inwards slightly below the crotch point.

BACK

1. Begin your draft as for the front. Mark the waist, hip, crotch line and hem. Draw horizontal guidelines at these points (*fig 21.18*).

2. Measuring to the left of the centreline on the crotch line, mark a point equal to one twelfth of the hip plus 1.8cm, then measure back to the right of this point and mark another point equal to one quarter of this measurement. At this point draft a vertical (CB) guideline upwards to cross the waistline.

3. Mark a point on this line equal to half the measurement of the body rise (*fig 21.19*).

4. On the waist, measure:

(*a*) 2cm to the right of the vertical CB guideline. Mark a point.

(*b*) Measure upwards 2cm and mark a point.

(*c*) Measure from this point to the right and mark a point on the waistline equal to the measurement of one quarter of the waist plus 4.5–6cm.

(*d*) Draw a sloping line joining the point to the mark on the waistline.

5. Crotch point:

(*a*) Measuring to the left from the left-hand point on the crotch line, mark a point equal to one-sixteenth of the hip measurement plus 1cm (*fig 21.20*).

(*b*) Measure to the left of this point by half of the above measurement again.

6. Draft the crotch curve from the CB waist point to this new point as indicated (*fig. 21.21*).

7. On the hip line measure to the right from the CB line and mark a point equal to one quarter of the hip measurement plus 2cm.

8. At the trouser hem, measuring from the centreline mark two points, one either side, equal to the measurement of one quarter trouser width plus 0.5cm.

21.20

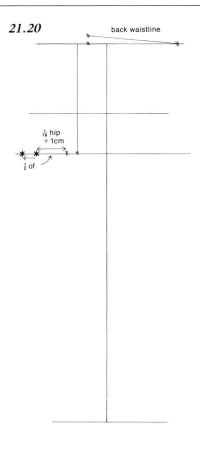

back waistline

$\frac{1}{16}$ hip + 1cm

$\frac{1}{2}$ of

21.21

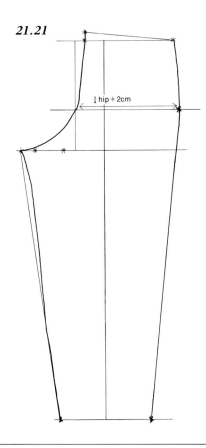

$\frac{1}{4}$ hip + 2cm

21.22

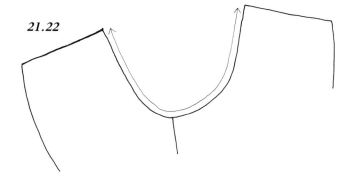

21.23

21.24

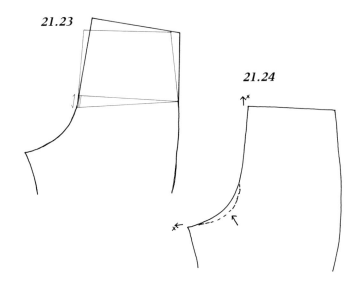

9. Draft the side seams, curving the inside leg seam inwards slightly below the crotch point.

When you have finished drafting the front and back of your trouser block, measure the crotch seam from CF waist to CB waist. It should match your check measurement plus 2cm for ease. You can also check that the width of your trouser leg at the upper thigh is greater than your body measurement (*fig 21.22*).

If you require greater ease in the crotch seam, you can add this by slashing the back block horizontally at the hip line and spreading the upper part of the block (pivot at the side seam hip point). You can insert a wedge of up to 3cm (*fig 21.23*).

If you wish to add only a small amount of ease, you can either raise the back waist seam, lengthen the crotch seam at the crotch point, or increase the scoop of the back crotch seam curve (*fig 21.24*).

22

Construction considerations

We must always remember that we are in control of constructing not only the garment but also the fabric from which it is made. It is possible to take a cut-and-sew approach to the fabric, but this is limiting. You should work from the inside of the garment outwards when you knit your fabric.

You can not only apply surface decoration, e.g. pictures as features, but also use different stitch patterns as features at selected points of interest, such as collars, cuffs and borders. You can affect the way in which the fabric is shaped and behaves, not only at the edges but from within the structure of the knitting itself e.g. in socks and gloves. This is *knitmanship*.

Having drafted your pattern, you must then focus on the construction – mapping out exactly how you plan to knit and assemble the garment.

You must remember to make allowances in your decision-making process for the special qualities inherent in the fabric you are constructing.

STRETCHABILITY

1.   Fibres. Cotton, silk, linen, etc. are not very stretchy yarns and do not produce a very elastic fabric, whereas some types of acrylic, etc., are much more elastic. The other factor which can affect the elasticity of the fabric is how the fibre is spun. If it is a tight twist, the fabric may be firmer.

Some yarns are also heavier. Silk and rayon in particular are quite heavy and can be very slippery. If you make a garment in these yarns, you must be aware of the fact that the force of gravity may make them 'grow' unintentionally.

2.   Stitch size. A fabric made in a loose stitch will be

more elastic and stretchy than a fabric made in a tight stitch size.

3.   Stitch pattern.

(*a*) *Single bed:* slip stitch, weaving and Fair Isle are less elastic than stocking stitch, tuck stitch, knit weave and lace.

(*b*) *Rib fabric:* the more zigzag the construction of the fabric (the more the yarn passes between the needles on the two beds), the more stretchy the fabric becomes (*figs 22.1, 22.2*).

THICKNESS

Weaving and tuck stitch produce thicker fabrics. The more tucking, the thicker the fabric. The thickness of the woven fabric depends on the thickness of the yarn used for weaving.

Fair Isle is two yarns thick, so it is really like a double fabric.

Lace fabric is usually thinner, but can be lumpy (or fall in 'hills and valleys') if a multi-transfer pattern is used.

Slip stitch can be either very thick (if it is used to create a three-dimensional or relief fabric) or thinner and used to create a fine texture. If used for multi-coloured work it will be thicker.

22.1

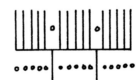

22.2

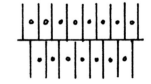

FABRICS AND FINISHING

1. The way the finished garment is treated can alter its appearance considerably. Acrylic yarn in particular can change character considerably when treated with steam and pressure. If acrylic yarn is steam pressed at a temperature higher than that it is subjected to when 'set' and treated in the factory, it will behave entirely differently. If you take a knitted fabric and 'set' it with a hot steam iron, it will behave more like a woven fabric, losing its elasticity and becoming much more stable. It will also become less resilient and bouncy and so be more amenable to draping, gathering, etc.

2. You can also alter the nature of any fabric woven in wool by subjecting it to a fulling or felting treatment. This can be done manually or mechanically.

3. Another very important consideration is how the fabric will hang on the body. If you plan to construct the fabric for your garment so that the knitting will hang sideways on the body, you must be aware that the garment may grow longer and shrink width-wise, and make allowances for this when calculating from your tension swatch.

Two samples of tuck stitch knitted in acrylic: the lower one is pressed

You can knit each section of the pattern in a different direction, or in several sections. You can assemble the garment when you have finished knitting all the separate sections, pick up and add on sections as you go, or knit sections within sections, such as gores, godets or inverted pleats.

Here are some of the possibilities. It is up to you to apply the ideas to your garments when you are planning them out.

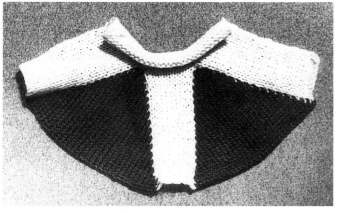

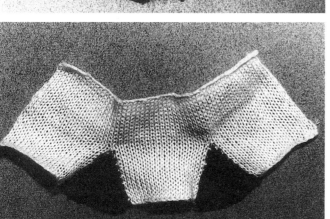

Inserts and gores

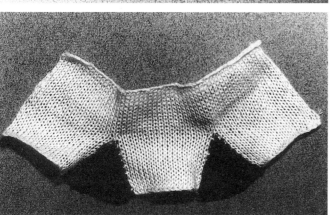

BIAS KNITTING

1. Lace

In lace, if you transfer stitches consistently in the same direction you will produce a fabric which will come out on a slant, in the direction the stitches have moved in.

(*a*) In the first sample the lace carriage consistently transfers all the stitches in the same direction. On Toyota and Brother machines you may use card **1** locked on any row. Always use your lace carriage from the same side of the machine and transfer a row of stitches. Then knit two rows. If you wish to reverse the direction of the bias, start the lace carriage from the opposite end of the needle bed.

On Knitmaster machines you can also lock card **1** on any row. Push one of your side levers back and leave the other forward. If you wish to reverse the direction of the bias knitting, reverse the position of the levers.

(*b*) For the second sample you will have to manually select your needles or use an electronic machine which can do one pattern on selected needles and another on other needles. The wider the pattern, the wider the bias sections will be. In this sample the needles on the left side of the needle bed were consistently transferred in one direction, while the needles on the other side were consistently transferred in the opposite direction. On a punch card machine your sections cannot be wider than 12 stitches (*fig 22.3*).

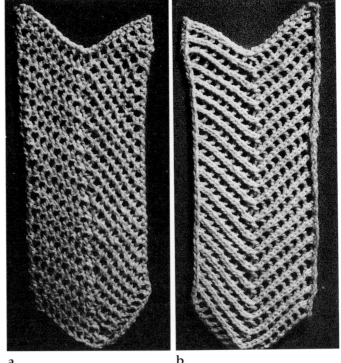

a   b

Bias knitting (a) front (b) back

22.3

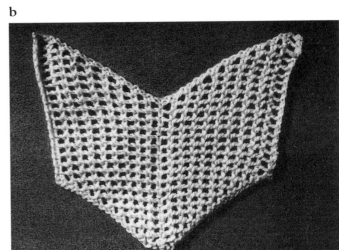

Pattern A + B

Brother electronic pattern

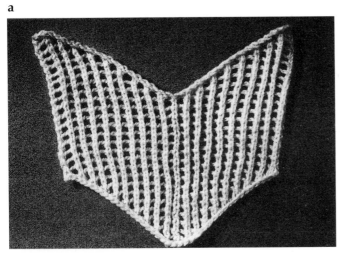

a

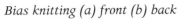

Bias knitting (a) front (b) back

b

2. Racked fisherman's rib

If you set up your machine to do racked fisherman's rib and rack the ribber alternately to the left and right *on every row*, you will achieve a bias fabric.

If the carriage is set to tuck when it moves from left to right on the main bed and the ribber is set to tuck when it moves from right to left, and you rack the ribber bed towards the carriage before you knit the row, the fabric will lean towards the right. If you rack the ribber bed in the same direction as the carriage is going to move before you knit the row, the fabric will lean towards the left (*fig 22.4*). So if you knit one row without racking and then resume racking every row, you will change the sequence and thus the direction of the bias knitting.

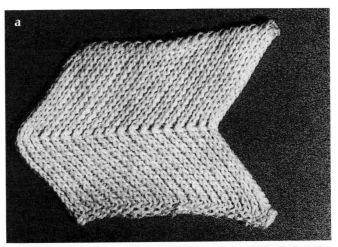

Racked fisherman's rib (a) front (b) back

22.4

Direction of fabric	Machine setting	1 Direction of racking	2 Direction of carriage
→▷	main bed TUCK →▷	→▷	◁—
	ribber ◁—TUCK	◁—	—▷
◁—	main bed ◁—TUCK	—▷	—▷
	Ribber TUCK →▷	◁—	◁—

3. Short row shaping

In short row shaping you can also create a bias effect. If you shape consistently in the same way you will get a bias effect in the fabric. It is a little harder to see what is happening because you are not knitting a straight piece of fabric as in the first few samples, but it will give a sense of movement to the skirt, peplum or ruffle if you are conscious of what is happening. It also gives a very interesting effect when knitting a tam-o'-shanter hat.

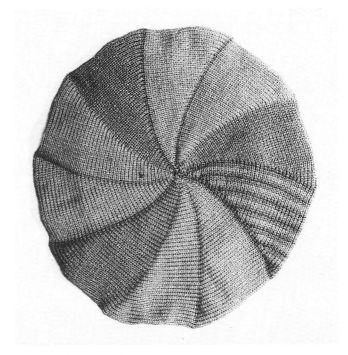

Tam-o'-shanter hat

DIRECTIONAL KNITTING

1. Short rowing

Short rowing can change the direction of your knitting within a section of the garment without changing the actual outside shape. You can use short rowing to exploit possibilities within the garment shape in terms of colour, pattern, etc. and still knit a 'brown-paper-bag jumper.'

2.   If you look at your pattern pieces as if they were jigsaw puzzles, you can divide them into sections and knit each separately. This will give you far greater scope for variation.

(*a*) You can knit two strips going in the same direction, joining the first strip to the second while you knit the second. Both strips can then vary in colour, stitch pattern or whether the stocking stitch or the purl side is on the right side. You can also shape either or both strips as you wish.

(*b*) You can pick up the edge of the first strip and knit the second in another direction.

(*c*) You can join two pieces of knitting using short row shaping on the in-between section.

Pick up the edge of the piece and knit outwards

Knit two strips going in the same direction

Gore insert

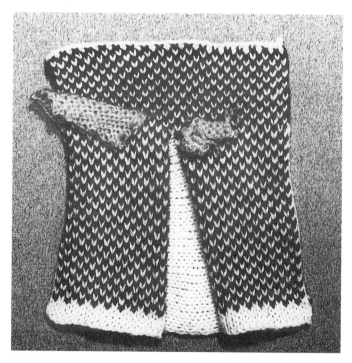

SHAPING WITHIN THE ROW

You cannot easily increase evenly across the row, *but* you can *decrease* evenly across it. In order to do this you may want to knit the garment and then turn it upside down to achieve the desired effect.

1.   You can decrease evenly either by removing the work on WY and replacing it on fewer needles, putting several stitches on selected needles, or by transferring the stitches and pushing empty needles to NWP before either putting the work onto WY or taking it off on a garter bar.

Gathered decreasing (a) front (b) back

2.   Pleats. You can obtain pleats by removing the work on WY and replacing the stitches on fewer needles but forming pleats as you do so. You will find that you have three stitches on every needle where you have a pleat.

Pleat

INCREASING (OR DECREASING) THE WIDTH OF THE FABRIC WITHOUT SHAPING AT THE EDGES

This will pertain to the measurement of the stitches.

1. You can alter the stitch size. The sample was knitted starting at T10/8/6/4/2. Each section was 10 rows.

2. You can alter the width (and length) of your fabric by altering the stitch pattern. The samples combine tuck stitch/stocking stitch (the fabric is wider where there is a stitch pattern) and slip stitch/stocking stitch (the fabric is narrower where there is a stitch pattern).

Altering the stitch size

Tuck stitch to stocking stitch

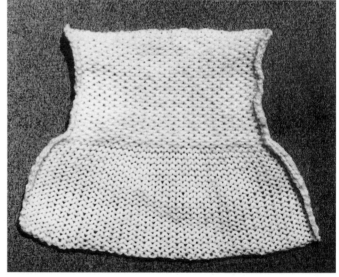

Slip stitch to stocking stitch (a) front (b) back

3. You can alter the needles in WP within the needle arrangement. In the sample every third stitch was transferred and the needle put into NWP.

Needles in NWP

4. You can make the fabric wider by dropping stitches and unravelling them after completing the knitting.

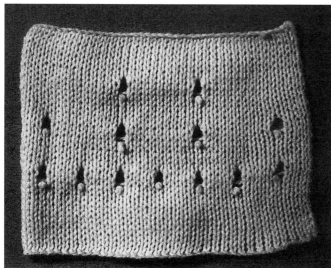

5. You can alter the width by changing from knitting a double-bed fabric to a single bed fabric, i.e. by introducing ribbing.

Dropped stitches

Ribbing

6. You can make the fabric narrower by introducing cables which will pull the fabric in.

7. You can narrow the fabric by knitting a simple Fair Isle pattern with Lycra or elastic thread.

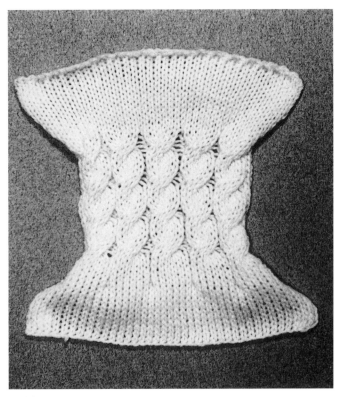

Cables

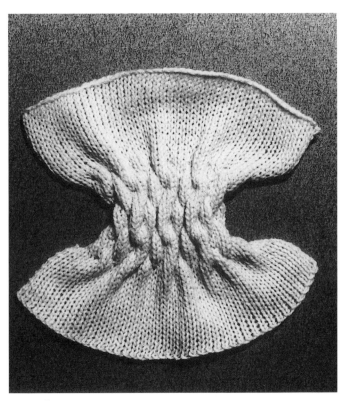

Knitted-in Lycra

These alterations have often been accompanied by an altering of stitch size (tension) as well as the other technique specified.

INCREASING (OR DECREASING) THE LENGTH OF THE FABRIC WITHOUT SHAPING THE EDGES

This will pertain to the measurement of the rows.

1.   Single motif patterns. If you knit your stitch pattern on only selected needles in WP you will find a different row measurement. The samples show SM tuck stitch. This can be done easily on an electronic machine but can also be done by selecting needles required to knit stocking stitch to HP manually on every row on a punch card machine.

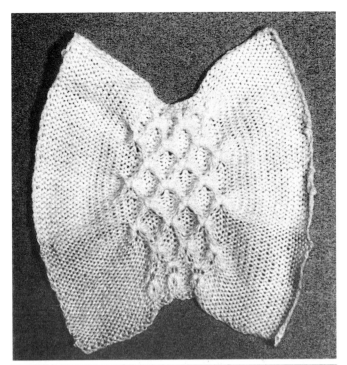

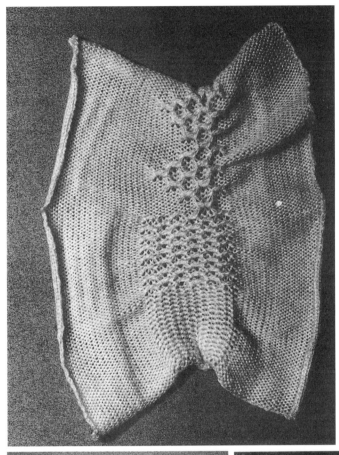

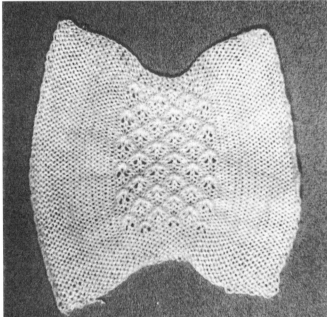

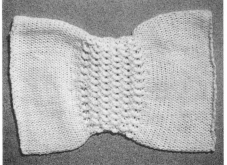
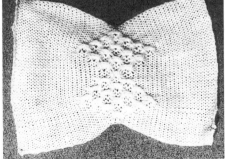
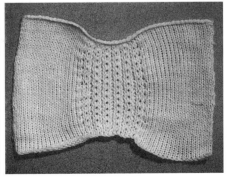

Single motif tuck stitch samples

2. Short row shaping. You can achieve this by increasing or decreasing the number of needles in HP on alternate rows. If you do this regularly you will achieve one effect, but you can also use it to arrive at more varied shaping effects.

(*A*) This sample was knitted pushing needles to HP and then knitting several rows over the remaining needles in WP before knitting all the needles back again. The yarn was wrapped around the last needle in HP next to the needles in WP on every alternate row. This resulted in a build-up of yarn on this needle, and led to a gathered effect.

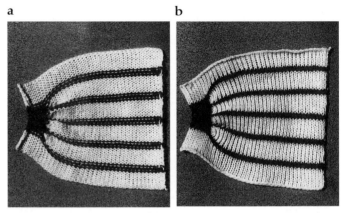

Sample A (a) front (b) back

(*B*) This sample was done by rapid shaping, moving only one needle on every alternate row, avoiding a build-up of yarn on the single wrapped needle. This will also result in a gathered effect.

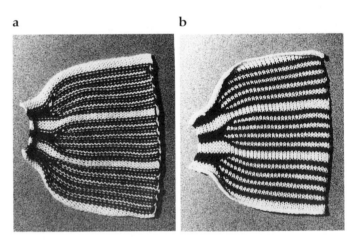

Sample B (a) front (b) back

(*C*) This sample was done in a more conventional manner, moving several needles on every alternate row. This shaping is also balanced so that needles moved to WP on the first half of the shaping were moved back into NWP on the second half of the shaping.

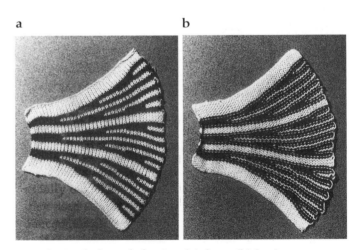

Sample C – balanced shaping (a) front (b) back

3. Dropped stitches. Some stitch patterns require stitches to be dropped after the knitting has been completed. A lot of these stitch patterns require a ribber or are done on a double bed machine. Included in this section are the Pfaff stitches called 'release stitches' or 'summer Fair Isle.' In summer Fair Isle a double-bed Jacquard is produced and then all the stitches on the main bed are dropped and run back. The effect is quite amazing, producing a fabric that looks like a single bed fabric but in which the stitches in any one row are not all the same size.

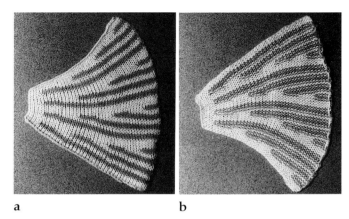

a   b

Sample in uneven shaping (a) front (b) back

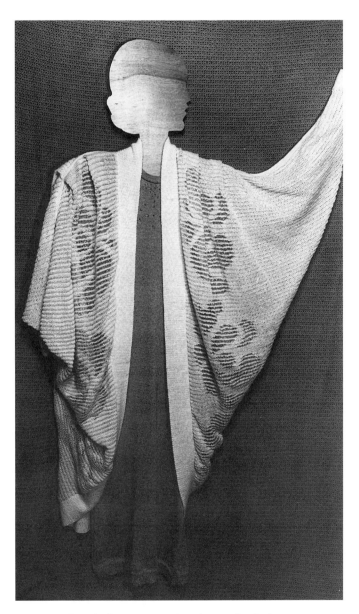

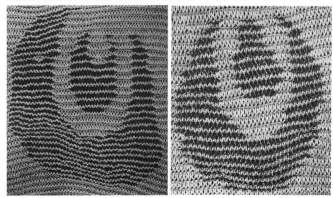

Garment in stitch pattern using dropped stitches.
(Right): Samples for garment

4. Smocking. This is a form of pick up which is done manually and will result in a difference of row measurement if it is not done evenly across the row. It is usually easier to use a change in yarn to mark the row to be picked up. In one sample there are little pleats; in the other a few stitches have been picked up selectively across the row.

I hope that these ideas have opened all sorts of doors; now there is no excuse for knitting ill-fitting brown paper-bag jumpers (unless you really want to!).

a

b

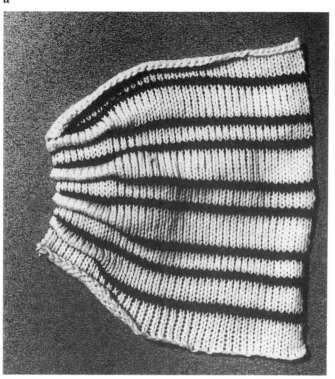
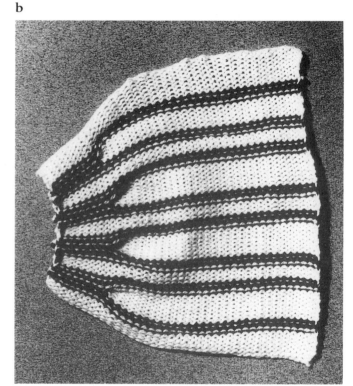

Picked-up pleats (a) front (b) back

a

b

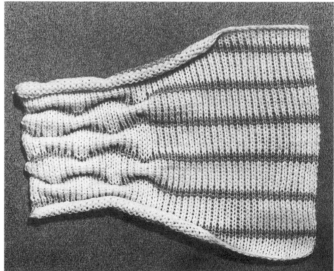

Picked-up smocking (a) front (b) back

23

Some additional ideas for designs

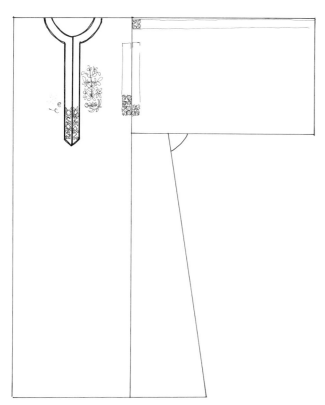

Gold thread on white linen

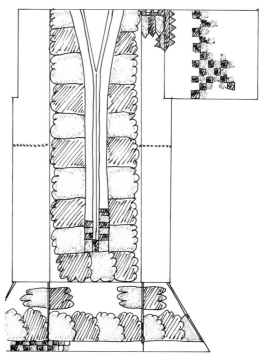

Man's coat dress – white linen embroidered in green rust and faded turquoise

Variations on simple shapes

Garment based on rectangles and squares

Poncho knit in two halves

Simple garments made from unshaped rectangles

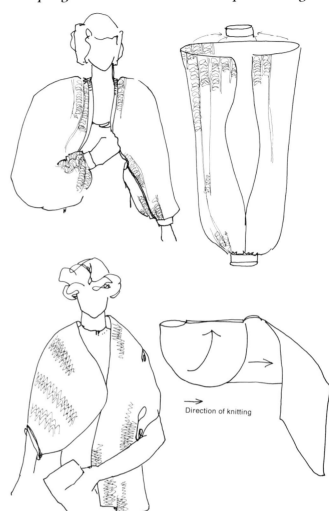

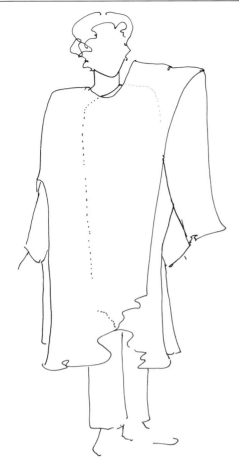

Direction of knitting

Wrap-over poncho

One-sleeved stole

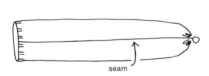

seam

seam

seam

**Hats and scarves
made from simple rectangles**

Index